Scarecrow Studies in Young Adult Literature

Series Editor: Patty Campbell

Scarecrow Studies in Young Adult Literature is intended to continue the body of critical writing established in Twayne's Young Adult Authors Series and to expand it beyond single-author studies to explorations of genres, multicultural writing, and controversial issues in young adult (YA) reading. Many of the contributing authors of the series are among the leading scholars and critics of adolescent literature, and some are YA novelists themselves.

The series is shaped by its editor, Patty Campbell, who is a renowned authority in the field, with a thirty-year background as critic, lecturer, librarian, and teacher of YA literature. Patty Campbell was the 2001 winner of the ALAN Award, given by the Assembly on Adolescent Literature of the National Council of Teachers of English for distinguished contribution to YA literature. In 1989 she was the winner of the American Library Association's Grolier Award for distinguished service to young adults and reading.

1. *What's So Scary about R. L. Stine?* by Patrick Jones, 1998.
2. *Ann Rinaldi: Historian and Storyteller*, by Jeanne M. McGlinn, 2000.
3. *Norma Fox Mazer: A Writer's World*, by Arthea J. S. Reed, 2000.
4. *Exploding the Myths: The Truth about Teens and Reading*, by Marc Aronson, 2001.
5. *The Agony and the Eggplant: Daniel Pinkwater's Heroic Struggles in the Name of YA Literature*, by Walter Hogan, 2001.
6. *Caroline Cooney: Faith and Fiction*, by Pamela Sissi Carroll, 2001.
7. *Declarations of Independence: Empowered Girls in Young Adult Literature, 1990–2001*, by Joanne Brown and Nancy St. Clair, 2002.
8. *Lost Masterworks of Young Adult Literature*, by Connie S. Zitlow, 2002.
9. *Beyond the Pale: New Essays for a New Era*, by Marc Aronson, 2003.
10. *Orson Scott Card: Writer of the Terrible Choice*, by Edith S. Tyson, 2003.
11. *Jacqueline Woodson: "The Real Thing,"* by Lois Thomas Stover, 2003.
12. *Virginia Euwer Wolff: Capturing the Music of Young Voices*, by Suzanne Elizabeth Reid, 2003.
13. *More Than a Game: Sports Literature for Young Adults*, by Chris Crowe, 2004.
14. *Humor in Young Adult Literature: A Time to Laugh*, by Walter Hogan, 2005.
15. *Life Is Tough: Guys, Growing Up, and Young Adult Literature*, by Rachelle Lasky Bilz, 2004.
16. *Sarah Dessen: From Burritos to Box Office*, by Wendy J. Glenn, 2005.
17. *American Indian Themes in Young Adult Literature*, by Paulette F. Molin, 2005.
18. *Gay and Lesbian Literature for Young Adults*, by Michael Cart, 2005.
19. *Karen Hesse*, by Rosemary Oliphant-Ingham, 2005.
20. *Graham Salisbury: Island Boy*, by David Macinnis Gill, 2005.
21. *The Distant Mirror: Reflections on Young Adult Historical Fiction*, by Joanne Brown and Nancy St. Clair, 2006.

The Distant Mirror

Reflections on Young Adult Historical Fiction

Joanne Brown
Nancy St. Clair

THE SCARECROW PRESS, INC.

Lanham, Maryland • Toronto • Oxford

2006

SCARECROW PRESS, INC.
Published in the United States of America
by Scarecrow Press, Inc.
A wholly owned subsidary of
The Rowman & Littlefield Publishing Group, Inc.
4501 Forbes Boulevard, Suite 200, Lanham, Maryland 20706
www.scarecrowpress.com

PO Box 317
Oxford
OX2 9RU, UK

British Library Cataloguing in Publication Information Available

Library of Congress Cataloging-in-Publication Data
Brown, Joanne, 1933-
   The distant mirror : reflections on young adult historical fiction / Joanne Brown, Nancy
St. Clair.
      p. cm.—(Scarecrow studies in young adult literature ; no. 21)
   Includes bibliographical references and index.
   ISBN 0-8108-5625-5 (hardcover : alk. paper)
   1. Historical fiction, American—History and criticism. 2. Young adult fiction,
American—History and criticism. 3. Young adults—Books and reading—United States.
4. Literature and history—United States. I. St. Clair, Nancy. II. Title. III. Scarecrow
studies in young adult literature ; 21.
   PS374.H5B76 2005
   813'.54—dc22

                                                                        2005019016

∞™ The paper used in this publication meets the minimum requirements of
American National Standard for Information Sciences—Permanence of Paper
for Printed Library Materials, ANSI/NISO Z39.48-1992.
Manufactured in the United States of America.

To our husbands, Milt and Steve,
with whom we share our respective histories.

"Novelists who depict their own age in the distant mirror of the past may offer a fresh perspective on the present."

David Cowart
History and the Contemporary Novel

Contents

Acknowledgments

*W*riting this book involved considerable research and raised some questions for which we wanted authoritative confirmation. For their assistance in lending us a hand (plus their knowledge and wisdom), we extend our sincere thanks to:

- Chris Crowe, Professor of English at Brigham Young University (Salt Lake City, Utah), who provided a wealth of invaluable information about the process of writing two of his most recent books, *Mississippi Trial, 1955,* and *Getting Away with Murder: The True Story of the Emmett Till Case.*
- Nick Proctor, Professor of History at Simpson College (Indianola, Iowa), who energetically and enthusiastically undertook the task of checking the early chapters of our manuscript for historical accuracy.
- Rabbi David Kaufman of Temple B'nai Jeshurun, Des Moines, Iowa, who answered questions raised in Chapter 5 about Jewish theology and ritual.
- Patty Campbell, our editor, whose support saw us through this project when its completion exceeded its due date by several months, whose editorial cuts and revisions were balanced by her comments of encouragement penciled in our manuscript's margins, and whose friendship we value as much as her editorial advice.

I

HISTORICAL FICTION AS GENRE

Portraits of the Past

History is a mirror, fiction a portrait.

Marc Aronson, *Beyond the Pale*[1]

$\mathcal{O}$nce upon a time not so long ago, young adult historical fiction was far from a popular genre. For many years, in fact, publishers shied away from it, viewing it as less in demand among young readers of fiction than novels of contemporary social realism. In 1980, Patty Campbell confessed to being convinced that

> young adults lack a sense of history to a significant degree. They will accept a good YA novel with a historical setting if the other elements of the story are appealing enough to overcome that drawback, but, in general, so-called historical fiction is sudden death on the YA shelf.[2]

Leon Garfield, the late author of many historical novels for young adults, echoed Campbell's perception eight years later when he described historical fiction "as being something of an embarrassment, like an elderly relative, to be tolerated out of a sense of duty and reluctantly supported in a condition of genteel poverty."[3] Teachers scrambling to find historical novels for their social studies classes had only limited choices.

THE RECENT POPULARITY OF HISTORICAL FICTION

That was then, this is now. And now, in the mirror of history, to borrow from Marc Aronson's metaphor, young adult novelists have found a rich source of material for their portraits. In 1996 Patty Campbell, reversing her earlier assessment regarding the popularity of historical fiction among young readers, noted with ironic humor, "[S]uddenly *historical fiction* is the magic phrase on every publisher's lips, beginning to replace . . . even—saints be praised!—*horror.*"[4]

Leonard Garfield has summed up the attraction with an apt metaphor:

> If history has any value beyond providing a livelihood for historians, it is to enlarge the imagination . . . . With the shrinkage of space to live in, individual freedom becomes much more an inward affair. Though we may scarcely swing a cat in our cities, we may still swing a dinosaur in our minds.[5]

Indeed, many contemporary writers of young adult historical novels have taken delight in swinging their own dinosaurs. Their fictional protagonists, almost always adolescents, occupy the marginalized position common to the central characters in much YA fiction, contemporary as well as historical realism. But although this pattern recurs frequently in adolescent literature, it gains particular effectiveness in YA historical fiction.

Katherine Paterson elaborates on this idea by noting the rebellious qualities inherent in the protagonists of YA historical fiction. "The characters in history or fiction that we remember are those who kicked against the walls of their societies."[6] These historical protagonists usually begin in a position of extreme vulnerability created not only by their youth, but also, variously, by race, creed, class, and gender. In confronting their respective circumstances and challenging the dominant structures of their society, each assumes more control of his or her life, gaining unanticipated strength. This storyline, a classic quest archetype, lends itself, as Paterson notes, particularly well to historical fiction and provides young readers with a vicarious sense of triumph. Given the satisfaction gained from this pattern, the question is not why YA historical fiction has enjoyed its current surge of popularity but why it ever lagged at all.[7]

HISTORICAL FICTION: MORE THAN AN ADVENTURE STORY

Not only has the genre increased in popularity, but it has shifted its emphasis. As an illustration of this change, the second edition of Nilsen and Donelson's *Literature for Today's Young Adults* (1985) limits its initial discussion of historical fiction to two paragraphs that distinguish the genre from other YA fiction purely by its "setting," defined as any narrative set during or prior to World War II."[8] A later discussion of five pages in the same text is part of a longer chapter titled "Excitement and Suspense: Of Sudden Shadows," a heading that underscores—as does the text itself—not the historical aspects of the genre but the page-turning attributes that might as easily be found in much fiction set in the contemporary world. While acknowledging that "we read historical novels because we are curious about other times and other places and other people," Nilsen and Donelson add that the *"most important* [italics ours] reason that readers are attracted to historical fiction is 'because we want adventure and suspense and mystery' (154). In other words, the genre's main attractions, as Patty Campbell noted in 1980, were the "other" elements of the narrative itself, with the historical aspects an almost incidental backdrop to the novel rather than integral to it.

A short sixteen years later—but generations in the publishing world—the sixth edition of *Literature for Today's Young Adults* (2001) devotes an entire chapter to the genre.[9] The sentence about "suspense and mystery" remains, but the longer discussion subordinates the suspenseful aspect of historical fiction to the genre's value in bringing the past alive for readers.

THE DEVELOPMENT OF HISTORICAL FICTION

In accounting for the rising interest in YA historical fiction, it is helpful to examine the development of the genre for adults, for its earliest forms, though not intended for young readers, were often enjoyed by them, and not surprisingly, YA historical novels have been shaped by their predecessors. Critics and scholars trace the beginnings of historical fiction as far back as ancient Greece, arguing that the mythological epics of such storytellers as Homer and Virgil mingled historical fact with fiction, a stance that positions the genre as one of the earliest of narrative forms. But as myth became more romantic and history became more factual, these two strands began to develop separately, although they remained connected by their common reference to the past.

By the eighteenth century, as the novel itself was first emerging, historical fiction took the form of what Barbara Foley calls the "pseudofactual novel,"[10] a narrative whose characters and situations are clearly invented but whose form mimics nonfiction. Thus, pseudofactual novels used memoirs, diaries, and letters to tell their stories. The term "history" or "historie" (followed by the name of the character or event central to the novel) often appeared on the title page, infusing another nonfiction element into the story. This documentary strategy is illustrated, for example, by Daniel Defoe's *Journal of the Plague Year*, written as a memoir. Although many of its details have sprung from Defoe's imagination, it reads as an actual historical document, despite the long episode about two London men who escape to the country and whose story is told in the third person, a break in the first-person narration that dominates the story.

Mimetic fiction has been appropriated in many historical novels for young readers. The novels in the popular *Dear America* and *My Name Is America* series are written as diaries. Karen Hesse's *Letters from Rivka,* a searing account of a young woman's experiences fleeing from Czarist Russia, takes, as its title indicates, the epistolary form of early documentary novels.

Parallel to the growth of documentary fiction, the early novels of eighteenth-century writers such as Samuel Richardson (who also used the epistolary form), Henry Fielding, and Tobias Smollett influenced the development of historical fiction, although they set their novels in their own times. Aiming to enlist the reader's belief, these novels introduced a note of psychological realism in the characters' responses to extraordinary events. This movement toward realism carried over into the nineteenth century, when the prevailing mode of the documentary novel shifted into what we know today as the historical novel. There was no pretense of narrating actual events; the tales were accepted as fiction but offered a credible perspective on the past. The term "historie" disappeared from the title pages of novels; the narrative, although set in a specific historical period, did not necessarily include authentic characters from the past, although their presence was not uncommon. When historic events entered the novel, they did so less to authenticate its absolute veracity or the writer's integrity than to persuade the reader to trust the writer's interpretation of a segment of history. And rather than convincing the reader through mimetic or documentary strategies, writers commonly used copious footnotes as testimony to the story's reliability.

THE INFLUENCE OF SIR WALTER SCOTT

The novels of Sir Walter Scott, who is often identified as "the father of the historical novel,"[11] used such an approach. His *Waverly* stories, for example, are thick with footnotes. Deriving most of his material from Scottish history and legend, he achieved an arresting ability to recreate the atmosphere of an age in all its pageantry and detail. He created a range of eccentric Scottish peasants and enlivened his stories with romantic subplots that involve aristocratic, if far less interesting, lovers. While Scott's historical settings are important to his plots, their significance lies more in providing a crucible in which his characters develop rather than convincing the reader of his novels' historical accuracy. The crucial interaction between character and the historical events of the era set a pattern in the genre—including young adult historical fiction—that has endured (to its advantage) down to the present. Novels such as Graham Salisbury's *Under the Blood Red Sun*, about a young Japanese boy living in Hawaii at the time of Pearl Harbor, or Ann Rinaldi's *Wolf by the Ears*, about the daughter of Thomas Jefferson's mistress Sally Hemmings, depend on their historical settings to create the story. Stripped of their historical elements, both stories would evaporate. The setting is integral to such novels, and is not merely a costumed backdrop. Katherine Paterson satirizes novels that merely use historical background as a peripheral backdrop as "bathrobe fiction" because the otherwise modern characters are simply dressed up in "pseudo-ancient dress."[12]

Historical novels for young adults are rarely if ever laden with footnotes, but many are prefaced by or concluded with notes by the author commenting on how the idea for the story evolved, on the research that the project necessitated, which characters and events are grounded in documented history, and how, in writing the narrative, the author gained a new perspective on the historical events and era covered in the story. Like footnotes, these comments help to strengthen the novel's credibility.

HISTORICAL FICTION IN THE UNITED STATES

Scott's influence traveled across the Atlantic to shape the novels of James Fenimore Cooper and his contemporaries. Cooper used native materials—the challenges of frontier living and the French and Indian wars—to dramatize the collision of opposing forces. Like Scott, he sometimes incorporated historical characters, most notably George Washington, whose presence struck a patriotic note and expressed Cooper's nationalistic ideology. In fact, Barbara Foley argues that all historical fiction expresses a particular ideology:

> Characters constitute a microcosmic portrayal of representative social types; they experience complications and conflicts that embody important tendencies in historical development; one or more world-historical figures enter the fictive world, lending an aura of extra-textual validation to the text's generalizations and judgments; the conclusion reaffirms the legitimacy of a norm that transforms social and political conflict into a moral debate.[13]

Cooper also injected Scott's romantic element into his narratives by creating characters such as a dashing rebel officer who falls in love with the daughter of a staunch loyalist. His portrayals of such relationships were insipid, but helped to further the tradition of historical romance. However, his novels are flawed by flat characterizations and overcrowded plots that also marked the work of his contemporaries and lent ammunition to later critics such as Mark Twain, who had little regard for Cooper, and Henry James, who expressed contempt for the genre. Many writers for young adults are aware of the risks of including in their novels too much information, however fascinating, that their research has uncovered. Elizabeth George Speare has explained that in deciding what research to include in a story, writers must ensure that every detail serves a purpose: "The fragment of history must take on a new color because it is seen through the eyes of a person and tinged with his emotion, or it must lend some of its own color to the character and be itself reflected in his thoughts and actions."[14] Joan Blos pokes fun at novels filled with too much detail as being written in "overstuffed sentences."[15]

Historical fiction in America received a critical validation with the work of Nathaniel Hawthorne, who found in Puritan New England an ideal setting to explore his near obsession with the consequences of sin. In 1850 he published *The Scarlet Letter*, his most successful novel. In this tale he developed more fully dimensional characters and thus infused genuine humanity into his protagonists. Can anyone read the forest scene between Hester Prynne and Arthur Dimmesdale and not be stirred by the subtle, yet intense passion between the lovers? Does not Dimmesdale's painfully public confession of adultery move one to empathy? The enthusiastic reception of *The Scarlet Letter* demonstrated that readers preferred becoming engrossed with the fate of believable characters to being inundated with a plethora of historical detail.

The publishing of historical fiction in America subsided during the Civil War era, but in the post–Civil War years, the genre gained popularity again. The plots of Cooper's novels that dramatized ill-starred couples from two families of conflicting political convictions or a single family divided within itself lent themselves well to a nation devastated by war and riven by politics. By now, historical fiction had created a romantic tradition. As in earlier decades, the post-Civil War novels were founded on historical assumptions that portrayed a clash between antagonistic ideologies—usually North versus South or pro-slavery forces versus abolitionists—represented by fictional characters, often lovers. By the final pages, the couple was usually united and the "sympathetic" historical force triumphed. Although ill-starred couples appear less frequently in YA historical fiction, the clash of opposing historical forces is a common element, e.g., slaves escaping from their masters, Jews trying to survive the Holocaust.

REALISM IN HISTORICAL FICTION

By the earliest twentieth century, realism became the dominant mode of fiction in general, a trend that impacted the historical novel. Stephen Crane wielded significant influence with his *Red Badge of Courage* by abandoning the structural trappings of historical romance, with its ideologically triumphant resolutions. Instead, he shifted the emphasis from the pomp and circumstance of glorified war to the ordeal of a young soldier as he faces his first battle. The lasting effect was to deglamorize and personalize the historical novel.

Crane's novel ran counter to the then-dominant paradigm for historiography, shaped largely by Thomas Carlyle's belief that history was the story of great men and their experiences. In the aftermath of *Red Badge of Courage,* the emphasis moved to a greater exploration of the experiences of ordinary people, to what historians call social history.[16] Faulkner, for example, accounts for the historical Southern mindset in his Yoknapatawpha County novels by using characters who represent historical significance but, with the exception of *Unvanquished,* little reference is made to famous generals or battles. Instead, these characters, ranging from the powerful to the oppressed, tell compelling stories of the pre– and post–Civil War South, often shifting narrative viewpoint from one character to another within a single novel.

The shift in interest from historical figures to commonplace individuals is evidenced in most recent young adult historical fiction, which tells the stories of "ordinary" adolescents. Even when historical figures enter the story, the focus is on the fictional young person. The legendary heads of state and their battles have receded into the background if they enter the story at all.

"ORDINARY" PEOPLE IN HISTORICAL FICTION

Novelist Kathryn Lasky calls the focus on ordinary people interacting with extraordinary events "keyhole history," an approach she has used often and effectively. When an editor at Scholastic Press requested a novel for the *Dear America* series, she asked Lasky "to delve into those moments of quiet dignity" in the life of an ordinary girl growing up in trying times.[17] Lasky, though pleased with the request, amended the proposition: she wanted also to include some "undignified" moments, such as "writing grocery lists, dealing with stomach aches, feeling frumpy, and being scared to death and mad as hell." Her request was anchored in a clear purpose:

> [W]hat I hope for young readers of my books is that they will see that history is not just reserved for great people or heroes or patriots . . . that there is distinction living an ordinary life with dignity, with hope and courage . . . that just being normal and ordinary had its own peculiar kind of grace. This is keyhole history.[18]

Although historical fiction has engaged readers and listeners for centuries, it failed to gain much impetus as a genre for young adults until the 1950s. There were some notable exceptions, such as Eric Kelly's *The Trumpeter of Krakow* and Carol Brink's *Caddy Woodlawn*, but in general the number of historical novels published for young adults was negligible. Not until the 1960s and 1970s did writers for adolescents begin to give the genre serious attention. Most of these earlier novels sprang from the imagination and careful research of British writers like Rosemary Sutcliff, Geoffrey Trease, and Leon Garfield, perhaps because historical fiction was a late-blooming genre in the United States. Harry B. Henderson offers a sound explanation:

> Initially, American writers felt that the nation had no history, no sense of the past comparable to that of European nations. Seventeenth- and eighteenth-century American writers saw the Past as something that existed only abroad, and if anything, America seemed to represent a break with the Past.[19]

Now, of course, American history has become an accepted subject for fiction, and young adult novels are no exception. As historical novelist Christopher Collier has said, "[T]here is no better way to teach history than to embrace potential readers and fling them into a living past."[20]

DEFINITIONS OF HISTORICAL FICTION

The stories that transport readers to Collier's "living past" are not easily categorized, for the genre labeled as "historical fiction" has been defined by various writers over time in various ways. Avrom Fleishman, in *The English Historical Novel: Walter Scott to Virginia Woolf,* excluded novels set less than two generations back in time, "novels without a number of historical events," particularly those in the public sphere—war, politics, economic change—and novels that do not involve "at least one . . . real person among the fictitious ones."[21] But these boundaries are too limited for most critics. David Cowart writes, "Historical fiction is fiction in which the past figures with some prominence. It does not require historical personages or events nor is it set at some specific remove in time. [It] is any novel in which a historical consciousness manifests itself strongly in either the characters or the action."[22] Geoffrey Trease, a prolific British novelist of historical fiction for young readers, has defined the genre as fiction set outside the time of living memory.[23] But historical novelist and essayist Thomas Mallon contradicts this definition by telling of writing *Aurora 7,* a historical novel he penned in 1988. This novel is set in 1962, during his childhood years that he remembers with great fondness: "I thought," he says, "that I was writing a book about childhood and change and the early days of space exploration," but realized as he worked that he obviously preferred living in 1962 to 1988. "I couldn't help but like being back in that personal Eden where the crabgrass was high and my mom was good-looking."[24]

As the above discussion indicates, there is no common agreement about the exact date or time period that separates "historical fiction" from other fiction. Young adult readers have not lived through events that constitute significant landmarks in the lives of older readers. In some years back, fiction set after World War II did not qualify as "historical." Now, of course, fiction written much more recently may qualify.

Amy J. Elias has offered a definition that is both concise and sufficiently encompassing. In *Sublime Desire: History and Post-1960s Fiction* she lists three primary characteristics that mark the genre:

1. specific historical detail, featured prominently, is crucial to plot or character development or some experimental representation of these narrative attributes;
2. a *sense* of history informs all facets of the fictional construct (from authorial perspective to character development to selection of place);
3. this sense of history emerges from and is constructed by the text itself.[25]

Because Elias's definition refrains from setting specific time limits, it helps to answer the question of how to categorize novels that are set in the present but whose main focus is on the past, with historical details portrayed perhaps in letters or diaries written by elderly or deceased characters or in conversations about the past by the contemporary characters. Elias would categorize such fiction as "historical." Her definition would also include such novels as *Little Women* and *Seventeenth Summer*. At the time of their publication, they were examples of contemporary realism but are set in what is now considered a "historical" period and meet Elias's criteria. Certainly, there is a distinction between fiction that from its inception is set in the past and fiction whose publication is contemporaneous with its readers; however, with the passage of time the latter involves readers in a historical period and imparts knowledge of it just as fiction does that is deliberately set in the past.

In fact, one could argue that all novels are "historical" in that they exist as artifacts of the era that generated them; thus, each of the above novels offers a clear (and historical) portrait of what was expected of adolescent girls in the 1860s (*Little Women*) and the 1940s (*Seventeenth Summer*): we learn about family loyalties, proper style of dress, relationships among peers and between the sexes during the time that each was published. Today's readers may be appalled or amused at the restrictions imposed on young women in earlier times, but the novels, ground-breaking when they first appeared in print, helped set standards of behavior for the young females.

Elias omits one final criterion that usually marks the genre: just as high fantasy involves a struggle between the forces of good and evil, historical fiction is marked by a clash between opposing socio-political powers. Samuel Taylor Coleridge, discussing the success of Scott's novels, maintained that the secret of his success was his subject—"the age-old contest between the forces of reaction and progress."[26]

This conflict is represented variously in young adult historical fiction that has been written as such, usually with reactionary characters pitted against a protagonist who signifies a more progressive element. And this criterion helps to distinguish between fiction whose authors have deliberately set their stories in the past and novels that gain the status of historical fiction only with the passage of time. Although the Civil War rages in the background of *Little Women,* it enters the story only peripherally. The central conflict lies in the four March sisters' attempt to conquer the obstacles that lie in the way of their maturing into "virtuous" young ladies. The struggles of Angie Morrow in *Seventeenth Summer* involve her skittish romance with the handsome Jack Duluth. Although the subtext of these novels touches on the issue of patriarchal hegemony, neither could accurately be described as a contest between reactionary and progressive forces. In *Little Women* Jo initially resists the constraints of her gendered role but develops into the "little woman" that nineteenth-century behavioral codes decreed. Of course, some novels with a contemporary setting may feature characters engaged in social or political issues (see discussion of *Mary Jane* in Chapter 2), but by and large, their struggles are less intense, more muted than those in historical fiction.

YOUNG ADULT HISTORICAL FICTION AS A BLEND OF GENRES

Complicating the issue of defining historical fiction is the fact that the genre includes a range of novels that differ as much from each other as novels of fantasy and contemporary realism. In fact, YA historical fiction often addresses the same issues as contemporary realism—e.g., family discord, maturation, death—and includes such widely diverse elements as horror, fantasy, romance, and adventure. For example, Kathryn Lasky's *True North*, set in 1858 and told from the alternating viewpoints of Lucy, a young and privileged Bostonian, and Afrika, an escaping slave, begins as a somber adventure story of Afrika's perilous journey north to freedom via the Underground Railway.[27] She must evade slave catchers and their dogs, slog through swamps, hide in a barrel beneath layers of smelly oysters and in a coffin beneath a corpse, and wade through a Boston sewer.

The initial phase of Afrika's journey ends when Lucy discovers the fugitive girl in a grandfather clock in the study of her deceased abolitionist grandfather. But a determined slave catcher from the South, posing as a refined businessman while courting one of Lucy's sisters, hopes to reap the monetary reward promised by the Fugitive Slave Act and is on Afrika's trail. Not yet out of danger, with Lucy's help, Afrika must escape to Canada.

Exactly who is this treacherous slave catcher? Detecting the answer to that question constitutes a mystery that winds through the novel, a mystery partially solved when his identity is revealed. But who has betrayed Lucy and Afrika to him? This question heightens the mystery and the suspense, and the girls' attempt to escape from him is the second part of their adventure.

True North also provides a social critique of the mid-nineteenth century. Flashbacks to Afrika's experiences on her owner's plantation paint a vivid and appalling picture of slavery: black children wrested from their parents and sold, black girls and women raped by their overseers and masters, slaves whose fingers and toes have been amputated because they were caught praying or learning to read, the brutal whippings, and humiliating slave auctions. Juxtaposed against the horrors of Afrika's life are the details of Lucy's life in upper-class Boston society that offer a scathing commentary on the rigid boundaries of women's lives, a theme also central to many YA novels set in contemporary times. Lucy is expected to spend hours embroidering monograms on her sister's wedding linens, a "cruel custom that yoked every female relative and every female servant in the bridal household to an embroidery hoop" (9–10). Unlike Afrika, who must endure daily heart-stopping dangers, Lucy finds her life boring. It is dominated by plans for her sister's wedding and her mother's careful adherence to what Lucy finds pointless social customs, for example the expectation that women keep their new gowns hidden away in tissue wrap for a full year before wearing them, lest they fail to show "proper" restraint. Given Lucy's longing for adventure and her resistance to the gendered constraints of her life, it is no surprise that her sympathies are readily enlisted to the cause of fugitive slaves.

Despite the accuracy of historical details in *True North,* this novel is not likely to have been written during the period that comprises its background. Like much recent YA historical fiction, it offers a revised perspective of the past. Contrary to the popular picture of New England as staunchly abolitionist, *True North* exposes the ambiguous political temper of antebellum Boston regarding the slavery issue. Many of Boston's leading families supported slavery, for the northern mills depended on Southern cotton planted, cultivated, and picked by slaves. As Lucy's father observes, "[L]iberal sympathies are going right out the window as they [mill owners] contemplate the future of their mills without a good steady flow of cotton" (66). And the novel makes painfully clear that the old mythic picture of happy slaves "down upon the Swanee River," as Stephen Foster's lyrics portrayed them, is a cruel misrepresentation of an abhorrent practice.

Caroline Cooney has also blended genres in her companion volumes, *Both Sides of Time, Out of Time,* and *Prisoner of Time.* They can technically be classified as historical fiction, for the female protagonist lives in the late nineteenth century, and her story offers details of upper-class life during that era. But the novels are primarily romances that incorporate fantasy—time travel—to rescue the doomed heroine from a forced engagement to a stuffy English lord. The contrast between the nineteenth- and twentieth-century lives of women provides, like *True North*, a comment on the constraints of women's lives and the rights that should be theirs. Cooney's novels stand in contrast to most of the romances written during the latter half of the nineteenth century, when "proper" women acceded to the demands of men, when propriety trumped personal desires. Also, some of the problems that trouble the heroine, such as the crushing bone stays of the female corset—de rigueur for securing the tiny waist so enviable among fashionably attired women—are, seen from the twenty-first century, as an outdated issue with little relevance to contemporary life other than as a symbol of patriarchal dominance.

THE WRITER'S PRESENT AS A PERSPECTIVE ON THE PAST

Thus, as much as readers might learn about the past from historical fiction, the genre also tells us much about the period in which the fiction was written, revealing writers' concerns about and attitudes towards the cultural tensions of their own times. Henry Seidel Canby noted this inevitability in 1927—almost 80 years ago—when he perceived that historical fiction is "more likely to register an exact truth about the writer's present than the exact truth of the past."[28] More recently, Katherine Paterson said, "I do not forget that it is my own twentieth-century identity that takes ancient events and sifts through them and creates the characters who allegedly took part in them."[29] In the same essay, Jill Paton Walsh agrees: "You often get highly contemporary attitudes, especially about trendy subjects, coming from characters in historical novels" (267).

Jane Tompkins echoes these attitudes in writing about the varying perspectives of actual historians. She observes that "if the experience of encountering conflicting versions of the 'same' events suggests anything certain, it is that the attitude a historian takes up in relation to a given event . . . [is] a function of the historian's position in relation to the subject."[30] If Tompkins' statement holds true for historians—writers whose interests lie mainly in rendering or interpreting past events with unerring accuracy rather than portraying fictional characters interacting with and responding to those events—then it is doubly true for fiction writers, whose imaginations create the characters who populate the past.

THE ATTRACTION FOR WRITERS OF HISTORICAL FICTION

Although contemporary realism remains the most popular genre among adolescents, historical fiction brings a unique dimension to their reading, and writers of the genre make a persuasive case for it. "Why write about the past when all our concerns are with the present?" asks Leon Garfield. "In fact, why bother with history at all?" He then answers his own questions with the hope that readers develop a deeper understanding of the present: "If the young discover that in the past they have been governed, led, abused, and slaughtered by fools and knaves, then perhaps they will look about them and see that matters have not greatly changed, and possibly they will do so before they vote."[31]

Similarly, Roberta Trites, concluding a book-length discussion of "power" in young adult novels in general, links her discussion to historical awareness, certainly an element that readers gain through engaging with historical fiction: "Part of creating more culturally aware readers is creating more historically aware students. Readers who . . . understand the historical context of what they read have a different understanding of a text than those who are isolated from such information."[32]

Erik Christian Haugaard makes a somewhat different argument, one drawn from his own experience of writing a historical novel when the war in Viet Nam was raging. Emotions ran high about the war, but Haugaard felt, lacking the distance of time, that this was no subject for his novel. Instead, he recalled a massacre analogous to the slaughter of Vietnamese civilians but that had occurred in a war between Denmark and Sweden. He opted to write a novel called *The Untold Tale,* for it was a subject "seldom or never" told but that would convey a similar story. He adds:

> I think one of the reasons I have been attracted to the historical novel can be found here. When you write a story that takes place in times long past, you are more free. Your readers have less prejudice and will accept your tale with open minds. You and your reader have less at stake, and thus you might get nearer the truth, possibly even to reality. For it is amazing how often sensitive, intelligent people can excuse or even condone the most despicable acts if perpetuated in the name of the politics they believe in or the nation they belong to.[33]

However persuasive these arguments for "historical awareness" or "truth," it is no easy task for an author to undertake the writing of historical fiction, a particularly demanding and problematic genre. Any writer who tells a story set in the past must negotiate the fine line between readers' contemporary sensibilities and historical accuracy. That writers continue to work in this genre, successfully engaging with the issues that define it, testifies to its value and viability. Reading these novels, we are reminded again and again that the issues of the past are inscribed on our own lives, that yesterday continues to impinge upon today.

NOTES

1. Marc Aronson, *Beyond the Pale* (Lanham, MD: Scarecrow Press, 2003), 62.

2. Patty Campbell, "The Young Adult Perplex," *Wilson Library Review* 55.3 (November 1980), 214.

3. Leon Garfield, "Historical Fiction for Our Global Times," *The Horn Book* (November/December 1988), 737.

4. Patty Campbell, "The Sand in the Oyster," *The Horn Book* (September/October 1996), 636.

5. Leon Garfield, quoted by Jo Carr in *Beyond Fact: Nonfiction for Children and Young People* (Chicago: American Library Association, 1982), 90.

6. Katherine Paterson, quoted in "In Their Own Words: Authors' Views on Issues in Historical Fiction," Lawrence R. Sipe, *The New Advocate*, 10.3 (Summer 1997), 243–58.

7. Chapter 2 examines this issue in more detail.

8. Alleen Pace Nilsen and Kenneth L. Donelson, *Literature for Today's Young Adults,* 2nd ed. (Glenview, Illinois: Scott, Foresman, 1985), 63.

9. Alleen Pace Nilsen and Kenneth L. Donelson, *Literature for Today's Young Adults,* 6th ed. (New York: Longman, 2001).

10. Barbara Foley, *Telling the Truth: The Theory and Practice of Documentary Fiction* (Ithaca, NY: Cornell UP, 1986), 107.

11. E. E. Leisy, *The American Historical Novel* (Norman, Oklahoma: University of Oklahoma Press, 1950), 8.

12. Katherine Paterson, "Where Is Terabithia?" In *Innocence and Experience: Essays and Conversations on Children's Literature*. Barbara Harrison and Gregory Maguire, eds. (NY: Lothrop, Lee, & Shepard, 1987), 227.

13. Foley, *Telling the Truth,* 160.

14. Elizabeth George Speare, Newbery Award Acceptance Speech, *The Horn Book* (August 1959), 269.

15. Joan Blos, "The Overstuffed Sentence and Other Means for Assessing Historical Fiction for Children," *School Library Journal* 32.3 (November 1985).

16. The need for such an approach is demonstrated in a comment by Henry Seidel Canby, then editor of the *Saturday Review of Literature*, when in 1927 he wrote, "The chronicles of the best known periods are full of gaps and silences. We know with a good deal of inaccuracy what men and women did, we know with much less accuracy of what they thought, we know still less what they were. . . . [In] history the great figures are recorded and almost nothing is known of the little ones, and hence over the historical novelist's story a spell of past greatness broods" ("What Is Truth?" *Saturday Review of Literature* 4.23, December 31, 1927), 481.

17. Kathryn Lasky, Presentation to the National Council of Teachers of English, November 1996.

18. Kathryn Lasky, "Keyhole History," *SIGNAL* 21.3 (Spring 1997), 10.

19. Harry Henderson, *Versions of the Past: The Historical Imagination in American Fiction* (NY: Oxford UP, 1974), 3.

20. Christopher Collier, quoted in Nilsen and Donalson, *Literature for Today's Young Adults,* 6th ed., 240.

21. Avrom Fleishman, *The English Historical Novel: Walter Scott to Virginia Woolf* (Baltimore: Johns Hopkins UP, 1971), 8.

22. David Cowart, *History and the Contemporary Novel* (Carbondale, IL: Southern Illinois UP, 1989), 5.

23. Geoffrey Trease, "The Historical Novelist at Work." In *Writers, Critics and Children: Articles from Children's Literature in Education,* Geoff Fox, et al., eds. (NY: Agathon Press, 1976), 42.

24. Thomas Mallon, "Writing Historical Fiction," *American Scholar* 61 (Autumn 1992), 604.

25. Amy J. Elias, *Sublime Desire: History and Post-1960s Fiction* (Baltimore: Johns Hopkins UP, 2001): 4–5. This last comment can be taken to mean that the historical aspect is not extraneous to the plot, not imposed upon, but "emerges" as an integral part of the story.

26. Samuel Taylor Coleridge, quoted by George Dekker in *The American Historical Romance* (New York: Oxford UP, 1987), 8.

27. Kathryn Lasky, *True North* (New York: Scholastic, 1998); hereafter cited parenthetically in the text.

28. Henry Seidel Canby, "What Is Truth?" 480.

29. Katherine Paterson, "Only a Lamp-holder: On Writing Historical Fiction." In *Innocence and Experience: Essays and Conversations on Children's Literature.* Barbara Harrison and Gregory Maguire, eds. (NY: Lothrop, Lee, & Shepard, 1987), 264.

30. Jane Tompkins, "Indians": Textualism, Morality, and the Problem of History." In *Ways of Reading,* 5th ed. David Bartholomae and Anthony Petrosky, eds. (Boston: Bedford/St. Martins, 1999), 685.

31. Leon Garfield, "Historical Fiction for Our Global Times," *The Horn Book* (November/December 1988), 738.

32. Roberta Trites, *Disturbing the Universe: Power and Repression in Young Adult Literature* (Iowa City, IA: University of Iowa UP, 2000), 147.

33. Haugaard, "Lamp-holder," 270.

· *2* ·

The Rise and Rise of YA Historical Fiction

> I had never thought of myself as a historical novelist: I didn't
> know that historical fiction was the bastard child of letters,
> respected neither as history nor as fiction.
>
> Katherine Paterson[1]

*K*atherine Paterson's statement is a reflection of the unexamined critical bias against historical fiction that dominated her early years as a young adult novelist and, indeed, much of the twentieth century. This bias has prevented a literary form, popular since its inception in the nineteenth century, from achieving "the place it deserves in literary history or the critical esteem it deserves," as Henderson argues in *Versions of the Past*.[2] He maintains that the problematic status of historical fiction is the result of two characteristics—its "impurity and vulgarity" (xv). Its "impurity" stems from the fact that it is neither fish nor fowl, neither pure history nor purely a product of the imagination. Its "vulgarity" stems from the fact that it tends to be viewed as middle-brow, popular, perhaps commercially successful, but lacking in artistic or literary merit (xv).

Jill Paton Walsh offers a similar explanation in more colorful terms: "Surely it has something to do with the fact that historical fiction is a mixed form, and open—as mixed forms tend to be—to devastating objections based on principle, very much like those of the man at the opera who objected, 'But people in danger of death don't sing!'"[3]

THE RISING POPULARITY OF YOUNG ADULT
HISTORICAL FICTION

The critical tendency to dismiss adult historical fiction has been evident in young adult historical fiction as well. But since 1986 when the Pleasant Company began publishing the wildly popular *American Girl* series, historical fiction has undergone a surge of popularity.[4] An appetite for these novels, one fed by the sophisticated marketing of a variety of accessories ranging from dolls to clothing for the young readers themselves, has left young readers, and often their parents, eager for more titles. And when follow-up series like *Dear America* or *Young Royals* sold enough to be considered solid successes, publishers were forced to revisit their notion that "Kids don't like historical fiction."[5] What they found involved economics as well as a redefinition and reassessment of the genre and a broader understanding of what constitutes acceptable subjects for the study of history.

MARKETING YOUNG ADULT HISTORICAL FICTION

The first of these, economics, is perhaps the most easily established. Markets breed markets, and publishers, seeing the success of the *American Girl* series, have jumped on the proverbial bandwagon and published their own series of young adult historical fiction. Patty Campbell has noted that the *American Girl* series was quickly followed by Aladdin's *American Diaries*, Avon's *American Dreams* and Scholastic's *Dear America*.[6]

Successful marketing campaigns have placed their products not only in bookstores but, more importantly, in the classroom as well. Promoted as viable supplements to whatever texts a teacher currently uses to teach subjects ranging from history to literature, publishers have, in effect, gained not just a captive audience, but more importantly, one made up of highly impressionable consumers with an increasingly large disposable income. Correlative to this explanation is that children and young adults read what is available to them. The appearance of these books in classrooms and bookstores not only provides a seemingly official endorsement but makes them easily accessible to young readers.

THE PSYCHOLOGICAL APPEAL OF HISTORICAL FICTION

Another explanation, one promoted by several authors of the genre, is that the past has an innate psychological appeal that publishers and teachers have for too long ignored in their rush to promote realistic fiction. Author Thomas Mallon, for example, maintains that the past has always had an appeal to readers that neither social realism nor science fiction can offer. Describing the past as "more familiar, cherishable than the future," Mallon maintains that the *known* past provides a comfort not available from the *unknown* future.[7] This is not to romanticize history but rather to suggest that to immerse oneself, however briefly, in a past world where conflict and strife occur and are resolved may provide comfort in an increasingly chaotic world.

Charles Frazier, author of the best-selling post–Civil War novel *Cold Mountain,* articulates a comparable explanation when he describes his own fascination with the past, particularly with its sense of "community" and "home," qualities he sees as absent in the "modern world."[8] Likewise, Kathryn Lasky, recalling her childhood reading tastes, describes the pleasure she has derived from historical fiction even more strongly: "I didn't want to be in the present. I wanted the past. It seemed more dramatic, more challenging, more eventful, more of a tapestry."[9] Recently, an increasing number of readers and writers have come to share Mallon, Frazier, and Lasky's attraction to the past.

NEW SUBJECTS FOR HISTORICAL FICTION

A final rationale for historical fiction's popularity may be that recent redefinitions and broadening of what is considered appropriate subjects for historical fiction have increased the choices for writers of the genre. Contemporary historians draw from a more diverse canvas than their predecessors: rather than follow Thomas Carlyle's narrow nineteenth-century focus on great men and their experiences, historians have developed what they call microhistory to explore a single village or individual. Viable subjects now include stories of domestic life, women, children, and slaves, so often invisible to the historian's eye in the past. Novelist Jane Smiley endorses this development: "Historians are not just doing the same old narratives of the same old wars. . . . Historians are doing different research, into mores and private lives."[10] The shift away from Carlyle's "great man" theory of history that Smiley so aptly describes is apparent when we compare two young adult novels set during the American Revolutionary war written almost a century apart.

The first, *The Quaker Spy: A Tale of the Revolutionary War,* by Lionel Lounsberry was published in 1889 as part of the *Boys of Liberty Library* series. The second, *The Winter of Red Snow: The Revolutionary War Diary of Abigail Jane Stewart,* written by Kristina Gregory, was published in 1996 by Scholastic as part of *Dear America* series. The titles alone suggest that the novels are directed toward different audiences, the first a male and the second a female. But the texts themselves suggest more significant, telling changes in the genre.

The inside cover's description of the *Boys of Liberty Library* series stresses the publishers' ideological goal as well as what they believe constitutes the books' appeal: "The stories are written in an intensely interesting style, and no boy can read them without being aroused to the highest pitch of patriotic enthusiasm."[11] To this end the writer presents the reader with characters that embody both gender and historical stereotypes. The main character, Adab Slocomb, a nineteen-year-old Quaker blacksmith, is heroic both in physical and moral stature. Like such heroes of mythical literature as Achilles or Beowulf, Adab's overall superiority to other men is revealed first through his superior physique. His "giant form . . . was made up of bone, muscle and hard flesh" (20). Though only nineteen, Adab shows a confidence and wit seldom found in one so young. When his mother objects to her Quaker son violating his peace testimony to join the "godless men of war" (6), Adab, not missing a beat, responds, "I go as a man of peace, not as a slayer of men, or a shredder of blood. There are many ways in which I can serve Friend George Washington, and my country, too, without placing a sword on my thigh or a musket to my shoulder" (6).

Like Adab, George Washington himself is depicted as confident, selfless, and oblivious to the physical privations he suffers at Valley Forge. The reader is intended to understand that a good part of his heroic stature is the result of his transcending the emotions ordinary humans feel under stress. When confronted with the despair of his fellow generals, he resorts to clichés that would hardly motivate a dispirited army: "Gentlemen, there is no excuse for such utter despondency. There was never yet a night without a day to follow it" (16). Washington's optimism flies in the face of military logic, for the enemy forces "now held a great part of Eastern New York and all of New Jersey" (15) and the American troops have been "lessened by two thirds by desertion and losses" (15).

Indeed, though there are moments of solemnity in *The Quaker Spy*, good cheer and the product of Adab's can-do spirit seem to prevail. The mercenary and theoretically blood-thirsty Hessians—referred to by minor characters as those "sassy Hessians," hardly a term to inspire fear—are easily killed by one of Adab's ruses. Early in the novel it becomes clear that though Adab risks his life as he takes on a series of missions for Washington, he will meet each challenge with aplomb and an adage bound to leave the adults around him slack-jawed with awe at his composure and wisdom. There is never a moment in which the reader doubts Adab's success even when he is confronted with execution.

A grimmer tone dominates *The Winter of Red Snow: The Revolutionary War Diary of Abagail Jane Stewart,* one of the *Dear America* series titles. Though young like Adab, Abigail shares none of his calmness or certainty that goodness will prevail. And the reader quickly understands why she doesn't. *The Winter of Red Snow* begins with a scene fraught with pain and anxiety: Abigail has been up since four in the morning, awakened by the cries of her mother who is in labor. Unlike Adab who, no doubt, would heat some water and simultaneously deliver both the baby and a sermon, Abigail feels all the fear and anxiety a young girl might be expected to feel seeing her mother in pain and knowing that the baby might arrive before the midwife: "I began to cry," she admits.[12]

Though the midwife does arrive in time to deliver the baby, Abigail's first diary entry does not end on a note of unmitigated joy. She notes that though her father laughs with joy at the arrival of a son, her mother "is as worried as I am" (4). We learn in the next diary entry the cause of that worry: Abigail's mother has already "birthed "nine children, three daughters and six sons, and "We have not had a brother live through the winter" (4). While the deaths of so many infants may not have the dramatic impact of Adab's potential hanging, those deaths do provide insight into the kinds of daily stresses and sorrows that characterized early Americans' lives. The significant shift in what is considered appropriate subjects of history that Jane Smiley described is vividly illustrated here. Childbirth and its risks as well as a young girl's emotional reaction to them provide a viable subject matter for a young adult novel.

This shift not only offers a broader choice of subject matter but pushes the reader to reconsider the nature of heroism and to see it not only in the acts of espionage or derring-do that Adab engages in but in the quiet acts of endurance experienced by those not previously considered worthy as subject matter. As *The Winter of Red Snow* unfolds, we recognize that Abigail is as heroic as Adab. We also see that she is a more fully drawn, nuanced character than he.

Finally, the postmodern blurring of genres and the consequent enthusiasm for hybrid literary forms suggests not only new subjects for the historical novel but new ways of writing it as well. Consider the status of Dan Brown's *The Da Vinci Code* for adult readers: the novel is set in the present but examines the past to reinterpret the Gospels of the New Testament to solve a complicated mystery, ultimately assigning a surprising role to Mary Magdalene; in YA historical fiction, there are such novels as *Out of the Dust*, a Depression-era story told in free verse, with each episode rendered in one- or two-page poems.

HISTORICAL FICTION AS SERIES NOVELS

Aggressive marketing by publishers intent on taking advantage of a profitable trend, a more comprehensive understanding of the nature of historical fiction, a broader acceptance of what constitutes appropriate subjects for historical study, as well as the psychological appeal of the past, interdependently explain the current popularity of historical fiction in general and of young adult fiction in particular. But for young adult readers the increasing popularity of this phenomenon cannot be separated from the popularity of the series novels. Indeed, the popularity of young adult historical fiction seems tightly connected to the marketing of these, and so we need to understand both the history of the series novel as well as its role in young adult historical fiction's recent popularity.

If historical fiction has, as a whole, suffered from a negative reputation, how much more problematic is the reputation of those books cursed by the double whammy of being both historical *and* series novels? One imagines them written, published, and read with the shame and embarrassment of the popular yellow-backed French novels of the eighteenth and nineteenth centuries. But no such thing. Young adults, their parents, and teachers—groups noteworthy for seldom sharing similar tastes—have enthusiastically embraced historical series such as *American Girl, Dear America, American Diaries, American Dreams*, and the *Young Royals*. If, as some critics maintain, the writing of these novels is "pedestrian" (Campbell 638), how do we account for the almost instant and continued popularity of these books among such disparate audiences? Beyond the undisputed profitability of these books for their publishers, what cultural work do they do, either overtly or covertly? And is that work of the sort that advances young readers' understanding of the world and their place in it? To answer these questions we need to understand the debates and tensions that have surrounded series novels in general and the different functions they serve for young adult readers and their adult counterparts. To do this, we also need to acknowledge that the category of "young adult reader" embraces a span of several years during which reading levels and interests vary widely. This alone suggests one explanation for the varying degrees in quality of the series novels.

Nancy Romolav, in her essay, "Children's Series Books and the Rhetoric of Guidance: A Historical Overview," convincingly argues that the "emergence of the public library movement . . . specifically the rise of children's services in the library"[13] was responsible for the creation of series novels. She further contends that public librarians, trained to view the library as a "moral force" (114), saw their particular "mission" as maintaining the distinctions between low and high culture (113). As a moral agent, the librarian's task was to promote high culture and to attempt to suppress low. Romalov argues that the popularity of series novels (as well as adults' ambivalence toward them) can be traced to the nineteenth century and parallels librarians' awareness that children were reading low fictions, such as dime novels and other sensationalist literature of the sort Jo March writes in *Little Women* before she falls under Professor Bahr's edifying influence. Such books, librarians believed, "incited readers to disrespect authority and created a taste for the sensational, the ugly, or the merely mediocre" (114). This realization led, first, to the decision to lower the age at which children would be admitted to the library and, perhaps more importantly, to the development of specialized children's services within the library. While librarians embraced the idea of exposing children to "high culture," their desire to do so was often curtailed by classist assumptions, especially as they applied to immigrant children who were, as one librarian maintained, "born and bred in the habitation of labor . . . cannot and will not read, as a rule, what I am willing to recommend."[14] For these lower-level and, one gathers, recalcitrant readers, popular books, such as those by Horatio Alger, were an acceptable choice (114). Mediocre as these books might be, their overt didacticism encouraged librarians to believe that, given the clear moral of the story, such texts might lead children to better things—if not a more elevated taste in literature, then a clearer understanding of appropriate behavior. Romalov notes that "one librarian even suggested that 'any book which showed a child from a poorer class of laborers how well-born people acted and spoke was of value even though it was neither a classic nor likely to endure'" (114).

Intent as librarians were on promoting literature that was "wholesome" (114), it is ironic that they resisted the series novels that began to be mass-marketed at the turn of the century. Advertisements for series novels, such as one for the Marjorie Dean series, promoted these products as "clean, wholesome stories that will be of great interest to all girls of high school age" (115). The cover graphics of such novels reinforced the publishers' contention that the books contained only the most wholesome fare. The covers for the *Motor Maids* series, for example, show four cheerful girls, either in or by a car, waving or pointing enthusiastically at an object of nature or a man-made marvel such as an early airplane. And a special effort was made to convince readers that these novels were free of the sensationalism that characterized their predecessor, the dime novel. The *Girl Scout* series promised to be "absolutely free from cheap sensationalism, yet legitimately absorbing, genuinely modern . . . the characters are modeled from . . . the highest ideals of girlhood" (116). In fact, a reader today would be hard pressed to find anything objectionable in these novels other than the relentless good cheer and the pluckiness of the characters. But librarians, unable to critique the moral content of series novels, instead focused on aesthetic concerns such as "the quality of the prose and the nature of the book's production." Romolav shows that much of "anti-series rhetoric is characterized by vague generalizations, name-calling, dire warnings and subtle pressures. If [librarians] could no longer confidently label these books as 'bad,' they would at least campaign against mediocrity" (115).

The aesthetic critique is still leveled at series books and, in particular, at historical series books. Patty Campbell describes the writing of the *American Girls* series, for example, as "earnest but rather pedestrian"[15] and the diary format of the *Dear America* series as "boring" (638). A perhaps more serious criticism, though, is that these books, though marketed as historically accurate, are in many respects inaccurate and promote stereotypes that reinforce the hegemony of the dominant culture while negating the experiences of historically marginalized groups. Certainly the marketing materials of some of the series suggest this is the case. Pleasant T. Rowland, founder and president of the Pleasant Company that created the irst historical series, *American Girl,* writes in her company's catalogue, "The *American Girl Collection* was created to give girls an understanding of their past and a ense of pride in the traditions they share with girls of yesterday."[16] The didactic lesire to instill a "sense of pride" in the readers of the *American Girl* series differs only in the degree of overtones from the goals of the *Boys of Liberty* series publishers, who in 1889 wished to rouse their readers to "the highest pitch of patriotism." While in each case the publishers' desire to instill pride and patriotism may be genuine, it is at the expense of reinforcing mainstream cultural narratives. It can also be viewed as an attempt to make palatable a literary form historically suspect. To further this end, each of the *American Girl* books includes a section titled "A Peek into the Past" intended to provide the historical context in which the protagonist's adventures occur. Yet, Daniel Hade, analyzing a single paragraph from a ection of the *Meet Kirsten* volume in the *American Girl* series, points out at least ix errors including "misspelled names, inaccurate routes, and misleading statements about what life in Sweden was like" (157). The inaccuracies Hade points out highlight one of the difficulties writers of historical fiction face. Their desire to create an emotionally engaging and credible fictional world may come at the expense of historical accuracy. Commenting on this tension, novelist Russell Banks says, "I assume . . . when a reader opens my novel, he or she will do so knowing that I have not written it as a biographer or historian."[17] Gary Jennings, another writer of historical fiction, is quoted in the same text, saying bluntly, "Shit. . . I was writing a novel, not a Ph.D. thesis" (19).

But Hade convincingly argues that the overall effect of all of these errors s "to support one of the great myths of United States history—that the United States was a land of opportunity, that it was the *new* world, a land of progress filled with new vitality, and new technology as opposed to a Europe that was old, tired, and behind the times" (158). He further argues that by promoting this myth, the *American Girl* books "put forth a romantic America, where all needs are met by opportunity, where poverty and oppression can be easily solved by the initiative of a young child" (163). Hade objects not to the fact that the *American Girl* books have an ideology (all texts do; some are simply more overt than others) but rather to the particular ideology of these series books, which he finds both naive and ethnocentric. But when one remembers the extensive product catalogue of dolls, doll furniture, doll clothes, as well as clothing for the readers themselves that are marketed as necessary accoutrements to the *American Girl* reading experience, it makes sense that the Pleasant Company would promote what Hade describes as a "feel-good, progress-oriented version of American history" (158). Feeling ashamed or guilty about one's historical heritage is unlikely to loosen the parental purse strings that need to be opened in order to consume all of the accessories necessary to have or share the experience of an "American Girl."

The huge success of the *American Girl* series led to the publication c other series such as Aladdin's *American Diaries,* Avon's *American Dreams,* Random House's *Ellis Island,* and Scholastic's *Dear America*, *My Name Is America,* an *Royal Diaries.* To what extent are these series prone to the same errors an damaging assumptions of their predecessor? To what extent are these problem inherent in the series format itself and, hence, unavoidable? To answer thes questions we need to examine both the history of the series novels in th twentieth century as well as criticisms leveled at them.

The Stratemeyer syndicate, responsible for some of the most popular se ries novels of the first half of the twentieth century—e.g., *Nancy Drew*, *Th Hardy Boys*, *The Bobbsey Twins*, and the *Rover Boys*—initiated the practice c having their books written by multiple authors and yet published under a sin gle pseudonym. This practice, coupled with strict authorial guidelines, facili tated the rapid production of multiple novels during the course of a single yea a practice clearly intended to increase profits as well as take advantage of youn readers' affection for a familiar cast of characters.

THE DIARY FORMAT AND YOUNG ADULT
HISTORICAL FICTION

Today's publishers no longer promote series novels as the work of a single au thor unless, indeed, they are, as in the case of Kathleen Duey's *American Diarie.* A quick survey of the *Dear America* novels shows only a few by the same au thors; Kathryn Lasky, Kristiana Gregory, and Barry Denenberg have writte several novels for this series. Though all of the authors in this series are con strained by the diary format, they nevertheless use it with varying degrees c success. Some authors work within the diary format better than others, and th suggests one explanation for the varying quality of the books. Critics have ar gued that the diary format is innately boring, unlikely as it is to employ th amount of dialogue that often moves plot in young adult novels, and the fic tive authors of these diaries are more likely to record external events rathe than to participate in them.

All of these assumptions can and should be challenged. While the diar may not offer the opportunities for dialogue or plot development of the nove in the hands of a skillful writer, say a Samuel Pepys or an Anne Frank, it ha provided the equally strong pleasures of taking the reader into a mind bein shaped by events outside of the author's control. Thomas Mallon writes, "Di aries were my first real love as a literary critic."[18] And when we consider hov many adolescents succumb to the marketing of blank diaries and the thrill c having a private place to keep their innermost thoughts, we are forced to chal enge the notion that diaries are innately boring. The popularity of the *Dear America* series suggests that young adult readers are drawn to a format that seemingly provides insight to another's most private thoughts.[19]

Rebecca Barnhouse, in *Recasting the Past: The Middle Ages in Young Adult Literature,* raises a more concrete, more understandable criticism of the diary format.[20] All of these books necessarily assume a relatively high level of literacy, an assumption that often strains credulity. In *Nzingha: Warrior Queen of Matamba,* one of Scholastic's *Royal Diaries* series novels, the reader is asked to believe that Nzingha has learned to read and write from a Portuguese priest, Father Giovanni Gavazzi, who lived in her father's court for years. While the presence of the priest in the tribe is verifiable and the source of much early information about Nzingha's life, there is no historical evidence to suggest that she was able to read or write. Commendably, the *Royal Diaries* series include significantly more historical context than other series: background on the characters, maps, photographs, and information on primary sources, and clear acknowledgements of when the author is speculating and when facts have been tweaked in order to accommodate the narrative. Nonetheless, the basic assumption that all of its subjects were capable of recording their thoughts is an inevitable, unavoidable weakness once a publisher commits to the diary format.

COMBATING STEREOTYPES IN YOUNG ADULT HISTORICAL FICTION

Perhaps more significant are the criticisms that historical series novels promote stereotypes of both character and ideology. These stereotypes, critics argue, are damaging to young adult readers' fundamental understanding of their place in the world and the extent to which that place has been shaped by historical forces beyond individual control. The accuracy of this criticism varies from series to series. Hade's criticism of the *American Girl* series coupled with Pleasant Rowland's comments in her company's catalogue suggest that that particular series does promote the dominant narratives surrounding the American dream in all of its feel-good glory. But can all the historical series be faulted on this count? A quick survey of some of the most popular—*Dear America, Ellis Island,* and *Young Royals*—suggest they do not and for a very good reason. Many of the books in those series are, unlike the *American Girl* texts, based on a specific historical event rather than a century.[21] Two of the titles from the *Dear America* series, for example, make this clear: *Voyage of the Great Titanic: The Diary of Margaret Anne Brady* and *A Journey to the New World: The Diary of Remember Patience Whipple.* Likewise, *My Name is America* series includes *The Journal of Douglas Allen Deeds: The Donner Party Expedition,* and the *Young Royals* series tells of *Beware, Princess Elizabeth,* and *Mary, Bloody Mary*. The authors of each of these titles, either by anchoring his or her character and plot to a particular or actual historical personage, is forced to work more closely within a verifiable historical framework than an author who chooses a broad period of time. A consequence of tying their characters and plot to a specific historical event is that authors are able to avoid the relentlessly upbeat and inaccurate ideology in the *American Girl* series that Hade criticizes. Other than the mere fact of survival, (which history precludes in some texts, such as Caroline Meyers' *Anastasia: The Last Grand Duchess* of the *Royal Diaries* series), one would be hard-pressed to find very much uplifting in the diaries of either the Titanic or Donner expeditions, events that do not lend themselves to happy endings. Each of the above mentioned diaries makes human fragility painfully clear. And in neither story is redemption found through the efforts of a child. In addition, the afterwords of each book make clear that the survivors of these events were permanently scarred by their traumatic experiences. Likewise, the stories of the two Tudor Queens Mary and Elizabeth I in Harcourt's *Young Royals* series—*Mary, Bloody Mary* and *Beware, Princess Elizabeth*—are both narratives of loss and suffering and, as such, are psychologically nuanced in a way that earlier series novels are not. Both young women, surviving events they cannot control, eventually rule England, but Carolyn Meyer, the author of these books, makes clear that they do so at great cost and are emotionally crippled by the various forms of abuse they survive. Like many books directed toward adolescent readers, these novels end when the characters are still adolescent. But because these books are based on actual historical personages, the authors must incorporate on some level those issues that color the adult life lived beyond the pages of the novel, even if only to imply them. The afterwords frequently do this and, in so doing, make clear that the happy endings of the *American Girl* series seldom occurred in the real lives of the characters about which authors such as Meyers write. Mary and Elizabeth achieved both wealth and power, but their lives were characterized by sacrifice, contradictions, and great complexity. Similarly, although removed in time and geography, the royal Anastasia died at sixteen, a victim of the brutal mass murder of her entire family.

Like any other form of literature, series novels have an ongoing, evolving history, one shaped by the material conditions and cultural narratives that give rise to them. Both of these factors provide a framework for analysis and critique that compels us to acknowledge that though early historical series novels for young adults were often characterized by formulaic plots, mediocre writing, and an unexamined commitment to reinforcing existing power structures, the genre has evolved, and those features, while they may exist, are no longer characteristic. Not surprisingly, these changes simultaneously reflect cultural shifts, and they pave the way for further evolution of the genre. The first of the young adult series, *American Girl*, emerged in the 1980s, during the

Reagan presidency, a time when the dominant political discourse was one of boundless optimism and a renewed belief in the rightness of all things American. It was a time when American people and values were seen as predominantly white and middle-class. The young adult series novels that emerged at that time tended to reflect a cultural narrative of success that can be traced back to John Winthrop's notion of the new world as a shining "city upon a hill," an idea reinforced by texts as diverse as the autobiographies of Benjamin Franklin and Andrew Carnegie and the novels of Horatio Alger.[22]

In this postmodern era, with its increased global uncertainties and emphasis on multiculturalism, there is a reluctance to replicate discourses that reinforce white privilege, an ideology implicit and unquestioned in early series. Current authors are more likely to contest the "feel-good "attitudes that characterized early series novels as well as the notion that individual effort and good will alone can shape social forces to desired ends that are demonstrably happy and in which justice is served. The more recent tendency of series novels to focus on events that have been disastrous (the *Island* series) or to explore the complex nature of the immigrant experience (the *Ellis* series), all depicting adolescence as psychologically complex, have resulted in novels that necessarily reflect the darker discourse that now dominates public life. As a result, novels are more thoughtful than their ancestors of the nineteenth and early twentieth centuries and better written than their antecedents of the 1980s because they *are* more complex, more complicated.

The more complex ideology that informs more recent series novels also allows for more complex portrayals of character, setting, and plot. The *Young Royals* series, for example, makes clear that being a princess involved more than outwitting wicked stepmothers and attending balls. Equally clear is that princesses are as capable of anger, hurt, and vindictiveness as the average human being. Consequently, the negative aesthetic judgments that were made about earlier novels are now suspect. Certainly, the contributions to series fiction by reputed young adult authors such as Carolyn Meyers and Kathryn Lasky raise the bar in terms of quality of writing and in so doing call into question the assertion that these novels are, across the board, poorly written. Likewise, their most common format, the diary or journal, is not in itself inherently boring and provides for many readers the sense of being invited into an inner life previously closed to them. Again, it is not the format that is a problem but rather how that format is handled.

Series novels have been a profitable undertaking for publishers since the nineteenth century. That readers can still purchase *The Bobbsey Twins*, *Nancy Drew*, and *The Hardy Boys* is evidence of this. The more recent incorporation of historical series novels into the curricula as educational supplements ensures ongoing commercial success while presenting educators with the task of separating wheat from chaff or determining literary dross from gold. The use of multiple authors presents both challenges and rewards. Some writers will be more adept at writing historical fiction than others, unavoidably resulting in uneven quality within any given series. But the use of authors with established reputations—reputations which these writers have an investment in preserving—may well result in a movement away from formulaic novels. Finally, the awareness that every literary text, whether historical fiction or contemporary social realism, embodies an ideology, provides teachers and other educators with the opportunity to hone critical thinking skills by making young readers aware of the ways in which ideology both manifests itself in a text and shapes our understanding of the past.

NOTES

1. Paterson, "Only a Lamp-holder: On Writing Historical Fiction." In *Innocence and Experience,* Harrison and Maguire, eds., 263.

2. Henderson, *Versions of the Past,* xv.

3. Jill Paton Walsh, "History Is Fiction," *The Horn Book* (February 1972), 17.

4. Campbell, "Sand in the Oyster," 637.

5. Campbell, "Sand in the Oyster," 636.

6. Campbell, "Sand in the Oyster," 636.

7. Mallon, "Writing Historical Fiction," 606.

8. Charles Frazier, quoted in "The Pinnacle of Success," *Newsweek* (April 6, 1998), 64.

9. Kathryn Lasky, "The Fiction of History: What Did Miss Kitty Really Do?" *The New Advocate* 3.3, (Summer 1990): 159; hereafter cited parenthetically in text.

10. Jane Smiley, quoted in "Recasting the Past," *Newsweek* (April 6, 1998), 65.

11. Lionel Lounsberry, *The Quaker Spy: A Tale of the Revolutionary War.* (Philadelphia: David McKay Publisher, 1889), frontispiece; hereafter cited parenthetically in text.

12. Kristiana Gregory, *The Winter of Red Snow: The Revolutionary War Diary of Abigail Jane Stewart, Valley Forge Pennsylvania, 1777* (New York: Scholastic, 1996), 4; hereafter cited parenthetically in text.

13. Nancy Romolav, "Children's Series Books and The Rhetoric of Guidance: A Historical Overview." In *Rediscovering Nancy Drew,* Carolyn Stewart Dyer and Nancy Tillman Romolav, eds. (Iowa City: University of Iowa Press, 1995), 113; hereafter cited parenthetically in text.

14. Deidre Johnson, "From Paragraphs to Pages: The Writing and Development of the Stratemeyer Syndicate Series." In *Rediscovering Nancy Drew,* Dyer and Romolav, eds., 21.

15. Campbell, "Sand in the Oyster," 637.

16. Daniel Hade, "Lies My Children's Books Taught Me: History Meets Popular Culture in 'The American Girls' Books." In *Voices of the Other: Children's Literature and the Postcolonial Context,"* Roderick McGillis, ed. (New York: Garland, 1999), 156.

17. Mark C. Carnes, ed., *Novel History: Historians and Novelists Confront America's Past (and Each Other)* (New York: Simon and Schuster, 2001), 19.

18. Mallon, "Writing Historical Fiction," 605.

19. So credible are these diaries to readers that teens often believe the *Dear America* series are actual historical documents—a misconception fostered by the publishers downplaying the real author's name on the cover. We would argue that this attempt at realism is misleading and should be clarified for the series' young audience.

20. Rebecca Barnhouse, *Recasting the Past: The Middle Ages in Young Adult Literature* (Portsmouth, NJ: Boynton/Cook, 2000), 9.

21. However, *My Heart Is on the Ground,* of the *Dear America* series, has been roundly criticized for its cultural inaccuracy of Native Americans.

22. Roger Betsworth, "The Gospel of Success in America." In *Social Ethics: An Examination of American Moral Traditions* (Louisville, KY: Westminster/John Knox Press, 1990), chapter 3.

· 3 ·

The "Truth" of Young Adult Historical Fiction

> So very difficult a matter to trace and find out the truth of anything
> by history.
>
> *Parallel Lives*, "Pericles," Plutarch

$\mathscr{P}$lutarch surely knew whereof he spoke. In writing about the famous Roman and Greeks who were his subjects, he described important events with immense skill but sometimes doubtful accuracy. His accounts are livelier for the dialogue he invented and the emotions he portrayed, but over 2,000 years later, writers and literary critics are still debating just how much freedom should be allowed to authors in developing their historical subjects. What is the line between fiction and fact? And what is a satisfactory balance between the two in historical fiction?

THE PROBLEM OF "TRUTH" IN HISTORICAL FICTION

Most readers of historical fiction usually assume that a historical novel, although fictitious, has a certain authenticity or that it conveys the "truth" about a certain period or event—if not a literal truth, then an emotional one. Yet writers of historical fiction must find a balance between historicizing fiction and fictionalizing history. Most responses to this issue stress the interpretative nature of both history and fiction. Along this line, Jill Paton Walsh, a British author who has written both history and historical novels for young adults, contends that more than careful research binds the two. She suggests that history is as much *fict* (Latin for "something made") as *fact* ("something done"). She adds that while evidence of history exists, it is itself "a construct of the mind," but adds that to be a good historical novelist, one has to be as good at history as any historian

32

Kathryn Lasky, prolific author of young adult historical novels, points to the myriad interpretations of what she calls "plain history" by historians, arguing that they rarely do it "plain" and that no history, whether within a novel or a history text, can be without bias.[2] In other words, for both the novelist and the historian, meaning lies not in a chain of events themselves but in each writer's interpretation of those events.

This argument is valid, but it ignores a major difference in the respective approaches of historians and novelists. The historian's methodology is necessarily broader and examines more historical complexities in tracking causes of events and their consequences. While historians may use digressions and footnotes to qualify and explain, successful historical novelists must forego the more expansive canvas in order to create characterizations and focused, forward-moving plot lines that arrive, finally, at resolutions often denied to history.

Margaret Atwood, in an essay exploring her experiences while writing a historical novel about an actual historical figure named Grace Marks, notes the necessity for minute details often ignored by the historian: "History may intend to provide us grand patterns and overall schemes, but without its brick-by-brick, life-by-life, day-by-day foundations it would collapse. . . . The shot heard round the world was fired on a certain date, under certain weather conditions, out of a certain inefficient type of gun."[3]

British historian Edward Hallett Carr has pushed this point further, maintaining that if history itself is a construct, the novelist may take the liberty to play with and even invent facts, to draw upon facts a historian would consider trivial. As an example, he says that historians may be interested in the fact that Henry VIII was a bad husband "only insofar as it affected historical events," but the novelist will view this king's repeated connubial executions as itself a historical phenomenon that may have affected history in "ways more subtle than whether or not the king made a poor decision after a sleepless night over a decapitated wife."[4] In other words, the novelist is interested, as Naomi Jacobs says in *The Character of Truth: Historical Figures in Contemporary Fiction,* not only "in what can be more or less proved to have happened but also in what *might* [italics ours] have happened, in this world or some amusing version of it."[5] Along the same line of reasoning, Atwood describes her "guidelines" in writing historical fiction: "if there was a solid fact, I could not alter it; . . . [but] in the parts left unexplained—the gaps left unfilled—I was free to invent" (1512). To which historian Jonathan Spence replies, "The historian is not free to invent whenever he finds gaps left unfilled."[6] So what is the "truth" of historical fiction? "Fiction," says Jacobs, echoing a line from Emily Dickinson, "tells its truth slantwise, like any mirror" (195), and the writer of historical fiction is bound to a "truth" that cannot contradict that which is "known" to be true—but is more free than the historian to "fill in the gaps."

Chris Crowe, educator and author, has, fortuitously enough, written two books on the same subject, the lynching of Emmett Till—one nonfiction, the other fiction. The nonfiction text is titled *Getting Away with Murder: The True Story of the Emmett Till Case*.[7] The historical novel is *Mississippi Trial, 1955*.[8] Both cover the same bleak facts: Emmett Till, a fourteen-year-old black youth from Chicago, came to visit relatives in Mississippi in the summer of 1955. He allegedly whistled at a white woman, Carolyn Bryant, in what was then the Jim Crow South. Consequently, he was kidnapped from his great-uncle's home by three men and a woman. Three days later, his horribly mutilated body was found floating in the Tallahatchie River. Two of the men, one the husband of Carolyn Bryant, were indicted for murder, brought to trial, and—despite overwhelming evidence of their guilt—were found "not guilty." The third man in the car was never identified, and Carolyn Bryant had been dropped off before Emmett Till was tortured and murdered. Despite their common core of facts, the two books are markedly different. Comparing and contrasting how Crowe has approached the story of Emmett Till's murder in his two texts helps to delineate the differences between history and historical fiction.

Getting Away with Murder: The True Story of the Emmett Till Case

Significantly, in the nonfiction *Murder*, the word "true" appears in the subtitle. Crowe is careful to stick to "what is known." However, the first chapter includes a vividly rendered scene in which Emmett Till is kidnapped, and here the writing borrows liberally from fictive techniques, providing the "brick-by-brick" details that Atwood describes. For example, Crowe sets his scene so well that the steamy, dark Mississippi night all but leaps off the page; e.g., "When the car engine shut down, the steady thrum of locusts resumed, filling the humid night air with a pulsing buzz" (15)—a skillful use of sensory appeal that effectively sparks readers' attention and immerses them quickly in the text. The scene is printed in italics, separating it from the more factual material that follows, and a footnote informs the reader that "This re-creation of actual events is based on statements made by those present and documents related to the case" (18).

In this book, there is no waiting to discover what happens to Emmett. His death is announced in the opening sentence of *Murder* ("In August 1955, a group of white men murdered a fourteen-year-old Black boy in the Mississippi Delta" [15]), and the first half of the text delineates the racial tenor of the times: in 1954 the Supreme Court decision in *Brown v. Board of Education of Topeka* had decreed that racially segregated schools were unconstitutional, a decision that inflamed white Southerners determined to maintain their Jim Crow way of life. The situation became even more heated when in May of 1955 the Supreme Court ordered that desegregation proceed "with all deliberate speed," and Crowe traces the rising tensions carefully, including the growth of the

White Citizens Council, a segregationist organization whose racial bigotry attracted members throughout the South.

In addition, Crowe fills in the larger historical background: telephones had been invented, industrial assembly lines were a major factor in the American economy, and motion pictures played in movie theaters across the country. The Second World War had ended ten years ago, Elvis Presley introduced rock and roll, and the newly founded McDonald's and Disneyland drew thousands of customers to their respective offerings. "It was," Crowe summarizes, "a turbulent, progressive year of unprecedented achievements and changes" (*Murder*, 37).

Crowe also offers background material on Emmett Till, and when he speculates about him, he is careful to use suppositional language: "he *may have* [italics ours] read" certain books; "he and his friends *probably* spent time" listening to the hottest new songs on the radio (*Murder*, 43). Crowe tells the reader that Emmett's personality was "brash" (*Murder*, 49), but although he discusses how the young man carried in his billfold pictures of white women cut from magazines and bragged to his Southern cousins that he dated them, we see little other evidence of the brashness that was Emmett's ultimate undoing. Crowe "tells" his reader about Emmett without "showing" the young man in action, entirely appropriate for his factual tone.

Balancing the "brash" side of his personality was Emmett's inclination to be obliging at home and around the neighborhood, hauling neighbors' groceries home in his wagon and shoveling their sidewalks in the winter. Family was important to the young man; he regularly spent weekends at his great-grandmother's home, helping her around the house and in her yard. This information creates a more sympathetic picture of Emmett Till, but is omitted in the novel because the white narrator would have no way of knowing about it.

The second half of *Murder* is devoted mainly to the trial; Crowe draws heavily on reported courtroom exchanges, newspaper articles from across the country, and factual descriptions of the crowds, both in and outside the courtroom. *Murder* is supplemented with many photographs, some of Emmett and his family, others of Southerners protesting the Supreme Court decision; there are photographs and drawings of the trial scene itself and of the two men indicted for Emmett's murder. One photograph near the end of the book shows the mangled corpse of Emmett Till. Crowe also uses material in *Murder* that would not have fit in his novel as he has structured it, in particular the later confessions of the two men in their interview for *Look Magazine*.

Mississippi Trial, 1955

In *Trial*, Crowe has used the same brutal tale of Emmett Till to create a coming-of-age novel with a fictional young white boy, Hiram Hillburn, at its center. Hiram has grown up in Greenwood, Mississippi, during World War II, living with his father's parents while his dad serves in the Navy and his mother works for the war effort. After the war, his father, repelled by Southern racism, stays in Mississippi only long enough to earn an advanced college degree in Oxford, then obtains a job as a college professor at Arizona State University in Tempe, Arizona. When he moves his family to the more liberal West, Hiram's grandfather, now a widower, vehemently objects. Hiram, still a child at nine years old, fails to understand the tension between his Grampa and Dad. Once in Arizona, he yearns for his idyllic years in Greenwood.

Each summer he begs to return to Mississippi, and each summer his father stubbornly resists Hiram's pleas. Then, when Hiram is nearly 16, Grampa has a small stroke, and Hiram is allowed to return for two weeks in August to help out. But his father's warning foreshadows what is to come: "Greenwood's not going to be what you expect, Hiram. You're older now, you'll see. And I'm sorry for what you'll see" (*Trial*, 44).

In the early part of the novel, Hiram is a naive, unreliable narrator. As a child, he witnesses scenes of racial bigotry and exploitation without making much meaning of them, but he idolizes his grandfather, who later becomes involved in the White Citizen's Council. "'God made Negroes to work the land,' the old man tells the child. . . . 'You're meant to be the boss, not the worker'" (*Trial*, 8). At the time, Hiram doesn't question the old man's pronouncement, and even when he returns to Greenwood as an adolescent, he is slow to refute his grandfather's perspective on race.

When he arrives from Arizona at the train station in Greenwood, he is met by his grandfather's long-time black housekeeper, Ruthanne, and introduced to her cousin's nephew, Bobo, later identified as Emmett Till. Ruthanne tells Bobo to carry Hiram's bags to his grandfather's truck, a demand that Hiram, not understanding that Southern blacks are supposed to serve whites, deems unnecessary. He insists that he can carry his own bags, but Ruthanne repeats her order over Bobo's objections. "I b-b-been on the train all the way from Chicago, Ruthanne," Bobo says, revealing a stutter that is not discussed in Crowe's nonfiction book. "I'm too tired to be carrying someone else's old b-bags" (*Trial*, 49).

Reprimanded by Ruthanne, Emmett finally picks up the lighter of Hiram's two pieces, but mutters to Hiram, "Ain't b-been raised to be nobody's old p-porter" (*Trial*, 49). The scene helps demonstrate that Emmett, raised in Chicago, has not learned how blacks are expected to behave toward whites in the South of the 1950s. As nonfiction, *Murder* includes no such scenes, but does report his mother's concern "that her son wouldn't know how to treat white people in the Jim Crow South" (*Murder*, 45).

Later scenes in the novel further emphasize this failure of understanding and show the "brash" aspect of Emmett's personality. Hiram has fond memories of fishing with his grandfather, and one hot afternoon he heads for a shady perch on the banks of the Tallahatchie. But once settled and enjoying the peaceful scene, he spots someone in the middle of the river calling for help, on the verge of drowning. Hiram dives in and uses the lifesaving techniques he has learned to rescue the victim, whom he recognizes as Emmett. Because Emmett struggles so, threatening to drown both of them, Hiram first punches Emmett in the jaw, then jams his knee into the victim's groin, finally loosening the boy's frantic grasp. Once on shore and recovered, Emmett shows little appreciation for Hiram's dangerous heroism. "You hit me," he says as soon as he recovers (*Trial*, 62). He also extracts a promise from Hiram to keep the incident a secret, not wanting his "country cousins" to know he can't swim. He explains that he inadvertently waded into water over his head to capture a snapping turtle in order to put it in his cousin's bed. Clearly, Emmett's "brash" and foolhardy behavior indicates a profound lack of judgment, but, unlike *Murder*, the reader does not know yet where his impetuousness will lead.

The next day, Hiram begins an education about the racial situation in the South when he accompanies his grandfather into town, where the old man stops at the county courthouse to do "business," a euphemism for his involvement with the White Citizens Council. He diverts Hiram by giving him a dime to purchase a treat at the concession stand in the lobby run by Mr. Paul, a friendly blind man whom Hiram remembers fondly from his childhood. From Mr. Paul, who is white, Hiram learns of the inflamed passions among Southerners generated by the Supreme Court decisions to integrate the public schools. Mr. Paul serves as Crowe's mouthpiece, conveying many of the historical facts about the inequalities between schools for the blacks and whites described in *Murder*. As Hiram listens, Mr. Paul vividly describes the deplorable conditions of the one black school he has visited and reveals facts about the discriminatory allotment of educational funding.

Hiram is already well acquainted with his grandfather's views on desegregation and has been influenced by them, and his response indicates the degree to which Grampa and Hiram's younger years in Greenwood have shaped his thinking. "What's wrong with people keeping to their own kind?" he asks. "Grampa used to say that's the way God wants it" (*Trial*, 74). Later, he reflects on the differences between Greenwood and Tempe, where "segregation never seemed to be a big deal" (*Trial*, 75), where no law kept the races separate. He is beginning to realize the damaging effect of segregation in the South: "The Jim Crow laws kept the Negroes pretty much stuck where they were—with no hope of things ever getting better" (*Trial*, 75).

Although Hiram is becoming aware of Grampa's staunchly segregationist views, he loves the old man. Crowe has developed Grampa as more than a stereotyped racial bigot. Hiram's grandfather sorely misses contact with his son and is often lonely. And there is no doubting his genuine love for Hiram. What

Crowe does not say in his history text he makes clear in his novel: without doubt segregationists espoused an abhorrent cause, but many at heart shared the same human emotions as their fellow citizens in both the North and South—they were capable of deep love for their families, grief at the loss of dear ones, fear of growing old and helpless alone.

Against this background of information about the angry racial tensions of the South, Crowe develops another scene on the Tallahatchie when, a few days later, Hiram goes fishing again. This time he is accompanied by R.C. Rydell, an old acquaintance whom Hiram remembers as a redneck bully. R.C.'s racial views and delinquent behavior spell trouble. In fact, they are trouble. R.C. tells Hiram of a humiliating trick he has played upon one of the Remington brothers, Grampa's two neighbors. Both men are shy, overweight, and socially inept. R.C. had offered Ralph Remington a ride home but instead drove him out into the countryside, demanded the terrified man's clothes, and left him stranded to walk home naked. Hiram is appalled. "It's one thing," he reflects, "to have a little fun with someone, teasing and stuff like that, but R.C. was just plain mean" (*Trial,* 84).

Later that afternoon, after eating part of the lunch Ruthanne has packed for Hiram, the boys fall asleep near the river, but Hiram is awakened by the sounds of splashing and laughter from upstream where the bank slopes into shallow water. Emmett is playing in the water with three of his cousins, but recognizing Hiram, wades out of the water and, to the concern and then amusement of his cousins, demands the remainder of Hiram's lunch. By now R.C. is awake and angry. "White folk don't share nothin' with colored, boy," he says, shoving Emmett in the chest. "Nothin'" (*Trial,* 91). What follows is an ugly scene. R.C. pins Emmett to the ground, slices open one of the catfish on his stringer, and forces the fish's guts down Emmett's mouth. Hiram is horrified but passive, only watching, although he later confesses to his grandfather that he "should have done *something*. . . .[Emmett] thought I was his friend" (*Trial,* 95).

This scene, of course, falls into the category of what *could* have happened, an entirely fictive incident but doubtless an echo of how many Southern whites treated blacks who failed to "know their place." And it operates to underscore Emmett's brashness and to demonstrate that people like Hiram, whatever their sympathies, are ineffective allies if they fail to act. As Edmund Burke once observed, "All that is necessary for evil to succeed is that good men do nothing." Hiram's story thus far, while the product of Crowe's imagination, portrays the "truth" of the Jim Crow South.

Grampa brushes off news of the incident: "Coloreds around here know better than to push themselves off on white folks. There is no friendship between whites and coloreds, never has been, never will be. Even a fool oughta known that" (*Trial,* 95). Hiram is no "fool," and he begins to understand his father's refusal to live in Mississippi.

Later, when he encounters R.C. again, he learns from him that a "strange nigger messed with a white woman up to Bryant's store," that he "talked ugly and whistled at her" (*Trial*, 105), and R.C. boasts that he's going with the "lady's husband" and some friends to teach Emmett how things work in the Delta. Alarmed and certain that the stranger is Emmett, Hiram calls the sheriff's office and tells a deputy about his concern. At this point, the reader, like Hiram, is still ignorant of Emmett's fate, a distinct contrast with *Murder*. The novel suspends the terrible outcome for several pages; both Hiram and the reader learn of Emmett's murder simultaneously, when the story makes headlines in *The Greenwood Commonwealth*. Two of the suspected kidnappers have already been arrested, and authorities are searching for the third. Hiram is convinced that the third man is R.C.

From here, the plot picks up steam rapidly. Hiram receives a phone call from the sheriff, who tells him he will have to stick around for the trial, longer than he planned. Then the body of Emmett is discovered floating in the Tallahatchie. He has been beaten so badly, his face so disfigured, that he is identified only by the ring his corpse is wearing. The trial itself duplicates much of the material in *Murder*, using actual court documents, interviews, and newspaper articles. The presence of Hiram and his grandfather, of course, are fictional elements, but Hiram's eyes, like Crowe's reporting in *Murder*, convey all the details of the trial and provide the reader with a sense of being there.

Both books make clear that bringing white people to trial for the murder of a black is in itself a landmark, although the two men are acquitted. The identity of the third person remains unsolved in the factual *Murder*, but *Trial* provides a fictive answer. Hiram has been convinced that the guilty party is R.C., but learns in an accidental encounter with him that R.C. was not even in town the night of Emmett's murder; his alibi is airtight. Then, to Hiram's dismay, one of the Remington brothers reveals that his grandfather had driven away in his truck with the accused men the night of the murder, returning unusually late. Adding to Hiram's growing suspicion is the fact that Grampa has traded his beloved truck for a new car. By now Hiram is certain that Grampa is the third man wanted for the crime. When he lets his grandfather know what the Remington brother has disclosed, Grampa's response confirms that the old man was involved in the crime: "The boy was alive when I left; they promised they were done with him when they brought me home" (*Trial*, 214).

Whether Grampa is guilty of murder, the reader can never know, but there is no doubt he was one of the men who kidnapped Emmett. Chris Crowe has gone well beyond "what is known" to "fill in the gaps." It is an imaginative and credible leap: somewhere in Greenwood, Mississippi, someone, still unidentified, participated in a heinous crime. He was surely someone's father, uncle, or grandfather. He might have been loved, perhaps a good person in many ways had he not been warped by the culture in which he was embedded. For Hiram Hillburn, his two weeks in Mississippi have changed his perspective forever. As he says to Mr. Paul, without revealing his grandfather's guilt, "[I]t's hard knowing that people can hide so much badness inside themselves, people you think you know and love. It makes you wonder about everybody" (*Trial*, 221). To which Mr. Paul replies, expressing what is surely Crowe's viewpoint, "Folks sometimes do ugly things, Hiram, but that don't necessarily make them evil. A lot of good folks just make stupid decisions or get themselves in the wrong place at the wrong time" (*Trial*, 221). As nonfiction, *Murder* is focused on only the facts; it makes no such apologies for the killers.

Murder, then, is about what its title implies: it is an indictment of the South of 1955, which set free two men who were guilty of kidnapping, torture, and murder of a child whose only offense was to cross the color line. But it credits the trial for the beginning of the Civil Rights movement, and the reader, given all the facts, is sure to cheer that the days of Jim Crow are over.

Trial, on the other hand, is primarily the story of Hiram Hillburn, a surrogate for all the actual youths who accepted the racism of the pre-Civil Rights South and only gradually (if ever) learned how much evil it fostered. In telling Hiram's story, Crowe is able to narrate the story of Emmett Till's murder, but it is Hiram's development that holds the narrative together.

THE PROBLEM OF BALANCE BETWEEN FACT AND FICTION

Adult readers of historical fiction may be willing to wait for the conflict to get underway while they absorb the minutiae of daily life that delineates a particular historical period and to take time for a satisfying resolution to present itself. However, young adult readers pose a challenge on this front. How many significant nuances and complexities should a writer for younger readers include? How many to exclude? Sheila Egoff, who has written extensively about children's and young adult literature, articulates the difficulties for writers for the YA reader, a label that includes a range of ages from twelve to eighteen: "The artistic problems inherent in the historical novel are increased in books for children. Here events must be more closely winnowed and sifted; character more clearly delineated, but without condescension or over-simplification. The [young reader] must be moved quickly into the consciousness of another time and his imagination stirred to it."[9] Her use of the term "children" implies that she is referring to readers at the younger end of the spectrum, for what a twelve-year-old may have difficulty handling, an eighteen-year-old might easily process, and what interests a twelve-year-old may bore an eighteen-year-old.

But countering the need to engage young adults "quickly" in the historical narrative is the genre's reliance on the accumulation of particulars that an author's research produces, the "brick-by-brick" details that Atwood has described. Writers commonly invest enormous time and energy sifting through archives, reading historical texts about the period, and visiting the sites where the action of the novel occurs. This research goes far beyond learning about particular events. A careful historical novelist conveys a sense of the period through minuscule details about such matters as clothing, food, transportation, and social customs. Atwood stresses this point by sharing more of her own experiences writing *Alias Grace:*

> History is more than willing to tell you who won the Battle of Trafalgar and which world leader signed this or that treaty, but it is frequently reluctant about the now-obscure details of daily life. Nobody wrote these things down because everybody knew them, and considered them too mundane and unimportant to record. Thus I found myself wrestling not only with who said what about Grace Marks but also how to clean a chamber pot, what footgear would have been worn in winter, the origins of quilt pattern names, and how to store parsnips. If you're after the truth, the whole and detailed truth, and nothing but the truth, you're going to have a thin time of it if you trust to paper, but, with the past, it's almost all you've got. (1514)

Thomas Mallon puts the case even more succinctly: "Only through tiny, literal accuracies can the historical novelist achieve the larger truth to which he aspires—namely, an overall feeling of authenticity." The novelist, like Marianne Moore's ideal poet, must stock his garden with real toads.[10]

Yet too many toads can overrun the garden. The very scope of an author's research poses a problem of balance. How does an author keep a narrative moving but also communicate the information necessary to bring the period alive? Many writers admit that having done the research, there is a real temptation to use too much of it.

> In commenting about his own research, Erik Christian Haugaard, author of many historical novels for young readers, offers insight into the problem. He says, "I try to keep all my reading material as close as possible to the period I am describing, making copious notes all the time, naturally. You will use only a fraction of the material you collect, but the rest is not wasted. It is used indirectly. It is this knowledge that makes you able to create well-rounded characters. Information you don't use in your novel is still part of your imagination."[11]

But using only a "fraction" of the material is easier said than done. Kathryn Lasky confesses, "There's this great temptation. You've done all this research. I really want to use it all. It's like nine-tenths of the iceberg is under water; it supports that brilliant tip that shimmers on top, so one way or the other it's there, but it doesn't all need to be there. That's a lesson I've learned over the years."[12] Indeed, Lasky's historical fiction has grown tighter; *True North* strikes just the right balance between fact and fiction. But writers can find it difficult to resist the temptation, cramming their plots with digressive details that serve mainly to display their copious research. Reviewers are critical when they perceive the imaginative content of the story submerged in historical facts, an imbalance that Hazel Rochman, for example, criticizes in Lasky's *The Bone Wars,* an otherwise fascinating account of paleontology in the nineteenth century: "The history overwhelms the fiction, but both are compelling."[13]

Chris Crowe has solved the problem of getting his novel underway quickly by initially concentrating on the tension between Hiram and his father. His opening sentence sets the tone and theme of the novel. "My dad hates hate," Hiram says (*Trial,* 1). He describes how he has had his mouth washed out with soap if he uses the word "hate," then adds with unintended irony a few sentences later, "I hated Dad when he acted like that" (*Trial,* 1). And by balancing the facts of Emmett Till's kidnapping and murder with the coming-of-age story of Hiram, Crowe has managed to weave historical detail (even the price of a candy bar in 1955) into his story without slowing or diverting his plot. *Publishers Weekly* criticized Crowe for taking "a bit too much time before arriving at the central action: the lynching of Emmett Till . . . and the nationally publicized trial, in which the murderers were acquitted," but one could argue that this criticism misses the point: *Trial* is primarily Hiram's story. His maturation hinges on his response to Emmett Till's murder and the subsequent trial, but—despite the novel's title—it is Hiram's slow process of growing into adulthood that moves the plot forward. *Booklist* acknowledges this focus in its review: "What moves this beyond docudrama is Hiram's relationship with Grandpa, which has always been strong, unlike that with his father."

Crowe's research, like that of most historical novelists, generated more material than he could possibly use in either *Murder* or *Trial.* He writes:

> I went to Mississippi on the very same day in August that Emmett Till had arrived, and stayed there for several days, visiting the sites he had been in the store where he insulted Carolyn Bryant, driving Old Money Road up to the Tallahatchie River. I spent hours in the Greenwood Public Library reading and photocopying microfilm from *The Greenwood Commonwealth* and *The Morning Star,* the two local papers that covered the case. I talked with people. I took photos. I read books in local libraries about Mississippi life and history. I took notes and made recordings to document how people in Leflore and Tallahatchie Counties acted, what things looked and smelled like, how Mississippi speech sounded.[14]

The challenge of researching the facts surrounding Emmett Till's murder was compounded because all the trial transcripts and most of the trial records were "lost" in the early 1960s. For testimony, Crowe had to rely on multiple newspaper accounts, and because the trial was covered by so many reporters, he was able to confirm the order of witnesses, events, and actual statements made in court. "If I couldn't find a statement reported in more than one source, I didn't use it," he says (July 16, 2004). He suspects that the transcripts were "lost" because of a master's thesis done on the trial in the early 1960s by a student at Florida State University. The student interviewed jurors, the killers, local authorities, and had full access to the transcripts and all other documents. Shortly thereafter, those records disappeared. Crowe assumes "that [the student's] research made Tallahatchie County authorities nervous about potential negative publicity from the case" (July 16, 2004). In fact, the novel portrays this resentment among Greenwood residents over the negative image conveyed about Mississippi racism in reports about the trial.

After writing *Mississippi Trial, 1955,* Crowe decided to use the material his research had generated to write a nonfiction text on the same subject: "I had tons of material about the case, and I was also familiar with many of the photographs that documented the trial and the weeks immediately before and after it. When I had finished the novel, I wanted to use all that research material and some of those fantastic photographs, so I proposed a nonfiction book about the case."[15] He thought that writing the straight history of the murder and trial would be "a piece of cake" because he had already done all the research for the historical novel. "I planned on stripping away the fiction from the novel, adding some photos, and "voila!" a nonfiction book would appear," he says (July 6, 2004). But the task proved far more difficult than he anticipated.

> I had so much material, I knew so much about the case that it was nearly impossible to write a word. I had assumed that a full knowledge of the case and the period would make it easier to write the book, but the information overload made it extremely difficult to distill the information into an accessible chunk for the book I envisioned. I had to cut and cut and cut and hang on tight to my chapter outline to get the book rolling. (July 6, 2004)

These comments illustrate, first, the difficulty of making coherent meaning from one's research, and, second, the difference between writing fiction and nonfiction. The winnowing of material in each case is specific to the genre, and while the research may serve both purposes, a writer cannot simply "strip away" the fictional elements of a completed novel to produce a historical text.

THE PROBLEM OF ACCURACY

However an author chooses to balance his or her material between history and fiction, accuracy remains a primary obligation. A fiction writer may "fill in the gaps" if the imagined material does not contradict what is known, but there is no margin for errors or anachronisms, either of which can reduce a novel's usefulness or interest. No serious writer of historical fiction takes this matter lightly, and writers who work in the genre tell rueful stories on themselves about their inadvertent lapses. Author Geoffrey Trease opened his *Mist over Athelney,* set in ninth-century England, with a scene in which the characters sit down for a dinner of rabbit stew. Only after the novel was published did an eleven-year-old reader spot a problem: There were no rabbits in England at that time.[16]

Usually a copyeditor catches and corrects these kinds of errors, but not always. Kathryn Lasky was tripped up when she allowed a character in *Beyond the Burning Time,* a novel about the Salem witchcraft trials set in seventeenth-century New England, to carry a kerosene lantern. Kerosene lamps were not used until the nineteenth century. Lasky accounts for this slip with an autobiographical detail. "I was writing the novel up in our summer place in Maine," she says, "where we have kerosene lamps, and I'm always worried that the kids could set the house on fire. So, even though my characters used candles in other scenes, I had kerosene on the brain when I wrote."[17]

Strict adherence to historical accuracy can also pose a problem if "accuracy" involves brutal or immoral behavior. What are the writer's options when the intended readers are young adults, an audience for whom some adults may desire a subdued version of historic events? Lasky has encountered this problem with two historical novels of the old West. The first, *Beyond the Divide,* follows a wagon train on its westward journey. In telling the story of Meribah Simon, who accompanies her father on the journey, the novel demonstrates how the pernicious greed for gold so corrupted many of the emigrants that they robbed and killed each other. The appalling toll of the Westward Movement not only on Native Americans but on the emigrants as well is clearly a major theme. Some reviewers, though, balked at the portrayal of mythic American pioneers as thieves and murderers. Dorothy Lettus writes, in *Voice of Youth Advocates,* "It is not appealing to read about mean, sordid characters, like those who people this book."[18] In the same novel, a young girl raped by outlaws is viewed as the guilty party and then shunned by most of the adults in the wagon train. When a critic protested such a response, wanting a more sympathetic reaction, Lasky defended the historical accuracy of the episode. "Hey," she said, "that's the way it was. There were no rape crisis centers back then."[19]

Lasky aroused similar criticism when she opened *The Bone Wars,* set in the nineteenth-century Old West, with a violent episode. Wrote Zena Sutherland, "Why the book begins with a scene in which five-year-old Thad is under a bed in which his mother, a prostitute, is being murdered by a brutal customer is not made clear."[20] Lasky defended the scene when she wrote, "It is a fact, verified though my extensive research, that a preponderance of women who went West alone were or became prostitutes. Despite this fact, we prefer to think of them as schoolmarms. Isn't that the nice, innocuous profession of all women? Well, guess what? There weren't all that many schools out there, and, brace yourself, I discovered the existence of more than a few schoolmarm/prostitutes."[21]

Like Lasky, Crowe has not shied away from the cruelty stemming from the racial tensions of the Jim Crow South. The scene between R.C. and Emmett is horrifying, and Crowe spares the reader no details of just how badly the black boy was tortured and killed. But had he muted the brutality, his story would have lost its power. It is precisely because of these details that the story of Emmett Till merits retelling fifty years later. However, he admits that the novel proceeded only with difficulty.

> [I]t was the hardest thing I've ever written. Historical fiction has restrictions that contemporary fiction does not. I had to stop my writing constantly to go back and double check the historical notes and facts, to make sure the historical elements in my novel were accurate and that I didn't unfairly blend fact with fiction. It was also hard to write because the details of Emmett Till's murder are so awful, so horrible that they weighed on me all the time. I know how important this case was, and I hope the book does it justice, but I was also glad when I was finished with it because it was so painful to work on. (July 6, 2004)

Crowe's careful work has paid off. Because of his frequent use of recorded documents and conversations, the novel has the ring of authenticity, reinforced by his note at the close of the story confirming his sources.

The dynamic nature of language poses another problem of accuracy. Vocabularies change from one historical period to another as new words slip into common usage and others become archaic. These transformations impose certain restrictions on dialogue, and writers of historical fiction cannot give their imagination entirely free reign in creating it. The language must not only ring true to the character speaking it; the author must also ensure that it corresponds to the vocabulary of the period while avoiding the temptation to sprinkle archaic words around just for the effect. Historical novelist Rosemary Sutcliff ridicules this use of archaic language as "gadzookery" and "writing forsoothly."[22]

Crowe has dealt well with the necessity of using a southern dialect in the dialogue spoken by many of his characters. He suggests the speech of Greenwood, Mississippi, by using a few regional expressions and colloquialisms (e.g., "peckerwoods," "you all," "more miserable than a crawdad in a stew pot") and syntactical constructions ("you done grown up," "ain't gonna be no harm done"). Although he drops some final g's, mostly in R.C.'s speech, he more frequently spells out the informal pronunciation, such as "gonna." These techniques, taken together, create the effect of Mississippi speech without distorting the language to the degree that it becomes inaccessible to the reader.

When a writer chooses to tell his or her story from the viewpoint of a first-person narrator, the issue of language comes even more critical. A narrator whose voice relies too heavily on outdated language, however historically accurate, is sure to lose the reader. But a narrator's vocabulary, like the dialogue for all characters in historical fiction, must be restricted to language in use at the time of the story. This dilemma can result in intriguing vocabulary lessons.

Writers John and Patricia Beatty tell of finishing their novel *Campion Towers,* set in the Massachusetts Bay Colony of 1651, when they began to suspect that their young first-person narrator was using some language that didn't exist in the 1600s. When they edited their manuscript to trace the history of any questionable words, their research validated their suspicions. They had to find substitutes for such terms as "mob," "aisle," "amazing," "bewildering," "chunk," "clunk," "carefree," and "complete."[23]

By creating a narrator who has been away from the South for years and speaks a more standard English, Crowe has avoided the problem of narrating his story in dialect. However, the rhythm of some of Hiram's speeches suggests a Southern influence, e.g., "Ruthanne had packed us a sack lunch better than most people's suppers" (*Trial,* 87). Occasionally, as Hiram comes to recognize the grim side of the South he has loved, he speaks in unconvincing paragraphs that sound more like excerpts from an essay than spontaneous language, and some of the other characters' dialogue verges on the didactic, especially Mr. Paul's. However, the overt moralizing is only occasional and not especially intrusive. It is the events themselves and Hiram's emotional reactions to them that convey the novel's meaning.

If the first-person narration is cast as a diary or journal, additional constraints are called into play, as author Joan Blos discovered in 1979 when she began to write *A Gathering of Days: A New England Girl's Journal.* She read several authentic diaries in preparation for writing the fictional one, learning that her choice imposed very particular limitations: "For example, dialogue would have to be used sparingly, as diarists tended to report the fact of a conversation, not its word-for-word content. Description would have to be limited to situations, objects, and persons of particular interest to the protagonist herself."[24] Of course, dialogue and description are two key elements in bringing any fiction alive, so the diary form was severely constraining. However, she stuck with it because, she says, it allowed her to be faithful to New England sensibilities— sensibilities often suppressed by understatement, without boring or disappointing twentieth-century readers accustomed to books whose protagonists announce their feelings clearly. Also, the highly personal voice of the diarist has emotional appeal for readers, especially younger ones.[25]

THE PROBLEM OF HISTORICAL CHARACTERS AS FICTIONAL CHARACTERS

From its beginning, long before "realism" became the dominant mode of fiction, the novel has demonstrated the urge to create the illusion of actual events. Along with what Naomi Jacobs calls "recognizable small truths" and the "baggage of realness"—real cities, streets, and parks; the minutiae of fashion, furniture, card games, slang, and music—historical figures, dead and alive, appeared commonly in early English novels and were treated with full fictional freedom.[26]

With the rise of realism in fiction came the assumption that such figures must be treated with objectivity and accuracy, a notion that posed creative difficulties for writers. But as recognition grew that complete objectivity was more a myth than a genuine possibility, writers have gained more liberty in using actual personages from history as characters in their novels. Now we are no longer surprised to see famous personalities forming friendships, romances, or adversarial relationships with fictional characters.

Naomi Jacobs explains this authorial freedom by pointing to the view that identity and what we call "reality" are no less constructs of language than are the most fantastic fictions (xvi). If, as she argues, there is no "real person"— if the public persona is itself a fiction, not an objective representation of a coherent individual—then fiction writers can improvise upon or reinvent the "facts" of a person's life (xvii). The result is a "plasticity" of historical figures that has liberated writers to incorporate them more freely, even veering from known facts. In *The Man Who Was Poe,* Avi, acclaimed author of many historical novels for young adults, creates a ghostlike character who pursues young Edmund through the dark streets of mid-nineteenth century Providence, Rhode Island. Some of Edmund's family have died; others have inexplicably disappeared, and the mysterious stranger, later revealed to be Poe, offers to find them—but only in return for something he wants from Edmund. There is no historical evidence to support this portrait of Poe, but the novel makes for a suspenseful and spooky story. Avi is a prime example of an author who has used a historical figure in a completely fictional context.

In Kathryn Lasky's *Alice Rose and Sam,* the author Samuel Clemens (Mark Twain) forms a close but imagined friendship with the young Alice Rose. Although much of what he says in the novel is drawn from his own work, Lasky created additional dialogue for him that welds seamlessly to Twain's actual words. She felt entirely confident inventing speeches for him because she felt she knew him so well. In an afterword to her novel, she describes how she read Twain's work as a child, identifying completely with the famous writer. "I loved Mark Twain so much I wanted to be Mark Twain, or more accurately, I wanted to be Sam Clemens."[27] When she wants to use a historical figure in her fiction but feels that she knows too little about the individual to be accurate, she invents a similar fictional character to serve in his stead.

Ann Rinaldi, who has also written novels in which historical figures play major roles, uses scholarly resources to create a foundation for her characters but does not allow the sources to limit her.[28] She "takes risks" in creating her historical characters such as Phillis Wheatley, the first African-American poet in the United States, and Harriet Hemming, the mulatto daughter of Thomas Jefferson and his mistress/slave Sally. Rinaldi wants her readers to understand such characters as "flesh and blood," fully human, "with complex motives and needs" (69). Both Lasky and Rinaldi are authors who "fill in the gaps" without straying too far from documented history.

Of necessity, Crowe uses many historical characters, such as the two men accused of kidnapping and murder, the attorneys and judge involved in the trial, Emmett's mother and great-uncle, and, of course, Emmett himself. With the exception of Emmett Till, he invents no scenes involving actual personages. Because all of their dialogue is taken either directly from documented sources or eyewitness accounts, Crowe has few "gaps" to fill in writing about these people. However, he hadn't planned on "the difficulty of teasing the nonfiction out of the fiction" (July 6, 2004). For example, the two murderers had five defense lawyers, too many for the readers to keep straight. Crowe reduced the defense to a single lawyer and gave him "all the outrageous comments in the closing arguments" (July 6, 2004).

THE PROBLEM OF THE WRITER'S PRESENT

Closely related to the problem of accuracy is the fact, as already discussed in the opening chapter, that any novel is filtered through its author's contemporary sensibilities. Affirming this, Canadian novelist Robertson Davies says, "We all belong to our own time, and there is nothing whatever that we can do to escape from it. Whatever we write will be contemporary, even if we attempt a novel set in a past age."[29]

Anne Scott Macleod elaborates on this issue in "Writing Backward: Modern Models in Historical Fiction." She says, "Writers of history select, describe, and explain historical evidence—and thereby interpret."[30] While stating that authors of historical fiction do not ignore "known historical realities,"[31] Macleod discusses how a writer's present can impact historical novels. First, "new social sensibilities have changed the way Americans view the past" (27). Macleod attributes these changes to feminist re-readings of history and insistence by minorities on the importance of their previously neglected experiences—and the differences of those experiences from the dominant culture. As a result, young women more frequently play central roles in the narrative with the emphasis on boys and men "modified" (27), stories feature more minorities and lives of ordinary people, and the "traditional chronicle of unbroken upward progress" (27) has been adapted to recognize the uneven advancement of the human race toward a better world.

However, Macleod also maintains too many writers omit or gloss over some ugly details of the past to bend their narratives to current social and political preferences. She criticizes the tendency of authors "stepping around large slabs of known reality to tell pleasant but historically doubtful stories" (27). She cites as examples the strong roles filled by young women of the past and criticizes "authors vaulting blithely over the barriers women lived with for so long" (28) as well as the happy but implausible outcomes awaiting these exemplars of feminine empowerment. Using as examples Patricia MacLachlan's *Sarah, Plain and Tall,* Avi's *The True Confessions of Charlotte Doyle,* Karen Cushman's *Catherine Called Birdy,* and Ann Rinaldi's *A Break with Charity,* Macleod discusses, in making her case, how these novels, though reaping many awards and favorable reviews, have ignored the unpleasant historical realities of farm work, patriarchal control, and slavery.

As a case in point, while conceding that Avi's *The True Confessions of Charlotte Doyle* is a "fine vicarious adventure story," she labels it as a "preposterous" one, as indeed it is. The reader must suspend disbelief to accept that in 1832, a thirteen-year-old girl from a sheltered, upper-class family, finds herself the only female crossing the Atlantic and joins a mutiny against the ship's captain. She emerges at the story's close not only sexually undefiled by any of the crew—a rough and tumble bunch—but as their captain! Avi took strong exception to any such criticism of his story, defending the novel as fiction and claiming that "it is a legitimate task . . . of fiction to re-invent the past, if you will, so as to better define the future. Historical fiction—among other things—is about today's possibilities."[32]

This seems a dubious defense at best, ignoring as it does a prime criterion of credibility demanded by good historical fiction. Perhaps an author writing to "better define the future" would do well to work in other genres, such as contemporary realism or science fiction. But to impose a current feminist ideology on a story set 150 years ago, particularly one whose carefully researched details about ships and sea anchors it firmly in the category of historical realism, is less than defensible. As Macleod says in "Writing Backward," "*Kirkus* called the book 'well-researched'—on ships, perhaps, but not, I think on probability theory, or even human development" (27).

Macleod also sees as unrealistic the rebellious quality that Ann Schlee and Katherine Paterson have deemed integral to historical protagonists:

> Most people in society are not rebels; in part because the cost of nonconformity is more than they want to pay, but also because as members of the society they share its convictions. Most people are, by definition, not exceptional. Historical fiction writers who want their protagonists to reflect twentieth-century ideologies, however, end by making them exceptions to their cultures, so that in many a historical novel the reader learns nearly nothing—or at least nothing sympathetic—of how people of a past society saw their world (32).

Other authors are critical of emphasis on literacy in much historical fiction. Rebecca Barnhouse, for example, takes issue with novels set in the Middle Ages that "allow modern attitudes [to] creep into the stories in the portrayals of reading and learning."[33] By explaining that in fourteenth-century France "a complete Bible cost the same as half a house, or forty sheep, or a team of hired assassins" (1), she defends her criticism that to an unlikely degree, "novels set in the Middle Ages feature characters who yearn to read or write" (ix).

Barnhouse also criticizes the way in which novels set in the Middle Ages portray Catholic characters who accept religious diversity in an era when any non-Christian was, at best, viewed with suspicion and, at worst, persecuted, exiled, or murdered. She offers up multiple illustrations of characters who, although indoctrinated with the Church's censure of Jews, Muslims, and heretics, encounter these outsiders with benign curiosity and tolerance.

Crowe has avoided most of these pitfalls, although, clearly, he is writing from a contemporary perspective that finds the Jim Crow South appalling. But Hiram is no rebel except in his relationship with his father; rather, he is very much the product of his childhood in the South and his sheltered environment in Arizona. And despite the fact that Crowe is writing for a young audience, he makes no attempt to gloss over incidents and language that might offend certain sensibilities: he uses the pejorative "nigger" in dialogue spoken by bigoted characters, he vividly renders the cries and screams heard from the barn where Emmett is being tortured, and he makes it a point to describe in detail the horribly mangled corpse that was once Emmett Till. It is these specifics, however unpleasant, that evoke the Jim Crow South of the 1950s and merit a retelling of Emmett's story.

THE ISSUE OF PROVENANCE

With some unusual exceptions, writers of historical fiction have no first-hand knowledge of their characters' experiences, but they can roam widely in their imaginations, setting their stories in distant times and places accessible only through research. No one would propose that authors be restricted to autobiographical material. Still, as we have gained greater respect for both the historical and contemporary experiences of cultures that have been all but neglected or distorted in earlier fiction, there has been some negative response to writers who have crossed cultural boundaries, particularly ethnic and racial ones. The debate is often heated, for the issue arouses powerful emotions and appears unlikely to resolve itself easily.

Some authors have been chastised for perpetuating racial stereotypes in work that had been initially acclaimed. William H. Armstrong's *Sounder*, published in 1969, is a case in point. Armstrong, a white writer, won the Newbery Medal in 1970 for his story about a family of Southern black sharecroppers. More recently, this same novel has been roundly criticized for its portrayal of the father as weak, submitting to racial abuse with little protest rather than fighting to protect his family. Critics have taken particular offense to Armstrong's failure to name the family members, a strategy originally interpreted as an attempt to portray its struggle as universal rather than personal.

Thelma Seto, a Japanese-American writer born and raised in the Middle East, has voiced strong opposition to writers appropriating material outside their own cultures. "I will not allow writers who do not have Asian ancestry to pretend to tell my story," she has asserted, objecting mainly to American writers of European descent "who subscribe to the belief that cultural thievery is quite acceptable."[34] Violet J. Harris, an African-American author of several articles and editor of a frequently cited text on multiculturalism, has endorsed Seto's position. While recognizing the "authorial freedom" of authors to choose their own subjects, she castigated in *The New Advocate* the "authorial arrogance" of some European and American authors "who demand freedom to write about whatever they wish without subjecting their work to critical scrutiny."[35] In the same article, she dismisses Kathryn Lasky's proposal for writing a book about Sarah Breedlove Walker, an African-American who made her fortune developing hair products for blacks. Harris charged that "the rhythm of text is likely to be Revlon, not Ultra Sheen, *Life* magazine rather than *Ebony* magazine, the milquetoast sounds of Pat Boone rather than the whoops and hollers of Little Richard" (114).[36]

Lasky is hardly one to let such a charge lie unchallenged. In a letter to the editor in the next edition of the journal, she argued that "this new insistence on certain rules for authorship and provenance of a story (who writes what or where) is indeed threatening the very fabric of literature and literary criticism."[37] She finds such strictures "not just verging on censorship; it is censorship. . . . The first criteria (sic) for publication should always be that the book is good literature" (6). To underscore her argument, she quotes W.E.B. DuBois, author of the seminal text in African-American studies, *The Souls of Black Folk*, as saying, "No human culture is inaccessible to someone who makes the effort to understand, to learn to inhabit another world."[38]

Others have sided with Lasky's viewpoint. Marc Aronson, for example, argues for eliminating what he calls "ethnic essentialism,"[39] and, of course, carried to its extreme, "ethnic essentialism" would preclude authors from writing historical fiction set in any country other than their own. Crowe has avoided any charges of "cultural thievery" by telling Emmett's story through the eyes of a white boy rather than a fictional black character living in Greenwood at the time of the murder. Reviews of *Murder* and *Trial* have been favorable, each winning many awards: *Murder* is a Jane Adams Honor Book, and *Trial* won the Jefferson Cup Award as well as an award from the International Reading Association. Both books received recognition as one of the Best Books for Young Adults from the American Library Association. As a review in the *School Library Journal* has said, "This book belongs in all collections to show young readers the full range of American history."

THE ATTRACTION OF THE PAST FOR WRITERS

Given the challenges and complexities involved in writing historical fiction, why do so many fine authors choose to write in this genre? Margaret Atwood offers a comprehensive answer, making clear that not all writers use the past for the same purpose:

> Some attempt to give more or less faithful accounts of actual events, in answer perhaps to such questions as 'where did we come from and how did we get here?' Some attempt restitution of a sort, or at least an acknowledgment of past wrongs. . . . Others . . . look at what we have killed or destroyed in our obsessive search for the pot of gold. Others delve into class structure and political struggles. . . . Yet others unearth a past as it was lived by women, under conditions a good deal more stringent than our own, still others use the past as background to family sagas—tales of betrayal and even madness. . . . Some might say that the past is safer. . . . With the past, at least we know what happened. . . . The Titanic may be sinking, but we're not on it. Watching it subside, we are diverted for a short time from the leaking lifeboat we are actually in right now.[40]

Various authors have offered their own accounts of their motives for writing historical fiction. Karen Cushman explains her fascination with the Middle Ages by saying, "The time period appeals to me because I think of the Middle Ages moving into the Renaissance as like a child growing into adolescence. At this point in history, people began to have concerns about identity and concerns about appearance. Men and women began to pay attention to how they looked, and all of a sudden, there were books written about manners. There were concerns about accountability and privacy. These are some of the same issues that today's adolescents face."[41]

Karen Hesse traces her interest in historical fiction to a library visit when she was eleven. She had wandered out of the children's section and plucked a copy of John Hershey's *Hiroshima* from the shelves. Here she found "people surviving under the most extreme adversity and behaving in a manner of extraordinary grace and dignity. I think you can hear the echo of *Hiroshima* in my work."[42]

Ann Rinaldi credits her interest in the past to her participation in historical reenactments, her "school of history." For example, she decided to write a historical novel, *Time Enough for Drums*, in 1981 after participating in a reenactment of the surrender at Yorktown.[43] She also gets ideas from her reading and research plus personal experiences whose emotions connect with something in the past.

Kathryn Lasky has always been fascinated with American history, and the old West of the nineteenth century holds special interest for her. However, she was wary of perpetuating the heroic myths that dominated television and Hollywood movies. "I've learned to smell a rat," she says about her skepticism toward the romantic stereotypes that obscure the uglier chapters in our nation's history,[44] and the rats have inspired most of her historical fiction. It has vividly portrayed appalling aspects of the Westward movement, the horrors of slavery, and the hypocrisy of prominent Northerners during the Civil War.

Chris Crowe was inspired to write *Mississippi Trial, 1955* when he was doing research for a book about Mildred D. Taylor, a noted African-American writer for adolescents who, in one of her autobiographical essays, referred to the impact that the murder of Emmett Till had had on her. Crowe was not familiar with the name, so he did some research in case the murder had influenced Taylor's writing and should be included in Crowe's book about her. What he discovered stunned him, and he wanted "American teenagers to know this story and its important place in American history" and its influence on the Civil Rights movement (July 6, 2004). He decided historical fiction would be the ideal vehicle for telling the story, but he wanted another component, something or someone ultimately affected by Emmett's murder but a story essentially separate from the murder.

Remembering his rocky adolescent relationship with his own father and parenting an adolescent son himself who, at the time Crowe was researching his novel, was pulling away into a more independent self, he felt that he had found the element that would shape his novel. The idea evolved into the relationships among Hiram, his father, and his grandfather. "Ending racism and discrimination matters to me very much," he says. "My own relationship with my son—and with my father—matter to me very much. This book gave me a place where all these issues could intersect" (July 6, 2004).

He also provides telling information about how he named his characters

> Hiram's first name comes from Senator Hiram Revels, an African American from Mississippi who was elected to the U.S. Senate in 1870. He was the first African American senator in U.S. history. Hiram's father's name, Harlan, comes from John Marshall Harlan, the dissenting Supreme Court justice in the famous 1896 Plessy v. Ferguson decision that legalized segregation in America. Their last name, Hillburn, is one I made up after looking through phone books from Leflore and Tallahatchie counties. Ruthanne is taken from my mother's name, Ruth Anne. R.C. Rydell is a Southern-sounding name I concocted using the old RC Cola, a drink popular down there in the 1950s, and Rydell, a macho sounding name that I patterned after the old Ridell athletic shoes. I also liked the sound of R.C. Rydell. (July 7, 2004)

As the above discussion indicates, historical fiction poses such a range of challenges to authors that it is difficult to generalize about their approaches They draw their ideas from a variety of sources and meet the challenges in way particularly suited to their respective work. However, it is safe to say that writers who take up the challenge of exploring history to create a fictional past are taking readers where they might otherwise never go. Margaret Atwood has expressed the value of the journey in eloquent terms: "The past no longer belong only to those who once lived in it; the past belongs to those who claim it, and are willing to explore it, and to infuse it with meaning for those alive today. The past belongs to us, because we are the ones who need it" (1516).

NOTES

1. Walsh, "History Is Fiction," 22.

2. Lasky, "The Fiction of History," 8.

3. Margaret Atwood, "In Search of *Alias Grace*: On Writing Canadian Historical Fiction," *The American Historical Review,* V. 103.5 (December 1998), 1505; hereafter cited parenthetically in text.

4. Edward Hallett Carr, *What Is History?* (New York: St. Martin's, 1961), 69–70.

5. Naomi Jacobs, *The Character of Truth: Historical Figures in Contemporary Fiction* (Carbondale, IL: Southern Illinois UP, 1990), 72; hereafter cited parenthetically in text.

6. Jonathan Spence, "Margaret Atwood and the Edges of History," *The American Historical Review,* V. 103.5 (December 1998), 1523.

7. Chris Crowe, *Getting Away with Murder: The True Story of the Emmett Till Case* (New York: Phyllis Fogelman Books, 2003); hereafter cited parenthetically in text.

8. Chris Crowe, *Mississippi Trial, 1955* (New York: Phyllis Fogelman Books, 2002) hereafter cited parenthetically in text.

9. Sheila Egoff, *The Republic of Childhood: A Critical Guide to Canadian Children's Literature* (Toronto: Oxford UP, 1975), 96.

10. Mallon, "Writing Historical Fiction," 64.

11. Haugaard, "Lamp-holder," 268.

12. Telephone interview, August 1996.

13. Hazel Rochman, review of *The Bone Wars, Booklist* 91.4 (October 15, 1994), 420

14. Chris Crowe, email correspondence, July 6, 2004; hereafter all email messages cited parenthetically in text by date.

15. Interview with Chris Crowe, www.penguinputnam.com/static/packages/us/vreaders-news/f;5–start

16. Trease, "The Historical Novelist at Work." In *Writers, Critics, and Children*, 46.

17. Quoted in "Historical Fiction or Fictionalized History? Problems for Writer of Historical Novels for Young Adults," Joanne Brown, *The ALAN Review* 26.1 (Fall 1998), 9; hereafter cited parenthetically in text.

18. Dorothy Lettus, Review of *Beyond the Divide. Voice of Youth Advocates* (October 1983): 204.

19. Kathryn Lasky, quoted by Brown in "Historical Fiction or Fictionalized History?" 9.

20. Zena Sutherland, quoted in *Presenting Kathryn Lasky*, 9.

21. Lasky, "The Fiction of History," 164.

22. Rosemary Sutcliff, "History Is People." In *Children and Literature: Views and Reviews*, Virginia Haviland, ed. (Glenview, IL: Scott, Foresman, 1973): 307.

23. John and Patricia Beatty, "Watch Your Language—You're Writing for Young People!" *The Horn Book* (February 1965): 115–116.

24. Joan Blos, "'I Catherine Hall': The Journal as Historical Fiction." In *The Voice of the Narrator in Children's Literature: Insights from Writers and Critics,* Charlotte F. Otten and Gary D. Schmidt, eds. (NY: Greenwood Press, 1989): 278.

25. See Chapter 2 for a more detailed discussion of this point.

26. Jacobs, *The Character of Truth*, xvii.

27. Kathryn Lasky, *Alice Rose and Sam* (New York: Hyperion, 1998), 249.

28. Jeanne M. McGlinn, *Ann Rinaldi: Historian and Storyteller* (Lanham, MD: Scarecrow Press, 2000), 69.

29. Robertson Davies, "Fiction of the Future," *The Merry Heart: Selections 1980–1995* (Toronto: Viking, 1996), 358.

30. Anne Scott Macleod, "Writing Backward: Modern Models in Historical Fiction," *The Horn Book* (January/February 1998), 26; hereafter cited parenthetically in text.

31. As the above discussion indicates, historical novelists feel increasingly free to stray from "what is known to be true." See, for example, Phillip Roth's *The Plot Against America,* in which he creates a novel revolving around the defeat of Franklin D. Roosevelt in his run for a third term and the election of Charles Lindbergh to the presidency. Nonetheless, however far from known events these novelists stray, they take pains to keep their stories believable.

32. Avi, "Writing Backwards but Looking Forward," *SIGNAL* 22.2 (Summer 1999): 21.

33. Barnhouse, *Recasting the Past,* 1.

34. Thelma Seto, "Multiculturalism is not Halloween," *The Horn Book* (March/April 1995), 172.

35. Violet J. Harris, "Continuing Dilemmas, Debates, and Delights in Multicultural Literature," *The New Advocate* 9.2 (Spring 1996), 113; hereafter cited parenthetically in text.

36. Harris's argument is marred by the fact that all of the "black" cultural artifacts she mentions here did not exist when Walker was alive.

37. Kathryn Lasky, "To Stingo with Love," *The New Advocate* 9.1 (Winter 1996), 6; hereafter cited parenthetically in text.

38. W.E.B. DuBois, quoted in *Presenting Kathryn Lasky*.

39. Marc Aronson, "A Mess of Stories," *The Horn Book* (March/April 1995), 167.

40. Atwood, "In Search of *Alias Grace*: Writing Canadian Historical Fiction," *The American Historical Review* 5.5, 1510–1511.

41. Stephanie Loer, Interview with Karen Cushman, http://www.eduplace.com/rdg/author/Cushman/question.html.

42. Carol Casey, "Carried by Creative Currents," www.childrenslit.com/f_hesse.html

43. McGlinn, *Ann Rinaldi*: 3; hereafter cited parenthetically in text.

44. Joanne Brown, *Presenting Kathryn Lasky* (New York: Twayne Publishers, 1998), 68.

II

HISTORICAL FICTION AS SOCIAL REALISM

· 4 ·

More than Skin Deep

[I]t inspires us with hope when we reflect, that our cause is not alone the cause of four million black men in this county, but we are intensely alive to the fact that it is also the cause of millions of oppressed men in other "parts of God's beautiful earth," who are now struggling to be free in the fullest sense of the word, and God and nature are pledged to their triumph.

Anonymous[1]

One of the most striking and positive consequences of multiculturalism has been its drive to tell the stories of those "millions of oppressed" referred to by the anonymous speaker at the 1865 Black Convention held in Charleston, South Carolina. In young adult historical fiction this has resulted in a plethora of novels that explore the less admirable and the morally reprehensible aspects of American history from the perspectives of those denied equal access to the elusive American dream of material success.[2] All of these novels, regardless of which specific historical events they build on, explore similar themes: the often misunderstood promise of equality in the Declaration of Independence, the pain of being labeled the outsider or the "other," the frustration of struggling for what white Americans view as their birthright, and finally, the awareness that equal rights can only be achieved through cooperative action. This latter theme's importance comes from its implicit rejection of an integral but dangerous component of the American dream, that success and happiness are the inevitable product of individual effort.[3]

The stories of marginalized and oppressed groups are not a new development; consider Harriet Beecher Stowe's wildly successful *Uncle Tom's Cabin*. What *is* new is the willingness to have those stories told from the perspective of the oppressed and to use that group's language and cultural milieu. To understand

59

the difference between early tales that positioned blacks, for example, as more contented in slavery than as free individuals, and contemporary novels that take as their subject the same antebellum period of the American South, one need only to compare two novels written a century apart.

Diddie, Dumps, and Tot or Plantation Child-Life

Louise-Clarke Pyrnelle's *Diddie, Dumps, and Tot or Plantation Child-Life*, first published in 1882 by Harper Brothers, is a nostalgia-driven account of life on a Mississippi plantation in the years preceding and after the Civil War.[4] The novel follows the adventures of three white sisters with the unfortunate nicknames of Diddie, Dumps, and Tot, and the admiring child slaves who apparently derive all of their satisfaction in life from attending to the white girls. The last chapter of the novel, titled "What Became of Them," makes clear the author's view that both the Civil War and, in particular, the emancipation of the slaves, was an unfortunate development for both blacks and whites.

We learn that the grand old mansion, that "happy home," has been burned down in the war and that the father of the white children "nobly died for Dixie" (234). In the aftermath of his death, his widow is driven to madness by "the agony of . . . the loss of her husband and her home" (235). Diddie's young husband dies on the Confederate "field of glory" (236), leaving his eighteen-year-old bride pregnant with their first child, and Dumps devotes her life after the war to teaching school and caring for her mother who resides in the State Lunatic Asylum. The youngest sister, Tot, is fortunate enough to avoid all pain and sorrow by dying young, before the war, and so is with the "bright band of angel children" (237) ready to greet her father when his "stainless soul" ascends to heaven.

Pyrnelle's clear sympathies for the lost Confederate cause lead her to represent the blacks who grew up on the plantation with the sisters in two ways, both of which deny them any complexity or, ultimately, any humanity. First, they are made to seem ridiculous by their attempts to use their status as free men or women to better themselves and others. The freed slave Jim becomes a politician under Reconstruction who "spends his time making long and exciting speeches . . . against the Southern whites, all unmindful of his happy childhood, and of the kind and generous master who strove in every way to render his bondage a light and happy one" (238). This passage fairly drips with contempt and willfully ignores the economic function of plantations and slavery. Significantly, Pyrnelle's contempt is not directed toward the slave owner but toward the ungrateful freed slave. Not only does she absolve the dead slave owner of any responsibility for his part in maintaining slavery, she actually commends him for making the best of a bad situation for which "he was in no way to blame," although he clearly profited from it. Jim is condemned not only for his lack of appreciation of his master's efforts to make his enslavement "light and happy" but, more importantly, for claiming the previously exclusive white privilege of using language—"making long and exciting speeches"—to effect social change.

Other black characters are depicted in equally demeaning ways, and, more often than not, are deeply nostalgic for their past lives as slaves on the plantation. From Pyrnelle's perspective, admirable black characters include Uncle Snake-bite Bob, who has the good sense "not to meddle with politics" (238) because he recognizes that doing so will impede his chances of getting to the "heb'nly sho." In the world of this novel, only whites who "meddle" in politics are absolved of sin for such activities. More interesting are the fates of Dilsey, Chris, and Riar, the former slaves who as children waited on and occasionally played with the title characters. These three are married now, with children of their own, and "nothing delights them more than to tell their little ones what "us an' de white chil'en usen ter do" (239).

Twenty-first century readers may find it unbelievable that former slaves had nothing better to recount to their children than their happy times with their white owners, but this narrative no doubt resonated with Prynelle's readers who subscribed to the narrative she constructed, still mourning the passing of slavery, resenting and resisting black attempts to claim full civil rights. The establishment of Jim Crow laws and the disenfranchisement of black citizens that persisted well into the twentieth century provide somber testimony to a receptive audience for Pyrnelle's novel.

Wolf by the Ears

Pyrnelle's notion of a "light and happy" enslavement is contested in Anne Rinaldi's *Wolf by the Ears*. Written as the journal of Harriet Hemmings, the illegitimate daughter of Thomas Jefferson and his long-time mistress and slave, Sally Hemmings, Rinaldi's novel represents slavery, even when accompanied by material comfort and love, as denial of another's humanity. In the first chapter Harriet explains that her journal was given to her by "Thomas Jefferson, my master"[5] who encourages her to write down what she feels because "it eases the heart" (9). Jefferson's recognition that Harriet's heart might need easing is possibly a reflection of his own heart's conflicted state produced by his ambivalence toward slavery. Author of the Declaration of Independence that guaranteed all men the right to life, liberty, and the pursuit of happiness, Jefferson was, nevertheless, very much a man of his time, one who saw those rights as exclusively the privileges of white men. He was also a conflicted slave holder, believing that new states should not allow slavery.

Rinaldi draws the title of her novel from a letter of Jefferson's in which he described the consequence of the United States permitting slavery: "Gradually, with due sacrifices, a general emancipation and expatriation could be effected. But as it is we have the wolf by the ears, and can neither hold him, nor safely let him go. Justice is in one scale, and self-preservation the other." This statement effectively signifies Jefferson's ambivalence toward slavery coupled with his desire to avoid conflict.

In *Wolf by the Ears,* his conflicted attitude toward slavery is reflected in his attitude toward the children he fathered with Sally. Rinaldi shows that although he loves them, he will not acknowledge them as his children. He promises them freedom when they turn twenty-one while desperately hoping they will choose to remain at Monticello, even though to remain is to accept servitude. All of his children by Sally have jobs on the plantation, but they are relatively easy ones compared to the onerous field work that his other slaves endure. Harriet and her brothers are all well-clothed and well-fed, taught to read and write, and encouraged to use his library. But Jefferson never acknowledges his relationship with Sally Hemings and their children. They all call him "Master," with the exception of his son Beverly, who calls him "anything I want."

When Harriet asks him if he will include her "mama" in his autobiography, in effect asking him if he will acknowledge the importance of a black woman in his life, Jefferson "smiled. But now his eyes were sad" (8). Later in the novel Harriet's pain at the thought of leaving Monticello is assuaged by her brother's reminder that Jefferson doesn't acknowledge them or their mother as anything but slaves: "Even if we're not his, even if you have doubts about that, you don't have doubts about what Mama is to him. But even she is on those slave lists" (213–14).

Harriet's gratitude for the journal Jefferson gives her at the beginning of the novel stems from her recognition that it is highly unusual for him to give a gift to "a nigra servant" (9). Recognition, however, is not to be confused with acceptance, and it is the material conditions of her life coupled with her confusion about Jefferson's relationship to her mother, and about whether he is, indeed, her father that creates much of the emotional tension fueling the novel.

The tension is also heightened by the silent tug-of-war over her future in which her parents are engaged. Harriet loves both her mother and her master. Each has a different plan for her future. Sally is determined that her daughter claim her freedom when she turns twenty-one. Jefferson is determined to keep her at Monticello, and Harriet is torn between their contradictory wishes: "I am my mamma's only surviving daughter. So then, you'd think she would not want to get rid of me. But she does . . . Master doesn't want me to go. Doesn't want my brother Beverly to go, either" (11–12). The illicit nature of her parents' relationship means that any plans they make for their daughter's future are

made covertly rather than openly. Harriet realizes that "Jefferson uses innocence as a weapon. He uses silence as a shield. He rules by kindness" (67). Sally
is more direct, arguing that "Freedom is all that matters" (18) and does everything in her power to ensure that if her children don't absorb this message from
her, they do so from others.

Harriet herself is reluctant to claim her freedom, writing in her journal,
"I don't want to leave here when I am twenty-one. And that is as big a truth
anybody can get past their lips" (13). Her reluctance has several sources. She
feels a sense of ownership of Monticello (36), however misguided it may be.
Her unwillingness can also be viewed as the emotional inheritance she has received from a mother and father who have been defined by the contradictory
pulls in their own characters as well as by their difficult relationship with one
another. Although Sally is determined that her daughter should claim freedom,
she herself rejected her own opportunity for freedom, and, so, like Jefferson, is
beset by conflicting impulses. Harriet describes Sally as a woman who has "this
sickness in her for thinking that if she'd had the sense of a hooty owl, she'd
have stayed in France years ago when she was there with the master. . . . She
was free in France" (18).

It was Sally's love of Jefferson, her desire to be with him, and his promise
that their children should be free that led her to reject the opportunity for freedom. Clearly, Sally still loves Jefferson, but her love doesn't keep her from recognizing his contradictions and raging against them: "He was president of these
United States. What's he done for our people besides all that fancy speechify-
ing?" (18). Sally knows her American history and uses that knowledge to further denounce Jefferson: "Sure he asks Congress to end the slave trade. Back in
1806. . . . But did he encourage them to pass a bill that would have banned slavery in all the states beyond the original thirteen?" (18). Sally is never depicted
confronting Jefferson with the contradictions in his behavior and, indeed, we
never see them in conversation, except in their roles as master and slave. But
her son Beverly, Harriet's older brother, does not hesitate to confront his father. Passionate in his desire to enroll as a student at the University of Virginia,
the university Jefferson is founding, Beverly challenges the man he knows loves
him, whom he knows is his father but who will not, cannot, bring himself to
openly acknowledge him as such:

> "You don't think I am smart enough to go to the university."
> "Beverly, I know you are smart enough to go to the university."
> "Then let me go. . . ."
> "I told you I can't," the master says again.
> "You can" . . . "It's your university . . . You built it. You were president of
> the United States! You can do anything" (41).

Beverly's declaration of "You can do anything" represents a child's faith in a parent's omnipotence. But Jefferson cannot do "everything" because to enroll Beverly would be to acknowledge that in his relationship with Sally Hemming, he has violated one of his culture's taboos. And to acknowledge that relationship would destroy his reputation. He tries to explain this to Beverly, tries to justify his unwillingness to tackle his culture's restrictions by telling the story of an old friend, another signer of the Declaration of Independence. George Wyeth openly acknowledged his relationship with his mulatto housekeeper and ended up murdered. The murderer, the dead man's nephew, went free. Jefferson draws a firm lesson from this story. "I am one man. I cannot change the way of things" (44).

Believing that he can do little for his children other than love them from a distance, Jefferson nevertheless hopes to keep his children on Monticello as long as he can, using what Harriet terms "the velvet trap of the master's love" (46), a term she acquires from an unexpected source, Thomas Mann Randolph, Thomas Jefferson's son-in-law and governor of Virginia. Sally, well aware of Harriet's reluctance to leave Monticello as a free woman, has contrived for her daughter to have a conversation with Randolph. Though the inhabitants of Monticello consider Randolph crazy, Sally dismisses this notion, telling Harriet, "Well, if he's crazy, that man, then I am the Queen of France" (19). During his encounter with Harriet, Randolph describes the situation Jefferson has created for himself and for his children: "My sainted father-in-law . . . here at Monticello he's laid a trap for himself . . . I'm talking about the traps we humans make for ourselves . . . Sometimes they are made of velvet . . . Are you making a trap for yourself here at Monticello, Harriet Hemings?" (27).

Harriet's reluctance to leave Monticello when given the opportunity is, as stated earlier, an understandable emotional consequence of the mixed messages she gets from her parents. But it also stems from her reluctance to accept the fact that in spite of all the material comforts of her life and the concern of her master, she is still a slave. Randolph asks her, "You like being a slave?" (26). And she is thrown into confusion, saying, "I am not a slave" (27). In response to her assertion, Randolph points out that despite the life she leads, despite the fact that "You're as white as any of them around here" (25), she is still a slave (27). Then, talking to Harriet as "no white person" (28) except Thomas Jefferson has, Randolph explains the nature of the velvet trap to her. Reacting to her assertions that she loves "Master Jefferson" and that he is "kind" to her, Randolph says:

> Kind, eh? Well kindness is not freedom. And security is not freedom. Freedom is often lonely. Nobody takes care of you. You take care of yourself. You think for yourself. You do dimwitted things, and you are sorry for them. You

pay for them. But there is no feeling in the world like freedom ... The way
you people feel around here is wrong ... slavery is wrong ... Look at my father-in-law. He can't make up his mind about slavery. Hates it yes. Says it's a
wolf America has by the ears. And that we can no longer hold onto it. But
neither can we let it go. (28–9)

Harriet promises to think about what Randolph has told her. But she resists his ideas even when other slaves tell her that if she stays at Monticello, she
will remain a slave, be forced to marry a slave, and any children she bears will
themselves be slaves. It takes an attempted rape by Mr. Randolph's son-in-law
to finally convince her to take her freedom while she can. Her decision to leave
is accompanied by another realization of equal importance: when she leaves
Monticello she will pass, that is, enter the larger world as a white woman. Randolph has told her that she "looks just like [Jefferson]," and it is those features
she shares with her father, white skin and red hair, that will make it easy for
her to pass as white physically, if not emotionally.

In the "Author's Note" to this novel Rinaldi writes that she wanted to
"do an historical novel about alienation" (x), and certainly there are many levels of alienation evident in *Wolf by the Ears*. Both Sally and Jefferson are alien-
ated from their idealistic selves by a complex of factors, she by her love for him
and her hopes for her children, he by his ambivalence about slavery and his
(convenient) belief that one man cannot affect significant social change. Once
Harriet makes the decision to leave Monticello and pass herself off as a white
woman, she experiences guilt, sorrow, and anxiety—guilt for leaving Jefferson,
who views her departure as an "attack" (225), sorrow because she knows she
leaves a man who, though he loves her, has made a conscious effort to ensure
that she, her mother, and her siblings have no record in his life as anything
other than slaves (214). Finally, she experiences anxiety because she knows that
in representing herself as white, she is cutting herself off, alienating herself from
the black community that has loved and supported her throughout her life.[6]

Sally adds to Harriet's confusion by telling her, "I don't know what it is,
keeping a family together. All my life I wanted for you and your brothers. That
we should be here together as family. Yet I only came back with him from Paris
because he promised me my children would someday be free. And that means
the end of my family" (225–6).

Sally's pain over losing her family is balanced by the joy she feels knowing
that her children will experience the freedom she has never had. She knows, as
all Americans of color have learned, that progress is slow and painful but that any
step forward made by a member of an oppressed group is occasion for pride:
"Point is, when [Beverly's] done and out there making something of himself ...
then he can come out and say he's part nigra ... And he'll be so proud because
he had to go the long way around but he got there just the same" (240).

Harriet strikes her own blow for equality as she leaves Monticello for the last time, a blow initiated by a suggestion from the white man she has agreed to marry. Though small, it is nevertheless an effective and necessary way of claiming her freedom. She resists it until she hears Jefferson's final words of advice to her, that if she should ever find herself "in difficulty and doubt how to extricate yourself, do what is right" (244).[7] Saying good-bye to the man she now knows is her father for the last time, Harriet does, indeed, do what is right: for the first time in her life she addresses him as "Mister Jefferson" rather than as "Master," thus claiming a more equal footing with him.[8] Her words cause "shock, confusion, even hurt" (247) in Jefferson's eyes, but they help Harriet break her "bonds" and leave her "singing" inside.

The notion of passing has typically referred to light-skinned black Americans choosing to represent themselves as white. Obviously, not all blacks have had this option, and many who have had the option have chosen not to use it. But it is possible to broaden the concept to include the pressure that has historically been placed on *all* minorities to assume behaviors and characteristics identified as white in order to "fit in." Curtis Chang, for example, in his essay, "Streets of Gold: The Myth of the Model Minority," convincingly argues that "the American public has historically demanded assimilation over racial pluralism."[9] Assimilation or "fitting in" would, in theory, chip away at white resistance to equal rights for blacks, and it was a practice advocated by many whites and black leaders like Booker T. Washington and reinforced by institutions such as the public library system (see chapter 2).

Mary Jane

The pressure to fit in as a tactic for claiming rights and opportunities provides a thematic framework for Dorothy Sterling's *Mary Jane*, published in 1959. Though it was written almost fifty years ago, the novel is worth exploring for two reasons. First, it is of historical interest, revealing strategies commonly used by blacks in their attempts to achieve civil rights. And, second, by virtue of its continued presence in libraries, it has become a novel that, though not intended to be historical, has achieved historical status. Initially, *Mary Jane* was important because it was one of the few novels published in the late 1950s to explore racism from a young person's perspective, using the experiences of a young black girl who takes on the challenge of integrating a high school. Clearly written as a response to the forced integration of Little Rock in 1957, Sterling's novel is a moving portrayal of an ambitious but naïve girl who glibly takes on the role of "foreign ambassador."[10] Mary Jane's glibness is in part the consequence of her youth but perhaps more so the result of living a safe, middle-class, but clearly segregated existence. Her decision to help integrate Woodrow Wilson High School is motivated by her desire to attend the "best high school" (6), buttressed by her belief that "I've got a right to go to Wilson" (7). Mary Jane understands on a theoretical level that there will be people who "might not like that pretty, cinnamon-colored skin of yours. Might be they could be mean to you" (15), but she is ignorant of the real effects of this hate.

One of the first consequences of her decision to integrate is a new awareness that the world is divided into "we" and "they" (26), and that they, the whites, have the power to influence such seemingly minor details as what she wears to school. Mary Jane learns this when she shops with her mother for new school clothes and tries, unsuccessfully, to convince her mother to buy her a red sweater. Her mother's rationale for refusing is racially based: "It's too flashy for school . . . it's just what they would expect you to wear" (26).

Ironically, Mary Jane's new-found awareness of the we/they nature of a racist culture is her introduction to a modality that has historically facilitated racism. Describing this phenomenon, theologian Cornell West has written: "How we set up the terms for discussing racial issues shapes our perception and response to these issues. As long as black people are viewed as 'them,' the burden falls on blacks to do all the 'cultural' and 'moral' work necessary for healthy race relations. The implication is that only certain Americans can define what it means to be American—and the rest must simply 'fit in.'"[11] Throughout the novel Mary Jane wears nothing but grey, navy, or white clothing, nothing that will reinforce any stereotypes about black affinity for bright, "flashy" colors. Under her mother's protective tutelage she does all that she can to "fit in." And, as West points out, it is Mary Jane, not her white classmates, who bears the burden of trying to achieve healthy race relations.

Not surprisingly, this burden is heavier than Mary Jane first imagines. She experiences all the manifestations of bigotry described so vividly by Melba Pattillo Beals' powerful memoir, *Warriors Don't Cry*, about integrating Central High School in Little Rock Arkansas in 1957. Like Melba, Mary Jane is verbally and physically harassed. Fellow students threaten to throw acid in her face. Her family receives threatening phone calls. And she suffers the pain of isolation. Though her girlfriends from her previous school don't deliberately exclude her from their activities, their different status as students in an all-black high school inevitably weakens their earlier friendship. Sympathetic to Mary Jane's experiences, her grandfather, a renowned biologist, suggests that white people's "dislike" of black people is based not just on hate but on ignorance as well: "Hate's part of it . . . and not knowing another part. They've got this picture of a Negro in their minds and they just don't know you" (15). Mary Jane's struggle, her challenge throughout the novel is to somehow get her classmates to "know" her, and, as a consequence of knowing, to accept her. She needs to move their knowledge from the realm of untested theory to that of tested experience.

Though her attempts to fit in don't shield her from her classmates' scorn and contempt, she does eventually achieve a limited degree of friendship and acceptance in ways that are familiar to readers of young adult novels: she befriends an injured animal and is herself befriended by another marginalized student, Sally, a white girl whose small size and childlike dress prevents her from being taken seriously by students her own age. On rare occasions she also shows anger, shoving back at students who shove her. Other times Mary Jane uses humor to undermine her teacher's tendency to stereotype: "In Social Studies when the teacher said 'your people' and the class turned to look at her, she craned her neck, too, and kept on doing it until some of the boys and girls laughed" (208).

Sally's friendship with Mary Jane supports Mary Jane's grandfather's contention that ignorance forms the basis of racism: "Until I got to know you I always thought . . . I always thought that all Negros looked alike and were different from whites somehow. But now I know—I mean, they're just people like anybody else" (151). Though both Sally and Mary Jane's parents are concerned about their daughters' friendship, allowing them to associate at school but not to visit each other's home, the girls persist. They ignore taunts from schoolmates and struggle to find ways to spend time openly with each other. Ultimately they succeed by finding a sympathetic teacher who helps them sponsor a science club that both can join. Once the science club is formed and its members are attempting to organize field trips, they must deal collectively with the problem of segregation when they learn that many of the places they wish to visit will not allow Mary Jane to accompany them. After a debate, one member suggests that the club "should not go anyplace where Mary Jane can't go" (206). A vote is taken and all but one student agree. Realistically, the conclusion of the book does not attempt to resolve all the racial issues raised in the narrative: Mary Jane is still not allowed to visit Sally, the Mother's League that protested her attendance at the school continues actively to oppose her, and many students persist in moving away from her when she sits down. Yet Mary Jane decides, even though she is still the subject of harassment, that "she was succeeding as foreign ambassador at Wilson High after all" (218). Obviously, this relatively happy ending is a function of the young adult genre. Nevertheless, the book's advocacy of patient persistence in the face of aggressive and active hate is a historically accurate rendering of black Americans' strategies for achieving civil rights when the book was published.

Written only two years after the Little Rock school integration episode that triggered it, *Mary Jane* is clearly of historical interest and provides us with knowledge of how issues of race were dealt with in the late 1950s, a critical time in the formation of the civil rights movement. Both Mary Jane and Sally, for example, are advised by their parents to "just be patient and things will work out all right" (137), an attitude toward civil rights promoted by both blacks and whites at this period. Mary Jane's mother's attempts to help her daughter "fit in" by rejecting any aspects of self-presentation that might be associated with black culture reveals her acceptance of the dominant white culture's right to determine what is normative.

Not only the character of Mary Jane and the novel's attitude toward civil rights in general, but the novel as a whole can be read as an attempt to "fit in," to make black people less of a threat by stressing their similarities to the implied reader. Mary Jane's grandfather, for example, is a retired college professor, a famous biologist who modestly eschews his earned right to be referred to as "doctor." Mary Jane's family is clearly a professional family; her father is a lawyer, and her brother studies to be one; yet her family claims none of the status of professional individuals. Likewise, the females in Mary Jane's family do nothing to threaten the hegemony of traditional gender roles: her mother is a "stay-at-home mom," and her sister is studying to be a nurse. Perhaps most telling, though, is the complete absence of anything that might be suggestive of black culture. In truth, if the reader were not told that Mary Jane was black, there would be nothing in the book to indicate it. Mary Jane's family lives in the South, but there are no linguistic markers in the book associated with either southern or, more specifically, black dialect. Nothing, in short, that would make a reader struggle with the notion of difference or suggest that difference might be something to celebrate rather than suppress.

The Watsons Go To Birmingham—1963

Such is not the case with Christopher Paul Curtis's *The Watsons Go To Birmingham—1963*, which, like *Mary Jane*, is a fictional response to an actual event, the September 15, 1963, bombings of the Sixteenth Avenue Baptist Church in Birmingham, Alabama, which killed four teenage girls. Unlike *Mary Jane*, Curtis's novel depicts an unmistakable black family and a black culture struggling with issues of class and generational conflict as well as racism. It is told from the perspective of ten-year-old Kenny, the middle child of the Watsons of Flint, Michigan, and much of the novel deals with the family's attempts to deal with the misbehavior of Bryon, who at thirteen is "officially a teenage juvenile delinquent."[12] Most of the action takes place in Flint with the family's trip to Birmingham occupying only the final five chapters.

The family's trip from Flint to Birmingham functions as an apt metaphor for a child's movement from the safe confines of home into the more complicated and, for black children, often threatening adult world. Curtis's text explores the different forms of racism found in the North and the South, and the epilogue delineates these differences. Curtis points out that "In the Northern, Eastern, and Western states, African Americans often faced discrimination, but it was not as extreme and pervasive as in the South" (207). He itemizes the institutionalized specifics of these differences: "discrimination in schooling, housing and job opportunities; prohibited interracial marriages; and enforced segregation by creating separate facilities for African Americans and whites" (207). As the novel unfolds, Kenny experiences first-hand the difference between northern and southern racisim.

For much of the novel Kenny is more often an observer than a participant in the action of the book. His perspective is complicated by his status as outsider. Though a black child in a black community, Kenny says he has "two things wrong with me" (21) that alienate him from his peers—his love of reading and his wandering eye. Each makes him an object of scorn to his classmates and earns him the status of outsider. The conflicts Kenny experiences in the first two-thirds of the novel occur within the family or in the school yard and have much less to do with race than with being a sibling or a student perceived by his peers as different. Because his world is a segregated one, these earlier conflicts are between blacks—between his parents and his older brother, or between Kenny and schoolmates. It is when his family takes their trip to Birmingham that Kenny learns about the multi-faceted destructiveness of racism. Though Kenny is often told by his teachers that "as Negroes the world is many times a hostile place for us" (23), his knowledge of racism is, like Mary Jane's at the beginning of her story, more theoretical than experiential. Yet unlike Mary Jane, Kenny does not experience pressure from his family to "fit in" by suppressing those features or aspects that are clearly black. In fact, the crisis that precipitates the trip to Birmingham occurs when Byron has his hair straightened or "conked." While parent-child conflict over hair may occur in white families, it usually has a larger cultural significance in black ones. In his autobiography Malcolm X describes his first conk as an indicator of his self-hatred, a self-hatred based on his acceptance of white standards of beauty.[13] And by the 1960s, when the "Black is Beautiful" movement was in its infancy, hair straightening, commonplace in Malcolm's youth, was seen as at best problematic, at worst as a sign of selling out. The Watson parents' anger at Byron's conk is a indication of this cultural shift:

> Momma sucked in a ton of air. "What have you done?" We all knew, though. She took a step back and leaned against the counter like if it wasn't there she would have fallen down. "Oh, my God, your father will kill you!" ... Byron had gotten a conk! A do! A butter! A ton of trouble! ... "Well," Momma said, "that's it; you are now at your daddy's mercy. You've known all along how we feel about putting those chemicals in your hair to straighten it ... What do you think now that you've gone and done it? Does it make you look any better? ... Did those chemicals give you better-looking hair than me and your daddy and God gave you?" (88)

When Dad comes home, he stays calm but takes Bryon to the bathroom where he cuts off the processed hair and shaves his son's head, then shows the results to his wife:

> "'Mrs. Watson,' Dad said, 'you can't possibly deny this is your child. You can tell this boy has got a ton of Sands blood in him, look at those ears!' . . . Momma put her hand over her mouth and said, 'Lord, don't blame this one on my side of the family, someone switched this child at the hospital'" (98).

Though Dad treats his son's action humorously, the conk is nevertheless the event that precipitates the family's trip to Birmingham. Their plan is to leave Byron with his maternal grandmother, and "if things don't work out he'll stay there for the next school year" (118). Both Momma and Dad are convinced "that there are some things that Byron has to learn and he's not learning them in Flint, and the things he's learning are the things we don't want him to" (122). Dad says, with unintended irony in light of the violence that is soon to occur, "Grandma Sands says it's quiet down where they are, but we think it's time Byron got an idea of the kind of place the world can be, and maybe spending some time down South will help open his eyes" (111).

But it is Kenny's eyes that seem to open the widest during the trip to Birmingham, and what he learns is that the scorn and contempt he has experienced from classmates in Flint is nothing compared to black Americans' experience in the South. Kenny's introduction to southern racism begins when Momma explains the plans she has made for the trip that include carefully scheduled stops. When Kenny asks why they can't just stop for a break whenever Dad is tired, his father imitates a redneck accent and replies "Cuz, boy, this he-uh is the deep South you-all is gonna be drivin throo. Y'all colored folks cain't be jes pulllin' up tuh any ol' way-uh and be 'inspectin' tuh get no room uh no food, yuh heah, boy? I said yuh heah what I'm sayin' boy?" (32). Again, Dad uses humor to convey an important message to his children about what it means to be black in America in 1963. He adds emphasis to his message when he resumes his parody, asking the rhetorical question: "Whas a matter wit choo, you think this he-uh is Uhmurica?" (132). It is noteworthy that Dad chooses to assign to southern whites the dialect that historically has been assigned to blacks as a racial linguistic marker rather than a regional one by authors as different in their perspectives as Harriet Beecher Stowe and Louise-Clarke Pynelle.[14]

The bombing of the church occurs in the last thirty pages of the novel, and while it shocks and frightens a "whole river of scared brown bodies" (184), Kenny goes into an emotional tailspin much greater than that experienced by the rest of his family, even that of his younger sister, Joetta, who has escaped from the church. Once back in Flint, Kenny retreats behind the living-room sofa, the place where family pets go when they need healing. To be healed, Kenny needs to find answers to a question: "Why would they hurt some little kids like that?" (199). Byron helps him realize there is no logical answer to Kenny's question (without acknowledging the logic of terror as an effective weapon), but that despite the injured kids, this one cannot withdraw from life:

> Kenny, things isn't ever going to be fair. How's it fair that two grown men could hate Negroes so much that they'd kill some just to stop them from going to school? How's it fair that even though the cops down there might know who did it nothing will probably ever happen to those men? It ain't. But you just gotta understand that that's the way it is and keep on steppin'. (203)

Just "keep on steppin'" can too easily be interpreted as just accepting and enduring, but Byron's advice echoes that of Sally Hemming's to her daughter. Placed in an historical context at the start of the Civil Rights Movement, Byron's advice is intended to help his brother survive in a world of violence against black Americans. He is trying to help Kenny accept that the world is not fair, especially to blacks, but learn that he must continue to endure, resting in the comfort of family love and support—all resources that marginalized groups have consistently drawn upon to survive in an oppressive culture.

Earlier we made reference to Cornell West's judgment that historically the burden for achieving equalitarian racial relations has been placed on the shoulders of the oppressed minority. Two recent young adult novels, Karen Hesse's *Witness* and Joyce McDonald's *Devil on My Heel*, wrestle with the question of white responsibility to confront racism even when that racism materially benefits them. Each novel explores bigotry from the perspective of white characters (though Hesse's novel is told by a whole cast of characters, black and white, young and old, Christian and Jew) whose eyes are gradually opened to an awareness of racism. In each novel the process of awakening to injustice occurs in a small, seemingly close-knit community and is accompanied by a need to help correct that injustice by those who arguably would benefit from its continuance. Finally, in each novel it is the white characters' friendships with members of a minority group and the empathy those friendships engender that awakens them to injustice. This process reinforces the contention made by the grandfather in *Mary Jane* that racism is based on "not knowing" a member of another race.

Witness

Witness is set in Vermont in 1924 in the months immediately preceding the election of Calvin Coolidge as president and the rejection by Vermont's secretary of state of the Ku Klux Klan's application to do "business here."[15] Hesse also reminds the reader of a larger culture of hate and intolerance with references to the D. W Griffin's silent film, *Birth of a Nation,* and events such as the murder of Bobby Franks by Leopold and Loeb. Structured as a drama in five acts, *Witness* touches on many of the social issues that have shaped the twentieth century: racism, anti-Semitism, fundamentalism, the sexual abuse of parishioners by clergy, and attempts of white supremacist groups to foster hate and bigotry. All of these issues are explored in the poetic monologues told by a cast of characters of different races, religions, genders, classes, and ages. But young adult readers are most likely to be drawn to the monologues of Leonora Sutter, a twelve-year-old black girl well aware of how race marginalizes her within her community; six-year-old Esther Hirsh, a Jewish girl from New York; and white eighteen-year-old boy Merlin Van Tornhout. Though all of the characters in the novel are pushed by its events into self-reflection, it is the story of these three young people, especially the transformations of Leonora and Merlin, that deals most directly with the alienating and destructive effects of racism and anti-Semitism.

Hesse begins with a monologue from Leonora, one that captures in striking visual images a moment of racism and the emotional alienation that results from it. Leonora describes a recent event when the girls in her class were asked to dance: "I don't know how miss harvey / talked me into dancing" (3). The consequence of Leonora's teacher's persuasion is that "i leapt and swept my way . . . / separated on the stage from all those limb-tight white girls / the ones who wouldn't dance with a negro . . . they told miss harvey they'd dance / but they wouldn't touch any brown skin girl" (3). Hesse then shifts to the perspective of Merlin Van Tornhut, who has witnessed the dance, and his reaction is painfully blunt: "i pushed the window up in school / to get the stink of leanora sutter out of the classroom . . . / no amount of air will get the smell of her out of my nose / the soot of her out of my eyes" (4).

Esther Hirsh's monologue follows Merlin's. She makes no reference to the dance, the behavior of the white girls toward Leonora, or Merlin's behavior in the classroom. The reason she doesn't can be found in Leonora's monologue: Esther, she says, is the only white girl who "didn't mind me being colored" (3). Esther's lack of concern over Leonora's race is perhaps the understandable reaction of a young girl who has not yet "learned" bigotry. But it is hard to ignore Esther's status as a Jew, another group that is the object of the Ku Klux Klan's hate. Surely, Hesse is deliberately suggesting that shared oppression can create bonds between the oppressed. The plot of the novel, which weaves together incidents of anti-Semitism and racism, suggests as much. The two girls form a bond of sorts after Leonora saves the younger Esther from being run over by a train.

Perhaps more significant is how the two girls effect for the better the lives of those around them. Esther and her father board with the farmer, Sara Chickering. Sara's growing friendship with Esther's widowed father coupled with her affection for Esther lead her to reflect on the transformative power of personal relationships:

i never thought much about it before.
if esther hadn't needed a place the last minute
with all those fresh air kids coming to town,
i would never think of it still.
i might have joined the ladies klan.
become an officer, even. . . .
i think a lot about it these days
the klan says they don't stand against anyone.
but a catholic, a jew, a negro
if they got arrested,
and the judge was klan
and the jury was klan
you can't convince me they'd get a fair trial.

it took having the hirshes here
to see straight through
to the end of it. (59)

As additional voices chime in, it becomes clear that this is a community where, as the sheriff says, "no one is too energetic about helping a colored man hereabouts, even if he is a neighbor" (8). And that subtle racism makes the community ripe for infiltration by the Klan. The increasingly active and aggressive presence of the Klan and the community's divided reaction to it allows Hesse to analyze the shared psychological roots of racism and anti-Semitism. Reynard Alexander, a newspaper editor whose initial stance toward the Klan is one of determined neutrality, becomes increasingly critical of it as he sees how it inserts itself into the community:

on arrival in a town,
the klan appears to serve the best interests of
the greater community,
"cleaning it up," keeping a vigilant eye out for
loose morals and lawbreakers
they deliver baskets to the needy,
money to the destitute,
but the needy the klan comforts are white protestant needy
the destitute white protestant, too. (69)

Though Reynard Alexander's shift from neutrality toward moral outrage is important, it lacks both the drama and narrative significance of Merlin Van Tornhout's movement into both self-understanding and greater tolerance. He is a young man who, as his name suggests, is torn in a variety of directions. Racist and anti-Semitic as he is, he nevertheless has an epiphany of sorts when he watches Leanora race to save Esther from an oncoming train and realizes that:

> i'm not saying she did anything i couldn't have done,
> but when i think on it
> maybe i didn't try because something
> something kept me in my place
> watching that colored girl run. (76)

What keeps Merlin in his place is an admiration, albeit grudging, for Leanora's speed and courage. Later, after he has fled the Klan and is on trial for attempted murder, he says of Leanora: "she was still a colored girl / but she wasn't *just* a colored girl" (150). He has, in effect, come to acknowledge her humanity. Merlin's admiration also makes him more empathetic to all of those he has bullied in the past, both black and Jew. When he is assaulted by a fellow Klansman whom he picks up on his way to a Klan meeting, he realizes "i never have been out bullied before . . ." The experience of being assaulted by one of his own group creates empathy for the young Jewish boy Bobby Frank who was killed by college-aged Jewish boys. Merlin was previously contemptuous of the victim because the boy "allowed" himself to be killed, but now he thinks differently:

> I thought about that boy in chicago,
> that bobby franks,
> and i looked at the drifter in my automobile,
> and i knew
> he would gladly do to me
> what leopold and loeb had done to that boy
> in chicago. (94)

Merlin's shifts, his realization that the world is not as easily understood as the Klan suggests, may seem small but they start a "roar" (115) in his head. That roar, a sign of moral confusion, makes it impossible for him to carry out the Klan's orders to poison Leanora's father's well. Unable to muster the courage to tell the Klan he has not followed orders, Merlin flees town. Later he returns and is wrongfully charged with attempted murder but is acquitted by Esther's testimony. At the end of the novel, when the Klan leaves the community, Merlin acknowledges that "i can't say I'm sorry about that" (153). And though Merlin, like his whole community, has suffered wounds that will take a long time to heal, both he and the town are better for being shocked out of their complacency.

Devil on My Heels

Joyce McDonald's *Devil on My Heels* is set in Benevolence, Florida, in 1959, and its events occur in the shadow of the attempts to integrate a high school in Little Rock, Arkansas. Late in the novel when one of the characters sardonically refs to the town as "Malevolence," the aptness of the misnomer has been well established by the plot. The narrator, Dove Alderman, is the daughter of a prominent orange grove owner. Her life at the novel's start is one of little care and much privilege. Her daily life has many of the qualities associated with situation comedies that nostalgically represent the 1950s, comedies like *Happy Days*, that portray life as a carefree time for adolescents, most of whom are white and middle-class.

The only child of a loving but distant widowed father, Dove is, at first glance, a typical fifteen-year-old girl: she worries about getting to the movies on time, bemoans a bad haircut, reads love poetry, and is beginning to think about her childhood friend, Chase, romantically. Her homelife is overseen by Delia, a black woman who has been the family's housekeeper since Dove's birth and is even responsible for naming Dove. All of these responses and characteristics resonate with those cultural representations that focus on the 1950s as a time of sweetness and light.

But as the plot of *Devil on My Heels* unfolds, the reader becomes aware of social turmoil caused by racial and economic injustice, turmoil that will disrupt the placid surface of Dove's life and call into question all of her assumptions about how her world operates. Gradually, too, a darker, more complex characterization of Dove emerges. She reads love poetry to dead boys, for example, in graveyards. She smokes cigarettes on the sly and sneaks out of the house late at night to make out with Chase. She is increasingly uncomfortable with the rigid class system that condemns her new friendship with the daughter of migrant farm workers. And she is sickened when classmates laugh at a postcard of a lynched black man. Delia, too, is more than the slightly befuddled, loving black housekeeper of media myth. She wears her dead husband's clothes to remind those who killed him that she hasn't forgotten the injustice of his death. She, too, reads poetry, but it is the poetry of black poets who rage against racial injustice.

Ultimately, Dove is forced to confront her classmates' hostility to an interracial romance between a white girl and a black boy, the mistreatment of Mexican farm workers by the manager of her father's orange groves and, worst of all, her father's membership in the Ku Klux Klan. By placing Dove's moral awakening in the context of larger social issues, McDonald contests those nostalgia-infused representations of the 1950s that skim over that decade's social problems. Family dysfunction as well as racial and sexual tensions all reveal the fault lines in the homogenous world previously presented as normative by the dominant culture. Dove's father is loving but distant. Delia makes little effort to suppress her anger over her husband's death by a hit-and-run driver. And Dove's favorite English teacher is likely to be fired for exposing her students to the beat poetry of Allen Ginsberg and Lawrence Ferlinghetti.

When a series of fires occur, caused by drought conditions, white men in Benevolence falsely attribute them to migrant pickers dissatisfied with their wages and work conditions. Dove is forced to recognize the injustice on which her life of privilege is built. She is also forced to recognize that to the workers who pick her father's oranges she is "the daughter of the enemy. I am not to be trusted."[16] Finally, she recognizes that she lives in a world where "there are two kinds of justice . . . justice for the white folks and a whole other justice for the coloreds" (120), and she resolves to do what she can to change this. Dove cannot accept the notion of two kinds of justice, and she refuses to accept Chase's contention that "whatever is going on, it's nothing you can do anything about" (126). After Dove learns the details of Delia's husband's death, she feels compelled to act, insisting to her father that we "owe Gus [Delia's husband] and Delia justice" (182). Dove's insistence on justice initiates a chain of events that are both physically and emotionally violent: Gator, a black childhood friend who has been organizing other pickers, and Chase are beaten by the Klan, and Gator almost dies. Chase is permanently estranged from his father, a Klan member, and Delia refuses to continue working for Dove's father. Whether justice is achieved in *Devil on My Heels* is arguable, but at the end of the novel Dove knows she has done some good: her father renounces his membership in the Klan, fires his racist manager, and improves both the conditions and wages of his workers. Still, the book ends on a melancholy note: looking out over her father's orange groves, Dove imagines she sees Chase and Gator as boys racing freely and joyously through the trees. But the knowledge she has gained makes her aware that those moments of easy camaraderie are unlikely to be repeated in adult life.

None of the books discussed in this chapter have the proverbial happy ending.[17] One could argue that the convention of optimistic endings that closed earlier young adult fiction is now an anachronism. And, perhaps, in a culture as racist as ours, the melancholy and ambivalent tone that characterizes the endings is the best, most honest ending readers can expect. Still, all of the novels are valuable to readers for the representation they provide into the American past. Young adults who read these books come away not only with a better understanding of the consequences of racism and bigotry but of the ways in which responses to them have been shaped by the culture that produces them.

NOTES

1. Quoted by Vincent Harding in *There Is a River: The Black Struggle for Freedom in America* (New York: Harcourt, Brace and Co, 1981), 318.

2. Racism in the United States, of course, affects people of many skin colors and backgrounds; however, because the issue of race is often tied closely to stories of immigration, this chapter will focus only on novels with protagonists whose stories are not immediately complicated by the problems associated with coming to a new land and culture. The struggles and triumphs of immigrant groups will be examined in Chapter 8.

3. Roger Betsworth, *Social Ethics: An Examination of American Moral Traditions* (Louisville, KY: Westminster/John Knox Press, 1990).

4. Louise-Clarke Pyrnelle, *Diddie, Dumps, and Tot or Plantation Child-Life* (NY: Harper and Brothers Publishers, 1882), 234. From the private collection of Professor Joan Gordon; hereafter cited parenthetically in the text as *Diddie*.

5. Ann Rinaldi, *Wolf by the Ears* (New York: Scholastic, 1991); hereafter cited parenthetically in text.

6. Rinaldi provides family trees for both Jefferson and Sally. Sally's tree makes clear the outrageousness of southern laws that defined anyone who had even "one drop" of black blood in them to be defined as black and, as such, a victim of all laws that oppressed blacks. Early in *Wolf by the Ears,* we learn that Thomas, an older brother of Harriet's, so closely resembled Thomas Jefferson that he was sent away from Monticello whenever guests arrived. The absurdity of those laws and the anxiety experienced by those defined as black as well as by those who chose to pass as white has been recorded in sources as varied as the nineteenth-century short stories of Kate Chopin (see "Desiree's Baby") and memoirs as recent as Shirley Taylor Haizlip's *The Sweeter the Juice*.

7. Jefferson's injunction to "do what is right" resonates ironically in Spike Lee's film on the nature of racism, *Do the Right Thing*.

8. The use of "equal" must be qualified by "more." As stated earlier, Jefferson was a product of his time. His assertion in the Declaration of Independence that all "men are created equal" was not intended to include either blacks or, for that matter, women. While he encouraged women to be educated, that education was intended only to enhance their roles as wives and mothers. He tells Harriet that he admires modesty in women and that he subscribes to the French view that married women should not dance.

9. Curtis Chang, "Streets of Gold: The Myth of the Model Minority." In *Rereading America: Cultural Contexts for Critical Thinking and Writing*, 4th edition (NY: Bedford/St. Martin, 2004), 377. In one of his notes to this essay Chang points out that "pluralism accepts ethnic cultures as equally different: assimilation asks for a 'melting' into the majority." He further points out that "the massive 'Americanization 'programs of the late 1800 . . . successfully erased Eastern European immigrants' customs in favor of Anglo-Saxon ones."

10. Dorothy Sterling, *Mary Jane*. (NY: Scholastic, 1959), 15: hereafter cited parenthetically in the text.

11. Cornell West, *Race Matters*. (Boston: Beacon Press, 1993), 3.

12. Christopher Paul Curtis, *The Watsons Go to Birmingham—1963* (NY: Bantam Doubleday Dell Publishing Group, Inc. 1995), 2; hereafter cited parenthetically in the text.

13. Malcolm X (with Alex Haley): *The Autobiography of Malcolm X.* (NY: Grove Press, 1964), 54. Malcolm describes his conk in the following passage: "How ridiculous I was! Stupid enough to stand there simply lost in admiration of my hair now looking 'white'. . . . This was my first really big step toward self-degradation: when I endured all that pain, literally burning my flesh to have it look like a white man's hair. I had joined that multitude of brain-washed Negro men and women in America who are so brainwashed into believing that the black people are 'inferior'—and white people 'superior'—that they will even violate and mutilate their God-created bodies to try to look 'pretty' by white standards."

14. This accent has also been associated with poor whites by many nineteenth-century novelists.

15. Karen Hesse, *Witness* (NY: Scholastic, 2001), 149; hereafter cited parenthetically in the text.

16. Joyce McDonald, *Devil on My Heels.* (NY: Delacort Press, 2004), 171; hereafter cited parenthetically in the text.

17. Obviously there are dramatically different reasons for Louise Clark Pyrnelle's unhappiness with how her characters' lives are resolved and that of all of the other authors discussed.

A Question of Faith

Faith may be defined briefly as an illogical belief in the occur-
rence of the improbable.

H. L. Mencken
Prejudices, First Volume

$\mathcal{A}$ confirmed cynic, Mencken was noted for his vitriolic attacks against established institutions such as religion. He excelled at framing insults that
elicited scathing retorts from those he labeled the "booboise." Yet there is a
kernel of truth in his definition of faith: belief in an unseen supernatural power
that requires—well, a leap of faith. Nonetheless, faith is universal. Every known
culture practices some form of spirituality and worship.

What accounts for this widespread need for a divine being? A recent
study, *The God Gene: How Faith is Hardwired into Our Genes,* by molecular biologist Dean Hamer,[1] claims that human spirituality is an adaptive trait, allowing the species to survive. Belief in a supreme power theoretically helps to rein
in our worst impulses and bring out our best. Hamer also argues that spirituality is part of the human genetic code; interestingly enough, his theory links
the genetic basis for spirituality to the neurotransmitters that regulate human
moods, a connection that would account for the sense of peace and well-
being that accompanies a spiritual experience. Predictably, the book has stirred
up stormy disputes among theologians, but religion itself—spirituality codified
into sets of laws meant to govern our behavior—has always been a lightning
rod for controversy. Although religion has historically served as a strong source
of identity and security, it has also been a continuing source of conflict. Mil-
lenniums of religious wars and persecution have left a bloody testimony to the
unholy consequences of holiness, but none of the conflicts, no matter how
brutal, has stifled the human need for faith.

Given this need, one might logically expect to find a sizeable number of novels for young adults with a religious theme. Yet there are relatively few. Nilsen and Donelson offer an explanation based on marketing factors:

> Books that unabashedly explore religious themes are relatively rare, partly because schools and libraries fear mixing church and state through spending tax dollars for religious books. Also, mainstream publishers fear cutting into potential readers and making others uncomfortable.[2]

Ironically, the earliest literature for young readers was entirely religious. Puritans in England believed that children were born sinners, and their beliefs traveled to the American colonies. Children frequently died young; the major concern, however, was not illness or death but eternal damnation. So stories for children warned constantly of the brimstone of hell, exalted the joy of death after a pure life, and tried literally to scare the hell out of young readers. The title of a text published in 1671 in England by the fiery Puritan preacher James Janeway and later adapted for the American colonies by the notorious Cotton Mather reveals the didactic nature of the stories between its covers: *A Token for Children: Being an Exact Account of the Conversion, Holy and Exemplary Lives and Joyful Death of Several young Children to Which Is Added: A Token for the Children of New England.* Janeway's statement of purpose is equally revealing:

> You may now hear (my dear lambs) what other good Children have done, and remember how they wept and prayed by themselves; how earnestly they cried out for an interest in the Lord Jesus Christ . . . O Hell is a terrible place, that is a thousand times worse than Whipping.[3]

Mary Lystad gives an overview of books for young readers during colonial times that echoes Janeway and Mather's religious fixation:

> [U]ntil about 1850, books containing adolescent characters and aimed at adolescent readers were written primarily to instruct young people in religious matters and other desired social activities. The religious behavior expected included piety, obedience, humility, and service to others, as well as prudence, hard work, and deference. By following such recommended behavior, a young man or woman would be prepared at any moment to die with a pure heart.[4]

Elsie Dinsmore

No female protagonist had a heart more pure than Elsie Dinsmore, the protagonist of a twenty-eight volume series created by Martha Finley over thirty-eight years. The first volume, *Elsie Dinsmore,* was published in *1867* and introduces the reader to Elsie when she is eight.[5] Her mother has died shortly after giving birth to her, and she lives on an antebellum Southern plantation with her paternal grandparents and their children. Her father had married impulsively, when both he and his bride were still in their teens, and his parents disapproved of the match. Elsie's father, still resentful of Elsie's role in his loss, travels in Europe. He has never seen his daughter. In fact, Elsie is one of the many abandoned-and-mistreated-children in literature. She is comforted mainly by her belief in Jesus, to whom she refers or prays on at least every other page. Still, she sorely feels the lack of familial love:

> [N]o one seemed to really care for her . . . . Mr. Dinsmore, though her own grandfather, treated her with entire neglect, seemed to have no affection for her, and usually spoke of her as "old Grayson's grandchild." Mrs. Dinsmore really disliked her, because she looked upon her . . . as the future rival of her own children. (43)

Her father's younger siblings, especially ten-year-old Arthur, taunt and tease her, but Elsie's only response is to pray and weep. Indeed, she is probably the most piously lachrymose figure in literary history. She can quote by heart long passages of scripture and professes her love for Jesus as often as she weeps. When Elsie is questioned by a visitor about how long she has loved Jesus, she responds with typically tearful devotion:

> "Ever since I can remember," replied the little girl earnestly; "and it was dear old mammy who first told me how He suffered and died on the cross for us." Her eyes filled with tears and her voice quivered with emotion. "She used to talk to me about it just as soon as I could understand anything," she continued; "and then she would tell me that my own dear mamma loved Jesus, and had gone to be with Him in heaven; and how, when she was dying, she put me—a little, wee baby, I was then not quite a week old—into her arms, and said 'Mammy, take my dear little baby and love her, and take care of her just as you did of me; and O Mammy! Be sure that you teach her to love God.'" (26)

Mammy has fulfilled that deathbed wish all too well. The pious Elsie, trying always to emulate her Savior, attempts to repress her anger or disappointment when treated unfairly and prays instead, wallowing in guilt over her failure to be as perfect as Jesus. When her father does finally return, he is stern and cold, making impossible demands and inflicting undeserved, humiliating punishments on her, a child whom most parents would consider uncommonly obedient and well-behaved. Clinging steadfastly to a love of her father despite his abusive ways, she blames herself—much like a battered wife—for his cruelty: "Oh! Why am I always so naughty?[6] Always doing something to displease my dear papa? How I wish I could be good, and make him love me!" (198).

Her father is the ultimate nineteenth-century patriarch. She must submit all her books to him for his approval, he holds the threat of corporal punishment over her head, castigates her for sitting on the floor with the other children to play jack-stones, punishes her one night by allowing her only bread and water for dinner, and forces her as to sit motionless on a stool for an hour because she was "naughty." There is almost no end to his stern fault-finding. When he finally develops some affection for his daughter, their relationship becomes even more disturbing because of its sexual overtones. Although Elsie now basks in her father's attention, he seems less like a father than a jealous husband:

> Her father treated her with the tenderest affection, and kept her with him almost constantly, seeming scarcely willing to have her out of his sight for an hour. He took her with him wherever he went on his rides and walks and visits to neighboring planters. . . . She felt grateful for all the kindness she received, and liked to visit with her papa; but her happiest days were spent at home on those rare occasions when they were free from visitors, and she could sit for hours on his knee, or by his side. (251)

A few pages later, he has locked them away together in his room, a punishment for her alleged impertinence to her grandfather. As he watches Elsie studying her Bible, he thinks, "The darling! . . . she is lovely as an angel, and she is *mine,* mine only, mine own precious one; and loves me with her whole soul" (268).

The turning point in their relationship occurs one Sunday when he orders her to sing some secular music for guests. Elsie refuses, explaining, "I *cannot* sing it to-day, I *cannot* break the Sabbath" (284). Despite the urging of several guests to let Elsie sing the song on the morrow, her father insists. "When I give my child a command, it is to be obeyed; I have *said* she should play it and play it she must" (284). Furious at his daughter's steadfast refusal, he demands that she sit at the piano until she complies. Hours pass as Elsie sits on the "high and uneasy" piano stool without playing or singing a note; finally, she faints. In the fall, she wounds her temple on a sharp corner of the furniture, narrowly avoiding an injury that would have proven mortal.

In the aftermath of this incident, father and daughter are again reconciled, but the reconciliation does little to staunch Elsie's constant flow of tears. She weeps when moved by her father's affectionate words, when she perceives disapproval in his glance, and when she learns that he does not love Jesus. In the final pages, she is overwrought when she hears the servants speculating about her father's romantic attentions to a visiting young woman and his possible marriage to her. "[B]ounding away like a frightened deer to her own room, her little heart beating wildly with a confused sense of suffering, she threw herself on the bed" (397). The novel ends on an ambiguous note. Her father, learning what troubles Elsie, flies up the stairs to his daughter's room, only to find her sleeping, her eyes tear-swollen. Although he "longs" to tell her that her fears are groundless, he refrains from waking her and leaves after kissing away her tears. Elsie sleeps on, unconscious of his visit. One can only assume that their relationship will continue its emotional roller coaster ride in subsequent volumes.[7]

Elsie Dinsmore clearly is stamped by the mores and attitudes of its time, when the virtues listed by Lystad—piety, obedience, humility, hard work, and deference—were demanded of the young. The racial attitudes in the novels are not only outdated but extremely offensive. The plantation on which Elsie lives is staffed by black slaves, euphemistically referred to as "servants."[8] Despite Elsie's piety, she is oblivious to the oppressed status of her beloved Mammy and the other slaves on the plantation, accepting the fact that slaves have reared her, that they dress her, cook for her, and drive her on her occasional outings in the carriage. She is concerned only that she and those she loves be "saved" to earn a place in heaven.

The slaves speak in the same demeaning dialect as the blacks in *Diddie, Dumps, and Tot*. For example, here is Pompey, who drives the family's carriages, exchanging gossip with the other slaves about Mr. Dinsmore's attentions to the visiting lady:

> If Marse Horace don't like her, what for they been gwine ridin' ebery afternoon? will you tell me *dat*, darkies? an' don't dis niggah see him sit beside her mornin', noon, an' night, laughin' an' talkin' at de table an' in de parlor? an' don't she keep a kissing' little Miss Elsie, an' callin' her pretty critter, sweet critter, an' de like? (396)

Mammy, initially nursemaid to Elsie's mother and now to Elsie, grieves in the same dialect for her dead young mistress: "'My darling young missus!' murmured the old nurse, 'my own precious child dat dese arms hab carried so many years, dis ole heart like to break wheneber I tinks ob you, an' 'members how your bright young face done gone away forever'" (384).

Not only does Elsie accept without question her privileged status as the recipient of slave labor, but she also expresses a deeply felt anti-Semitism. When a family friend questions why she is weeping over her Bible, her answer reflects the intolerance of the day towards Jews. "'O Mr. Travilla!' said the little girl, 'does it not make your heart ache to read how the Jews abused our dear, dear Saviour?'" (297).

Given these outdated attitudes (and all of Elsie's tedious weeping), one might reasonably expect the *Elsie* books to have faded into oblivion, however popular they once were. But no. The series—all twenty-eight of them, following Elsie from girlhood through adolescence, marriage, parenthood, widowhood, and grandmotherhood—have been reissued with the boast that they are not "abridged or modernized."[9] In addition, an eight-volume set about Elsie has been published between 1999 and 2001[10] under the umbrella title *A Life of Faith,* "based on the best-selling classic by Martha Finley." These novels follow the same trajectory of Elsie's life, but only from childhood to widowhood, using incidents similar to or the same as in the original. Readers can purchase a study guide lest they miss the urgent message of the stories, that is, as Elsie quotes, "If any man love not the Lord Jesus Christ, let him be anathema, maranatha,' accursed from God" (297). Another volume, *The Character of Elsie,* presents an analysis of Elsie's virtues so that she might serve as a role model for young girls today. Other supporting material has also been published: a *Dear Elsie* volume of advice to young female readers, an Elsie diary for readers to record their thoughts, and an Elsie doll. These texts are widely available at Christian bookstores.

Although it is not uncommon for books published in earlier centuries to attract contemporary notice and republication, the Elsie phenomenon is unusual in that a character from such a problematic novel as *Elsie Dinsmore* has been appropriated by a group, in this case the religious right, to sustain its agenda. In addition, there are two sets of spin-off volumes, also published under the *A Life of Faith* umbrella, some written by Martha Finley, others adapted from her characters and written by contemporary authors. One series features Millie Keith, a friend of Elsie's, the other her daughter Violet Travilla. Both sets, like the *Elsie* series, come with their own paraphernalia such as dolls and study guides.

The *Elsie* volumes, both the original version and the adapted series, represent examples of YA historical stories with a religious theme, albeit a more heavy-handed one than most. Broadly speaking, this body of fiction can be divided into three categories:

1. Novels in which characters profess their faith at the outset and rely on it to see them through life's rough patches. *Elsie Dinsmore* is an extreme example of this group.
2. Novels whose protagonists know little of spiritual matters or reject what they do know, but who develop a strong faith during difficult times and emerge spiritually triumphant.
3. Novels whose characters are based upon tales from either the Old or New Testament and which freely extrapolate from the original, in some cases expanding upon the original texts, in other cases standing them on their respective heads.

In My Enemy's House

Because religion has proved such a source of bloody conflict, many YA historical novels with religious themes have narrated predictably, stories of persecution.

Much of this fiction falls into the first category, stories in which the protagonists survive mainly by clinging to their faith. Such a novel is Carol Matas' *In My Enemy's House*.[11] Told in the first person by fifteen-year-old Marisa Ginsberg, the novel opens with the Nazi occupation of her Polish town. The daughter of devout Jewish parents, Marisa is blond and blue-eyed like her father, a contrast to her dark-eyed, brunette mother and siblings. She is timid, easily frightened, and now terrified by the humiliations and public killings inflicted by the Nazis on the Jews of her neighborhood.

She wonders whether God is punishing them, rationalizing that "if everything is God's will, then this must be a punishment" (5). Things get predictably worse. Her father is taken from the family and loaded onto one of the notorious freight trains; the Nazis isolate the Jews, forcing them to wear armbands with the Star of David and conducting "actions"—mass arrests of Jews who are killed or transported out of the city. Without Papa, Mama cannot cope. As the oldest child in the family, Marisa must take charge, and she calls upon her faith to comfort her sister Fanny and gain strength for herself: "God will take care of us. Either He will spare us or He will take us; either way we're in His care. Don't be afraid" (20).

But there is much to fear. The sisters witness a particularly brutal action in which a truckload of Jews is unloaded by a ravine and shot, their bodies dropping into the gorge. Having survived the massacre, Marisa and Fanny return home to find their mother and younger siblings safe, but Marisa cannot erase the horror of the scene that she has just seen. She wishes she were dead a thought that haunts her throughout much of the novel.

The girls are forced to labor for the Nazis under brutal conditions. One night, Fanny vehemently declares that she "hates" God. She then amends her statement: "No, I don't hate Him. You can't hate what doesn't exist." In response, Marisa quotes the Baal Shem Tov[12]: "In the struggle with evil, only faith matters" (32). Fanny replies that she has no faith; that if there is a God He who made the world also made the rules, and He could have made different ones. Marisa is thunderstruck.

> What if Fanny and Sophie were right? It had *never* occurred to me to question God. *What if he is so cruel?* I thought. Or *could it be that He hates us? Or is He punishing us? Or . . . or . . . He doesn't even exist?* (33)

Later, when Marisa is unsure about the whereabouts of her mother and younger siblings, she puts these doubts aside: "*There is a God. There is a God And He has spared them. He has spared them*" (34). Her response raises another philosophical question: If, indeed, there is a God and He has spared Marisa's family, how to account for the deaths of so many others? One could argue that Marisa's insistent faith at this point is blinkered, though understandably so

Then she learns from a Polish neighbor that her mother and younger siblings have all been taken away on a train. He adds that the Nazis have created a ghetto to which all remaining Jews must move. The neighbor tells Marisa that with her blond hair and blue eyes, she "could be one of us" (35) and explains how he could arrange for the paperwork to give her a new identity, a non-Jewish Polish one.

Marisa resists the idea, but Fanny urges her sister to accept. "Someone from our family has to survive," she says (36). But Marisa's heart has turned to ice and she does not want to live. Before she drops off to sleep that night, she considers saying that she will take the train to Germany to work as a Polish slave, but instead will throw herself on the tracks. As she sleeps, she dreams that her father appears to her and quotes the Baal Shem Tov: "'When God wants to punish a man, He deprives him of faith.' But God will not punish you so. 'The righteous shall live by his faith.' I will be with you, Marisa. And God is always with you. . . . You must never think of taking your own life" (44).

Marisa receives another lesson in faith from her friend Shmuel, with whom she has a romantic relationship, when she prays for the safety of Fanny and her oldest brother, Yahuda. Now both are missing. "Oh God, please God, don't take them, too. Please God," she pleads (62). Her plea demonstrates that she still clings to her faith, but Shmuel discourages this expression of belief: "Marisa, if you pray to God to save them and He doesn't, then eventually you'll lose your faith. And that's all you have. I won't let you lose it" (62). Although Shmuel has wrestled with the problem of whether God exists, he understands one thing very well, that Marisa cannot beg God for personal favors. Instead, she can thank Him for what she has. Marisa is incredulous. What do they have? Shmuel answers that they have love, not hate, in their hearts. He insists that even they lose each other or their lives, they will still have love, love the Nazis cannot take from them, and that is enough reason to give thanks.

Marisa protests that she won't have love, that she hates the Germans and to Shmuel's response that she does not have to harbor such hatred, she retorts that she cannot choose how she feels. "You just feel," she insists. Shmuel's answer is key to Marisa's survival: "You *can* choose," he says. "You can and you *must*" (63).

Marisa's ability to keep love in her heart is tested when she at last decides to assume a Polish, non-Jewish identity. She is instructed to take the train and report to a work center in another Polish town. As the Nazis move through the aisle checking the passengers' papers, Marisa remembers Shmuel's admonition and realizes that there *was* something to thank God for. "*Thank you God, I said to myself, for not making me like them*" (73).

Once at the work center and assigned to a barracks, Marissa must make another crucial decision. The first night, in the dark with hundreds of other girls, most of them asleep, she hears one cry out from a dream—in Yiddish.

Risking her life, Marissa wakes and warns the girl, then scurries back to her own cot just as the supervisor returns. "Why did I do that?" she wonders, knowing that her actions have revealed her Jewish identity. But her faith continues to guide her. "The Talmud said, 'A person is always liable for his actions, whether awake or asleep.' My breath slowed down. *I did the right thing,* I thought, *made the right choice. The outcome is for God to decide*" (74–75).

After a humiliating physical examination, she is put on another train, this time for Germany. At first she works for an abusive German farmer, where she is one of several "filthy Poles" there. The only bright spot of this interlude is Helga, a German girl serving out her mandatory year working for the state and who helps Marissa learn German; she also admires Marissa's fair looks, speculating that if Marisa were a German girl, she would be the Aryan ideal, treated with respect as a producer of beautiful German babies.

The compliment goes momentarily to Marisa's head as she imagines herself in that role: "For a moment I *was* a perfect German girl, ruler of the universe. A shudder passed through me. . . . How easy it was to be seduced" (85).

Marisa is learning some painful lessons about the appeal of power. Then she is subjected to a different kind of "lesson," this time about deception, when she is transferred to another farm, this one in Weimar and owned by a Herr Reymann, a high-ranking Nazi officer. Once there, Marissa thinks, *"I really am in the belly of the beast"* (90). But this family treats their Polish workers well, making Marisa initially feel secure. The wife is pleased with Marisa's now perfect German, the children are "cheerful, polite, and relaxed," and fourteen-year-old Charlotte seems to take a special liking to Marisa. But the illusion of a kind family is shattered when Charlotte invites Marisa to watch as the children play a board game. As a Pole, she is not permitted to play with the German children, but the invitation pleases her—until she understands the game: "Jews Out." The first player to get the most Jews out of town wins. Although appalled, Marisa can say nothing.

One of the children brags about their uncle, who "has gotten rid of thousands of Jews. Maybe *ten* thousand!" (91). He then proudly shows Marissa photos that this uncle has sent home. She is shocked by what she sees:

> German soldiers, their guns aimed at naked men, women, and children, standing over a large pit; a naked woman, holding a small child against her chest, a soldier aiming at her; a long shot of a deep pit full of dead bodies. (92)

Again, she can give no sign of her distress, express no condemnation. As the children return to their game, Marissa is left to ponder the irony of the world she has just entered:

> The children seemed so nice. Their parents, too. They were the kind of people who would probably never cheat or lie or steal. They were "good"

people. And yet they could murder, or condone murder, with no problem. I had to conclude then that they saw Jews as not even human. They had to believe that lie so deeply that murder was no longer murder; torture and cruelty no longer held the same meaning. (93)

She is jolted to recognize that evil in people can masquerade as "normal." Unlike the brutal and bestial Nazis in Poland, the Reymanns are refined and cultured, but they harbor the same murderous hatred against her people. She is all alone among people who would want her dead or imprisoned if they only knew her true identity, and her thoughts turn once more to suicide. The nicer the family is to her, the more she hates them. Schmuel's lesson about keeping love in her heart fading, Marissa finds her only pleasure in deceiving the Reymanns. One afternoon, as she is helping Charlotte with geography, she casually fabricates great-grandparents who came from Berlin, adding that this fictitious grandmother married a Pole, tainting the family bloodline. The lie grows: her mother, Marisa says, married a German, but all the documents were lost in a house fire. Charlotte and the family accept the lie, and Marissa rises a notch in their estimation.

This lie exacts a price. Believing that Marisa is mostly German, Charlotte invites her to attend a meeting of the League of German Maidens, an evening that proves distressing. The girls are asked to check a large pile of clothing to make sure that no buttons are missing, no hems torn. Marisa realizes that when the Nazis have forced the Jews to strip in public, there has been a pragmatic side to their cruelty. The Jews' clothing will be used by German citizens. She is overpowered by hopelessness and anger. Why have none of the Germans resisted Hitler? How can Charlotte believe that ridding Germany of Jews is "like killing rats who only breed disease" (103)? She thinks,

> They will *succeed in wiping us out, each and every one of us. And the few like me who might survive—what would be left of our Jewishness? Nothing. . . . Was I still a Jew if I couldn't be a Jew?* (103)

Marisa's questions touch on a central concept of religion as a collective, not individual, pursuit in Western culture. Certainly, people may and do pray alone, but worship, in the Judeo-Christian tradition, requires congregational participation. Religion derives its strength as a source of identification from membership in a group who all share the same rituals and beliefs.[13] Marisa's dilemma also raises a difficult issue. She has denied her identity to save her life. History is full of martyrs who refused to succumb to such temptation. Has she made the correct moral choice?

Because Marisa is brave and resourceful under the most difficult circumstances imaginable—an innocent victim of insane cruelty—the implied reader wants her to live. But one deception leads to another. Charlotte persuades Marisa to accompany her on a late-night, furtive meeting with Charlotte's boyfriend Georg, who belongs to an anti-Hitler gang. Although the gang beats up Hitler Youth Group members, they hate Jews, and Marisa's fears of being discovered grow. When they return home, Charlotte's mother catches them sneaking in, and although she promises not to tell her husband, Marisa is terrified.

She faints, and when she regains consciousness, Charlotte's mother is bending over her, her hand on the girl's forehead. Has the woman been genuinely concerned? "'Maybe she [is] simply a good person,'" Marisa thinks. "*But how could that be? She [is] a Nazi!* That meant she was evil through and through. Didn't it?" (120). Marisa "cannot understand the world" around her. She remembers her father's teachings as absolutes, but the world is complex. Bewildered, she is finding that some people are not entirely good or evil, nor are they easily identified as such. Rather, they are capable of great kindness to those they care for and great cruelty to those they have been taught to despise. It is small wonder that Marissa is confused.

More fearful than ever of being identified as a Jew, Marisa violates her father's teachings by planning another deception, this one a betrayal of Charlotte. She tells Herr Reymann of Charlotte's involvement with Georg, confessing that she accompanied Charlotte one evening—only one—but that Charlotte has continued to sneak out. She professes to care about Charlotte's welfare and her secret involvement with the anti-Hitler gang, although her actions are motivated only by self-interest.

Afterwards, she "felt horrible, somehow dirty. And what if Herr Reymann went after the whole [anti-Hitler] group? Had I given them all up to ensure my own safety?" (125). Her safety, however, is fleeting. "We always think we know what the future will bring but we have no idea," she muses (127), and she is right. Because she is fluent in both Polish and German, she is sent to a factory in Berlin, where the Germans are desperate for people to translate German work orders to their Polish slaves. There she makes friends with a Polish girl her age and survives the Berlin bombing by the Allies. Huddled in a shelter as the bombs fall around them, she suddenly realizes "something quite wonderful." She no longer wants to kill herself. Instead, she is making plans for finding work in another city, planning a way to say alive. Although she doesn't speculate on the cause of this change, the reader can infer that her faith has seen her through the nightmare of the Holocaust. Eventually she returns to Weimar where Herr Reymann finds her and brings her back to his farm to help Frau Reymann with her son Hans. Hans has been wounded and is now paralyzed from the shoulders down.

Marisa's reunion with the Reymanns reignites the old ambiguities. Charlotte waits for her outside, throwing her arms around Marisa when she arrives.

et part of Marisa feels cold, feels nothing. "After all, I was still only a servant, stupid Pole, worse if she knew the truth, so why should I have felt anything or her?" (157). But another part melts in response to Charlotte's affection. She experiences similarly mixed emotions towards Hans. She feels truly sorry for im, but "Wasn't this the same child who played Jews Out when I first arrived? Who couldn't wait to go fight and kill Poles and Jews?" (159). How can she still e a Jew if she harbors such ambivalent feelings, if she cannot go to *shul* and ray with other Jews, if she cannot remember the words of the sacred Torah?

When she lies down to clear her head and rest, she again dreams of Papa. He ssures her she is still a Jew. She does remember the Shema, the prayer central to ewish worship; it means that all people are part of God, even the Nazis she is living with. Papa reminds her of Shmuel's admonition to keep love in her heart: Love is God. And God can only exist if you let him into your heart" (160).

When Charlotte comes to her room, weeping because she does not want o be forced to conceive babies for the Reich, Marisa puts her arms around the obbing girl, feeling "almost like [she] was embracing a land mine" (162). Then a huge hunk of ice" in her heart starts to melt away, and she remembers a line rom Ezekiel: "I will take away the stony heart . . . and I will give you a heart of flesh" (162). Again, Marisa recalls her father's wise words: "It is better for my nemy to see good in me than for me to see evil in him" (163).

Inevitably, the war ends and Marisa leaves the Reymanns, despite their leas that she remain. At a DP camp she finds her parents' and younger siblings' ame on a list of the dead, but Fanny and her brother's names are missing. Are hey alive or dead? Neither Marisa nor the reader knows. But Marisa does find hmuel's name on a list of the living, and he is in a camp not far from hers. She emembers snatches of the Psalms they recited while hiding in Poland: "Happy s the man who has not followed the counsel of the wicked . . . He is like a tree lanted beside streams of water . . . and whatever it produces thrives" (168). She ows to become a scholar and to document all that has happened to her, but he is also determined never to forget the most important lesson she has learned: My scholarship must never take second place to my heart, because only there oes God truly reside" (168).

In My Enemy's House underscores the sustaining power of faith and the oll of hatred. But it hardly touches on the morality or consequences of denying one's faith, even for the sake of survival. Kathryn Lasky's *Blood Secret* explores that issue in more detail.

Blood Secret

Jnlike Marisa, many protagonists of books with a religious theme discover r affirm their faith only after experiencing difficult, even traumatic events.

Blood Secret follows this plot structure, but with a twist that depends on the fantasy of time travel.[14] Fourteen-year-old Jerry Luna, raised a Catholic, has been shuttled from one Catholic Charities home to another after her mother disappears when she is eight. Her father, Hammerhead, is dead after deserting his wife and baby when Jerry was only three weeks old, and her mother "had hung out with a lot of potheads and druggies" (5).

Jerry can provide no help in describing what her mother was wearing when last seen or anything else about her, for since her disappearance, Jerry has stopped speaking. She has buried the longing for her mother in silence, suffering from what her records label as "selective mutism." Yet she understands everything that other people say and is a "good student," even able to read Spanish and write it fluently. She is uncertain about her name. Is she Jerry Moon, Jeraldine de Luna, or Jerafina Milagros? Is she Jerrene Hammerhead?

Although her exact name remains unsettled and, by implication, her identity, a search has discovered a great-aunt, Constanza de Luna, who lives in the Albuquerque area, where Jerry goes to live. Although Constanza is in her nineties she is very active, a professional baker with a thriving business, and the breads she serves at meals are delicious. At first Jerry thinks that her aunt is a vegetarian because there has been no meat at any of the meals. But on the third evening, her aunt prepares a roast. To Jerry's surprise, she is not allowed to drink milk with her meal, although she has been allowed to do so on the other nights. Constanza explains that mixing meat and milk is "terrible" for her digestion, but Jerry has regularly drunk milk with her meals of meat at the Catholic homes.

Nor is that the only odd custom her aunt practices. On Friday night, before dinner, the old woman exchanges her thin cotton dress and old felt hat for dressier clothes, replaces the oilcloth table covering with a nice cloth, and sets the table with her good pottery and cloth napkins. When Jerry comes into the room on the first Friday night of her stay, she sees her aunt, her head covered with a shawl, standing before two candles that she has lit. A practicing Catholic like Jerry, she explains that these are Lenten candles, kindled to "remember the death of Christ" (40). Jerry recalls no such custom in either Catholic home where she has lived, but she is intrigued by a sense of "mystery" at the heart of the dinner. "It was more than a mystery, really. It seemed as if it might be a well of some sort that could ensnare them. There was something almost ritualistic in the way Constanza lifted the wineglass to her mouth" (41).

That is not the only mystery. Before baking her bread, the old woman takes a pinch of dough and throws it into one of the ovens to burn to ashes. Why this waste of dough? Jerry is puzzled. Still, she finds that she and her great-aunt have one thing in common: they each rub the top of their heads at moments of stress. Constanza has created a bald spot at the back of her center part from years of rubbing. Other than this strange habit, the two relatives bear no resemblance to each other. The "deep, deep reddish brown" of Constanza's skin contrasts with Jerry's "dark olive complexion" (25); Constanza is "tall and skinny," with "high cheekbones" and a nose that sat "as bold as a knife-back ridge on her face" (26). Jerry is "stocky," her face "pudgy" (25). Jerry is sure that her aunt has Indian blood.

As the days pile up, Jerry begins school, makes a friend, learns to drive Constanza's truck, and begins to speak—a little. Most important, she begins to explore the basement of Constanza's house by flashlight. Drawn by the mysterious sound of children's voices floating on the air, she descends the steps when she wakes at night and is fascinated by the amber glow of light there that emanates from the red New Mexican earth of its walls. In the basement, she discovers an old, camel-backed trunk, and inside she finds an assortment of objects:

> Some were shallow boxes; some things were wrapped in ancient-looking tissue paper, some in Spanish newspapers. There were odd bits of fabric, a picture frame with no picture, a Bible, a cup tarnished nearly black with age, something that looked like a corncob with a bit of worn fabric wrapped around its middle. . . . She sensed that she had at her fingertips the fragments of a puzzle. An extraordinary kind of three-dimensional jigsaw puzzle, a puzzle of time and space. (63)

The remainder of the novel unravels the puzzle, a piece at a time. Each object that Jerry lifts from the trunk transports her back centuries, to trace the beginning and spread of the Spanish Inquisition. The scenes from the past, rendered in first person from the perspective of the character central to that particular segment of time, require a steadfast suspension of disbelief on the part of the reader, but they successfully convey the pain and terror the Inquisition inflicted on the Jews and the strategies the Jews developed to stay alive without giving up their religion. Lasky says in an Author's Note following her novel that "if I was to tell this story, I would have to tell the whole story—the centuries upon centuries saturated by blood. This story could not be told as a day in the life of the Inquisition, nor could it be the story of simply one family within one generation. The crushing weight of time would have to be as significant as any character" (246). It took her ten years to figure out how she could encompass such a span of time within a single novel.

The first object Jerry lifts from the trunk is a piece of lace with a "dull stain" towards its center. As she examines it more closely, "time began to bend," and she is transported to Seville, Spain, in 1391, where she becomes a silent observer of Miriam's story. The Jews in Seville have been confined to the Jewish Quarter, the result of a decree by the "bad friar Martinez" (65), who has ordered their conversion. He has also "created a monster of evil for Jews" by whipping the "little people" into a frenzy of anti-Semitism. This section demonstrates the ease with which a malevolent leader can incite mob violence against "the other," a minority perceived as not only different but inferior.

Miriam's mother is the finest lace maker in the city and is working on a piece of lace for the archbishop's sleeves. But the lace is never finished. The protective gates surrounding the Jewish quarter are burned, and a family friend is killed as the mob shouts, "Death to the Christ Killers" (75). Miriam faints, then awakens in a church. She is being baptized by the evil friar, who sprinkles holy water on the top of her head. She is now a New Christian with a new name, Maria, after the Virgin Mary. Mama's lace is on her shoulders, stained with the blood of their friend. Mama and her other daughter have also been converted, but once home, Mama takes the lace and scrubs the top of Miriam/Maria's head so hard that it burns, then throws the lace onto the floor. Miriam keeps touching the place on her head, a gesture that survives down through the ages, and retrieves the lace from the corner where Mama has thrown it. She vows to keep it "forever and ever" (79).

Jerry's experiences in the cellar affect her behavior in the present. She is again mute: her few "words were creeping back down into the cellar, through a trapdoor" (81). Each time she visits the cellar, she handles another object in the trunk and learns more about the persecution of the Jews. She is transported to Toledo, Spain, in 1449, when Spain passes the "pure blood" laws. Under these laws, those with Jewish ancestry are considered New Christians, even though they have been faithful Catholics for three generations. Many are suspected of being "Judaizers," Jews who secretly practice the old religion.

When Jerry makes other forays into the past, she follows descendants of Miriam as they flee to Granada, back to Seville, to Toledo, and to Portugal, each move motivated by increasingly ruthless persecution. The family has produced a long line of devout Catholics, including priests and nuns, but they remain suspect because of their ancestry. The Inquisition sets up more and more laws to separate the New Christians from the Old Christians, to prevent those of "pure blood" from marrying the "Conversos," even those who can trace their identity as Catholics back many generations. The persecution, as Lasky presents it, is motivated more by politics than religion. The Old Christians are jealous of the successful New Christians, many of whom occupy enviable high positions, which the "pure blood" laws will prevent them from holding in the future.

The Church carries out executions in which those suspected of being secret Jews are burned in public squares while those of "pure blood" celebrate around the fires. Some of the Conversos have abandoned the Church in the face of such horror, asking, "What kind of religion is this where they . . . persecute us, often violently, and try to exclude us?" (117). They become clandestine Jews, rejecting Catholism because it preaches such hatred. Instead they try to preserve the rituals of their ancient faith, banding together as small congregations in carefully guarded secrecy.

Jerry finds the words to share what she has witnessed about the Inquisition with her aunt. As she continues her exploration of the past through items in the trunk, she learns that Constanza's Lenten candles are in fact *Shabbos* candles, lit by Jews at sundown on Friday to welcome the Sabbath; she also learns that her aunt's refusal to mix meat and milk stem from Biblical dietary laws that forbid Jews to boil a kid in its mother's milk. She discovers the origins of Constanza's ritual of tossing a bit of dough into the ovens to burn into ash: The bread was once offered as a sacrifice to remember the destruction of the Temple in Jerusalem, "to diminish our joy" (158) in the face of historical sorrow. Jerry imagines these traditions "like remnants . . . smashed on the desert of what once had been a rich faith, then picked up again, perhaps unrecognizable and patched into something else" (170). Jerry's newly acquired insights confirm that "when a custom, a tradition, is cut off from its roots or practiced so long in secret, it begins to disintegrate. It becomes lost or turned into something it was never intended through some strange process of denial" (167).

And she learns of more persecution, more horrors. Rumors of Jews "tearing the heart out of a Christian child they had crucified on Good Friday" (163)—the wild tales known as "blood libel"—drove the Jews to the Yucatan Peninsula in Mexico. This very trunk has been sent to a Mexican ancestor. But even there, the Inquisition follows them. Trying to escape the persecution, the Jews flee to Mexico City, where as *Marranos* they practice their religion in secret but, when caught, are strung up on racks in the torture chambers beneath the Holy Office of the Inquisition. Down through the centuries, in the face of such torment, some of Jerry's ancestors buried the sorrows of their heritage in silence, much as Jerry has. Eventually, many of the *Marranos* immigrated to New Mexico, where they have intermarried with people of Navajo and Pueblo blood.[15] But their religion survives. In one episode set in historic New Mexico, she observes an ancestor nailing up a *mezazuh*[16] to the door frame of their home and learns that dirt must never be swept through a door on which a *mezazuh* is nailed. She also learns of a female ancestor with the given name of Jerusalem.

Rather predictably, by the end of the novel, Jerry is speaking fluently, and Constanza accepts her Jewish heritage and renames Jerry Jerusalem. Past and present converge in an upbeat ending. Jerry has discovered and claimed the faith of her ancestors and all is well. But while the novel offers, like Lasky's previous historical fiction, fascinating, if horrifying, details of the past, *Blood Secret* raises some troubling questions about faith. Is belief a matter of "blood"? Should people like Constanza or Jerry, who have both been faithful Catholics, abandon a religion that, whatever its cruel past, they have practiced all their lives because they discover that they have "Jewish blood"? Such a position would seem to support the Inquisition's insistence that "blood" governs one's faith. Or should one derive from this novel the resilience of the Jewish faith and its survival in the face of incredible odds? The healing power of one's ancestral religion? It is possible to construct any of these interpretations from Lasky's novel. However, despite the statement by one of the characters that "You can have the purest blood, but with a bad heart, it is worth nothing" (202), the final, if unintended, message seems to be that "blood," not belief, is the ultimate religious determinant.

Preacher's Boy

On a much lighter note, but still exploring questions of spirituality and belief is Katherine Paterson's *Preacher's Boy,*[17] set in rural Vermont during the summer of 1899. Ten-year-old Robbie Hewitt, the preacher's boy of the title, hears a visiting evangelist hint that the end of the century may also mark the end of the world. By his own admission, Robbie is a "rapscallion of a boy," a literary descendant of Tom Sawyer. In fact, *Tom Sawyer* is one of his favorite books, and he speaks in a non-standard dialect that echoes Twain's own rapscallion. He is a prime example of what Leslie Fielding has called "The Good Bad Boy" of American literature, "crude and unruly in his beginnings, but endowed by his creator with an instinctive sense of what is right."[18]

If the world will end in just a few months, Robbie wants "to make hay" while the sun still shines (22). He is tired of trying to live up to what is expected of a preacher's boy. "People just have unrealistic expectations if your pa happens to be a preacher," he complains (10). To add to his frustration, none of the other children in his family are troubled by such standards. His older sister Beth takes pleasure in being a "lady-in-training" (74), a role that entitles her to condescend to him. His retarded older brother, Elliot, is too simple-minded to be held responsible for his actions and, worse, as Robbie sees it, is his father's favorite; his little sister Letty is off the hook by virtue of her age.

"I ain't got the knack for holiness," Robbie confesses (20), and he decides to become "a heathen, a Unitarian, or a Democrat, whichever was most fun" (21). His antics draw criticism from the pious townspeople, who are quick to judge. Robbie's father, minister of the town's Congregational Church, has also attracted the town's censure: his sermons lack the fire of brimstone, and even more scandalous, Pa is reading Darwin's *The Descent of Man*. Robbie can hardly believe that his father would study such an unholy book. "It was the worst thing you could do, even if you weren't a preacher—to believe that man wasn't created by God on the sixth day but had descended from the apes" (106).

When he confides to his friend Willie that he has become "a convert to disbelief" (22), Willie tells him that he's an "apeist . . . one of them there heathens who don't believe in God" (41). Robbie dislikes the designation, but is resigned to it because "if I was going to be an unbeliever, I had to be an apeist whether I liked the notion of monkey granddaddies or not" (41). Still, the habit of prayer dies hard. Robbie longs to ride in a motorcar before the world collapses in dust and ashes, and he slips in a "to-whom-it-may concern prayer" (34) to say that he would sure like to ride in one—just once. And he misses the sense of belonging that accompanies religious identification. "It seemed lonely to be an apeist," he says at one point (60).

At first, his misbehavior is fairly innocent, boyish pranks that range from stringing a pair of girl's bloomers up the town flagpole to sending a spider down the back of a parishioner's dress during church services. Then, in a more serious incident outside the church after services, he lands a blow on the face of his nemesis Ned Weston. Ned and his brother Tom, sons of the mayor and the town's wealthiest man, are making fun of Elliot. Robbie's motive here is less mischief than angry defense of his brother, but, as usual, he acts without considering the consequences—his father's stern displeasure.

The real trouble begins one afternoon after he and Willie fall asleep after skinny dipping. They wake to the jeers of the Weston brothers, who are treading water in the middle of the pond and holding aloft Robbie and Willie's stolen clothes. The naked boys swim out to grab their clothes, but Ned and Tom toss the garments in the water. Willie is quick enough to grab his before they sink, but Robbie is not so lucky, and his clothes disappear into the depths of Cutters Pond. To add fuel to Robbie's fiery temper, the Weston boys taunt him about his brother Elliot and his father's study of Darwin, calling the boys "Monkey sons! Monkey brothers! Monkey papa!" (101).

In blind fury, Robbie swims over to Ned and shoves him face down in the water, nearly drowning him. Ned is saved only because Willie, appalled at his friend's actions, rescues the boy, who scuttles off with his brother. Willie dresses in his sopping clothes, about to abandon his friend, but Robbie clambers ashore, imploring Willie not to leave him. "I wouldn'ta killed him. You know that" (102).

Willie isn't so sure. "How can you know what a feller will do? One who don't have to pay no mind to the Ten Commandments?" (103) he asks before he begrudgingly gives Robbie his shirt to wear temporarily; it is barely long enough to cover Robbie's "privates."

However, Robbie is hardly a lost soul. In fact, his conscience is so active that he repents immediately for his rash actions. "A flood of horror washed over me. I *had* meant to kill Ned Weston," he admits to himself. "I could deny it to the day I died, but I knew I'd felt the rage boiling in my head that proved me kin to every murderer in history from Cain to Jack the Ripper" (103). Clearly, to handle his explosive temper Robbie needs the divine guidance that his "apeism" has denied him.

From this point on, the plot moves rapidly. Robbie has previously discovered a homeless girl, Violet (or Vile, the name she goes by) and her abusive, alcoholic pa, Zeb, living in an abandoned miner's cabin that he and Willie had claimed for their secret clubhouse. Unwillingly, Robbie has been drawn into their lives: first he steals vegetables from his home to help feed them. Then, in hiding from what he knows will be his father's anger over the incident at Cutters Pond, he conspires with Vile to simulate his own kidnapping. Robbie figures the scheme will serve several purposes: it should net them some money from the ransom fee, deflect Mr. Weston's certain fury over the near-drowning of his son, and create a flood of worry to dissolve Pa's anger at Robbie. But the plan backfires when Zeb, thoroughly drunk and vicious and with Robbie's phony "HELP" note in his pocket, whacks Robbie over the head with a broken whiskey bottle.

At home much later, his head bandaged and a fever raging from his infected wounds, he is so dizzy he can hardly stand and the days pass in a blur. Only later does he learn from Vile, who pays him a surreptitious night visit, that her father has been apprehended with the incriminating note in his pocket, charged not only with kidnapping Robbie but attempting to murder him. Already in custody, Zeb will go to court to stand trial for his life. He is destined to hang, and Vile pleads with Robbie to set things straight in the courtroom.

Because of Robbie's precarious condition, Pa has gone to the court house in Tyler, ten miles away, to testify on his son's behalf that Zeb is guilty as charged. Robbie, although a self-declared apeist, is haunted by the commandment not to bear false witness, and he imagines his father, his hand on the Bible, swearing to tell what he believes to be the truth. When his mother leaves him alone with Elliot to go to her sewing circle, "All of a sudden it seemed God was clearing the way" for Robbie to set things right (162). As the saying goes, there are no atheists (or apeists) in foxholes. He starts off for the courthouse in Tyler, weak and dizzy, when a motor car nearly runs him down. Ultimately, both he and Elliot get to ride in that motorcar, all the way to Tyler. It is what he had prayed for, and he rejoices in his good fortune: "And do you know? From that very moment I stopped all pretense of being an apeist and signed on as a true believer for all eternity. How could I not? God had worked a personal miracle especially for me" (172).

Robbie, of course, had never been much of a confirmed "apeist." His temporary lapse is more adolescent rebellion than philosophical rejection of God, and his return to the fold is more boyish high spirits than spiritual enlightenment. Still, although Robbie has an instinctive knowledge of right and wrong, he needs divine assistance to stay out of trouble, and his reclaimed faith redeems him when he saves Zeb from the hangman's noose, confessing the truth to his startled father. Months later, when December 31 rolls around and father and son ring in the New Year together in the church bell tower, the "joyful welcome" to the new century signals that God is indeed in his heaven and all's right with the world—which shows no sign of ending.

The Garden

God is also in his heaven in *The Garden,* a first novel by Elsie V. Aidinoff based on the Biblical Genesis, but the divine presence in this tale is less than reassuring.[19] Aidinoff is hardly the first writer for young adults to use the Bible as a source,[20] but unlike most such writers, she has not so much extrapolated from a Bible story as she has deconstructed it. In Aidinoff's version, the Old Testament God is more a grumpy old man than a divine presence. He is pleased with the world he has created, like a child with a new toy, but he is too arrogant to be a wise parent to Adam, whom he is raising while the Serpent raises Eve.

The characterization of God, Aidinoff explains in an author's note, grew out of a visit to New Mexico, where she became interested in the development of the atom bomb: "The brilliant scientists who created the bomb were passionate about their work—totally absorbed, exhilarated, drunk on intellectual excitement. But. . . they never considered the moral implications of the bomb or the suffering it would bring" (402). She began to see similarities between them and the Old Testament God, "choleric and impetuous," impatient to make his creation work as planned with no understanding of the human cost. As Eve says of the Creator, "he had no interest in any opinions but his own and did not like us to think for ourselves" (75). She also questions why God teaches all those hymns of adoration. "We know," she says, "he made the sea and the dry land and all the rest. Why does he have to hear it over and over again?" (88).

It is an interesting question, typical of Eve, who demonstrates a natural ability for critical thinking. She is curious about everything, including the creation of the world, and the Serpent supplies two versions, the Biblical myth and the scientific theory of evolution. "Each has its truths and realities," it says, but without resolving the contradictions (12–14).[21] Eve is also artistic. When the Serpent sees that Eve has made a series of little serpent sculptures, it is delighted. "You have brought humor into the world—an attribute God overlooked in his Creation" (18). This is one of the first clues that God cannot predict or control all that happens in the world he has fashioned.

The Serpent is a beautiful and versatile creature, with prominent ears, iridescent skin that can change colors, and emerald eyes. It can wind itself into a small feathered coil or stretch its body as high as a tree, and is able to heat or cool its body at will, using its tail to warm food and its entire body to cool the air on sultry days. It implies that it existed before Creation and tells Eve that it has many names, Wisdom, Justice, and Reason among them (105). These are qualities that

God obviously lacks. Its attempts to describe God to Eve are like those of a wise parent helping a child understand a temperamental, eccentric relative.

In many ways, the Serpent is the hero of this book, a Promethean figure who teaches Eve to question and to value her ability to exercise free will. This, of course, leads to her eventual expulsion (along with Adam) from the Garden, but the Serpent in this version is to be credited, not condemned for the Fall. Otherwise, the human race might have loitered in the Garden forever, never making use of the brainpower with which God has endowed them, never knowing the satisfaction that comes only through hard work and imagination.

When God meets Eve, he is taken with her physical beauty, pleasantly surprised that such loveliness could come from Adam's rib. He is less pleased with Adam, who has "run off" somewhere and doesn't respond to God's summoning whistle. God describes the boy as his "first try, so he's not perfect" (45). Indeed, Adam displays a classic case of Attention Deficit Disorder: he is inattentive during his lessons and apparently hyperactive, wiggling his toes and playing with his hair when he should be sitting still. "And," complains God, "for some reason I can't fix him by waving a finger" (45), an admission that not everything in his Creation responds to his wishes.

When Adam does appear, he seems an immature child. He has forgotten that Eve was coming and spent much of the day chasing the animals in the Garden. He has, however, brought flowers for Eve, but the blooms have been ripped carelessly from their stems and the petals are torn. Eve, always respectful of all life in the Garden, is appalled—and later learns that Adam feels free in the Garden to take whatever he wants. Unlike Eve, he has no concept of living in harmony with nature, an ancient case of careless consumerism versus gentle environmentalism. But Adam is "a joy to behold," graceful, muscular, with the same golden hair as Eve (50), and the Serpent reflects later that he is a "nice boy. . . . More to him than first appears" (54).

Eve overhears God confide to the Serpent that Adam will "be good for strong bodies. Eve has the brain" (61). Only later, to her sorrow, does she comprehend what God "can hardly wait to see" when God decides that "now is the time" for Adam and Eve to "procreate" (95). When God orders Adam to mate with Eve, the act amounts to a rape. Despite Eve's screams of pain and Adam's reluctance to finish the act until, against his will, he is carried away by lust, God's only reaction is pleasure at how well his planning "worked" and insistence that "There's no harm done" (100). In her Author's Note, Aidinoff says that "it always seemed wrong that, in religion as in mythology, woman is so often blamed for the introduction of sin into the world" (401). The rape scene makes clear that in Aidinoff's view, Eve is far more sinned against than sinning.

The scene culminates with the Serpent ordering God and "that foolish misguided boy" to refrain from coming near Eve "until the moon has filled and aded six times" (106). Protesting but finally acquiescent, God obeys. In the intervening months, Eve and the Serpent venture outside the boundaries of the Garden, clambering over the barriers that God has erected to fence them in. With the Serpent as a guide, Eve discovers a volcano, the ocean and the desert, mountains and snow. With each visit, they are threatened with a natural disaster—an erupting volcano, giant ocean waves, a tornado. Eve worries that God is punishing them for leaving the Garden, but the Serpent has doubts, uncertain even that God created these destructive forces. "[God] hasn't left the Garden in ages," the Serpent explains, "and I don't think he realizes what's going on" (147). Eve is fascinated: "The idea of God losing control of the world was terrible—but there was something exciting about it too" (148). Nor, the Serpent tells her, is nature's violence aimed specifically at her. "Most of the time it's not; you just happened to be there when it's happening" (185), a comment meant to redirect the way humans imagine themselves at the center of the world.

The world outside the Garden, away from God's presence, becomes more intriguing with each visit. Each time Eve brings something back from their excursions: a clot of earth, a rock, a scoop of sand. From these materials, she fashions a bowl with a little serpent on its rim and sets it out on a small mound to harden in the Garden. Mysteriously, it disappears, but where it had been, a small, unusual tree begins to grow. This is, of course, the Tree of Knowledge of Good and Evil. In contrast to the Biblical Genesis, which specifies that God created this tree and points it out to Adam and Eve, in Aidinoff's story the tree grows without God's knowledge. When he discovers it in the Garden, he forbids Eve and Adam to eat its fruit, then attempts to destroy it. Without his knowledge, one apple survives the wreckage.

That Eve and Adam will eat from this apple is foreshadowed in their resistance to God's will. Earlier, God has begun to recognize that he has little control of Eve; Adam, too, is becoming more independent, and God reacts like the frustrated parent of two rebellious adolescents. "Eve," he says at one point, "I don't want to have these arguments with you. Why have you become like this? Adam, too, doesn't want to do things the way I'd planned" (246). God is especially angry that his plan for procreation as a "joy" hasn't gone as he expected, and he finally dismisses Eve from his presence, furious over her reaction to the sexual act: "Go away! I have no use for you" (247).

The Serpent in this version of Genesis is no tempter. Rather, it tries to explain to the young couple the consequences of eating the apple. They may no longer be protected by God and may fall victim to "disease, poison, death" (300). Later, the Serpent explains the necessity of death as a way of making a place for children. Without death, it says, "You could not have a succession of beings progressing through life, each generation learning and growing and giving in its own way" (332). Adam and Eve, of course, have never seen children;

they have never *been* children. The Serpent assures them that "[c]hildren are wonderful! The essence of joy!" Then he adds, "Wait and see" (332).

But when the Serpent tries to explain the concept of "evil," his view contrasts sharply with God's view. The Serpent explains that "evil is hurting something, with the *intent* to hurt. Willfully harming another being: flora or fauna. Taking from others because you yourself need what they have. Or want it . . ." (302). God interrupts. Evil, according to him, "is one thing and one thing only: disobedience to God!" (302). When Eve asks about the importance of "being kind and good," God acknowledges those virtues, adding that he is putting together some "commandments" about how he wants people to behave (303). With the Serpent's prompting, he recites the Ten Commandments, at times to Eve's bewilderment. What is a neighbor, a manservant, a dultery (which Eve takes as two words)? Other things puzzle her, too. Alone with Adam, she considers whether God is evil. She cannot forget the pain of being raped. God has harmed her, and she says she can never love him again.

Aidinoff cannot stray too far from her source. Eve is destined to become the mother of all humankind, a role that she has resisted, but Aidinoff helps Eve accept her destiny by letting her experience the joy of sex. (Aidinoff is kinder to Eve than the God she has created.) Thus, the Serpent takes the guise of a man and makes ecstatic love to her, preparing her to live with Adam as his wife. Finally, Eve decides to eat a bite of the apple, and she does so of her own free will, not because the Serpent has tempted her, although at Eve's request, he does fetch the surviving apple from the top of the tree, committing what God has defined as sin: disobedience to Him. Eve knows the exact consequences of eating the apple—expulsion from the Garden—but prefers to live freely outside the Garden, with all the risks implied, rather than remaining in it always under God's control. Adam, too, chooses to eat from the apple. He cannot imagine life without Eve and couldn't possibly stay in the Garden without her.

When God discovers what they have done, he is furious. (No surprise here.) Shouting "Traitor" and "Treachery" at the Serpent for giving the apple to Eve, albeit at her request, God uses the phrasing from the Biblical Genesis to curse the Serpent, then Eve and Adam. To the Serpent he says, "On your belly you shall go and you shall eat dust all the days of your life." To Eve, "In pain you shall bring forth children, and your husband shall rule over you." God likewise condemns Adam: "You will toil all the days of your life, and bring forth thorns and thistles, and in the end return to the ground" (389–90).

The Serpent protests that banishing the couple from the Garden is enough punishment for their disobedience, reminding God that there is not only justice, there is mercy. "You taught these children to pray to a just and merciful God. Be merciful now!" (393). God is impervious to the Serpent's plea. "They have defied me!" he shouts. "They are *evil, evil!*" (393). Then God adds that he will make an exception for the Serpent, allowing it to remain in the Garden, for he will be lonely without Adam and Eve. But the Serpent chooses to go into the wilderness with the couple, having no wish to stay with the god his old friend has become.

When chaos descends on the Garden and the animals stampede, Eve is guilt-stricken at what her actions have wrought. But, as always, the Serpent is there to reassure her:

> "You and Adam chose freely, both of you, and it was brave. Never doubt that it was the right choice: in the Garden you would have been God's chattels forever. This"—it nodded at the chaos around us—"is not your doing. It is God's." (396)

When Eve and Adam leave the Garden, they come upon a grove of apple trees with the distinctive petals they had seen on the Tree of Knowledge. Adam recalls that God had thrown apples from the Tree over the falls, and he recognizes the grove as springing from "God's apples." Eve turns to Adam in the closing sentence, correcting him. "*Our* apples," she says. "*Our* trees" (400). The couple has claimed a world of their own, beyond God's absolute control. The reader knows that they will experience both joy and sorrow, peace and war—for this story is a reflection on the compromises the human race makes when it chooses freedom over blind obedience.

Aidinoff's tale casts the novels discussed earlier in a new light: What kind of a god is it in which people place so much faith? Is faith the "illogical belief" that Mencken claimed? Has God remained in his Garden, impervious to what is happening beyond its borders? What are the boundaries of human free will? How do we explain the problem of evil, the suffering inflicted on innocent people who have not disobeyed God? There are as many answers to those questions as theologians debating them. That these issues have found their way into young adult literature demonstrates their eternal significance—to fiction writers as well as philosophers—and reinforces the centrality of spirituality and religion to the human condition.

NOTES

1. Dean Hamer, *The God Gene: How Faith is Hardwired into Our Genes* (New York: Doubleday, 2004).

2. Nilsen and Donelson, 6th ed., 165.

3. James Janeway, quoted in *A Guide to Literature for Young Adults,* Ruth Cline and William McBride. (Chicago: Scott, Foresman, 1983), 17.

4. Mary Lystad, "The Adolescent Image in American Books for Children." In *Young Adult Literature: Background and Criticism,* Millicent Lenz and Ramona M. Mahood, eds. (Chicago: American Library Association, 1980), 27. Although Lystad uses the adjective

"adolescent," this period of development was not differentiated from adulthood until the early twentieth century. Michael Barson and Steven Heller, authors of *Teenage Confidential* (San Francisco: Chronicle Books, 1998), point out that there was not even "a name for them [adolescents] before the 1920's."

5. Martha Finley, *Elsie Dinsmore* (Chicago: The Saalfield Publishing Company, nd): 43; hereafter cited parenthetically in text. Although the plot of *Elsie Dinsmore* unfolded in a contemporary setting at the time of its publication, with the passage of more than a century since then, it has assumed the status of historical fiction, much like *Little Women* and *Diddie, Dumps, and Tot.*

6. "Naughty" is a word she applies frequently to herself, even for the most minor infraction of her father's rules.

7. Actually, Elsie enjoys a less troubling relationship with her father in later novels; there are other matters over which to shed abundant tears. Her father nearly dies, the Civil War and its aftermath tries her faith, and she must deal with the heartbreak of widowhood. In fact, every volume confronts her with trauma that occasions fervent prayers, tears, and the fainting spells common to women of that era.

8. The Southern antebellum setting is made clear in subsequent volumes.

9. Nashville, TN: Cumberland House Publishing, 2000.

10. Franklin, TN: Mission City Press.

11. Carol Matas, *In My Enemy's House* (New York: Aladdin, 1999); hereafter cited parenthetically in text.

12. The Baal Shem Tov was a noted Hasidic scholar of the fifteenth-century, famous for his tales that ended with a moral. His stories survive today in the body of significant Jewish literature.

13. In orthodox Judaism, the branch to which Marisa's family belonged, communal prayer requires the presence of at least ten men, a *minyan.*

14. Kathryn Lasky, *Blood Secret* (New York: HarperCollins, 2004); hereafter cited parenthetically in text.

15. The family lines become so complicated that Lasky provides a multi-page family tree at the back of the book.

16. A *mezuzah* is a decorative object to be nailed to the doorframe of a Jewish home. It is hollow, its chamber containing in Hebrew the command to keep God's words constantly in one's mind and heart by, among other ways, writing them on the doorposts of one's house.

17. Katherine Paterson, *Preacher's Boy,* (New York: HarperCollins, 1999); hereafter cited parenthetically in text.

18. Leslie Fielding, *Love and Death in the American Novel* (New York: World Publishing, 1960), 268.

19. Elsie V. Aidinoff, *The Garden* (New York: HarperTempest, 2004); hereafter cited parenthetically in text.

20. See, for example, Donna Jo Napoli's *Song of the Magdalene* (New York: Scholastic, 1996), Beatrice Gormley's *Miriam* (Grand Rapids, MI: Eerdmans Books, 1999), and Gloria Miklowitz's *Masada* (Eerdmans Books, 1999).

21. Throughout the novel, the Serpent is referred to as "it," neither male nor female.

· 6 ·

Class Matters

We are all animated with the spirit of industry which is unfettered
and unrestrained, because each person works for himself. . . . We
have no princes for whom we toil, starve, and bleed: we are the
most perfect society now existing in the world.

J. Hector St. John de Crevecouer
Letters from an American Farmer[1]

One of the United States' most cherished cultural myths is that we live in a
classless society. Historically this notion has allowed us to differentiate ourselves
from other, older cultures while functioning as a tool to both incite and measure individual achievement. Biographies by men as varied as Benjamin Franklin
and Andrew Carnegie have imprinted on our national consciousness the optimistic belief that, unfettered by class restrictions, we are a land of endless opportunity and that anyone who works hard enough will achieve success. More
often than not, success has been measured by the accumulation of wealth and
accompanied by the assumption that those who are rich deserve to be so. Ben
Franklin, for example, suggests that "He that gets all he can honestly, and saves
all he gets . . . will certainly become rich."[2] In other words, wealth will surely
arrive if one just works hard enough. If it doesn't, well then, it's because one
simply hasn't put forth *enough* effort. Failure to thrive materially is never a cultural or social failure but always an individual one.

But though we celebrate classlessness, the reality is that we are and always
have been a stratified society, one in which some are rich, many more are not, and
individual effort is only one of the many factors that *may* lead to material success.
Classlessness and wealth are uneasy bedmates, for contrary to Ben Franklin's assumption, hard work and frugality do *not* inevitably translate into riches. Historian Peter Gay, commenting on what he has termed "success literature," argues

that narratives such as Franklin's and Carnegie's are more "self-deluding fictior than tough-minded reportage. Its prolific authors [of success literature] stress the cheerful side at the expense of gloomier examples in a very complicated story."' Horatio Alger, often mistakenly celebrated as the guru of rags-to-riches narratives in young adult literature, made this quite clear in *Ragged Dick*: "If you'll try to be somebody, and grow up into a respectable member of society, you will. You may not become rich,—it isn't everybody that becomes rich, you know,—but you car obtain a good position and become respected."[4] Alger makes clear what most u recognize to be true, that wealth will not come to all of us, matter how hard we work or hope for it.

The national tendency to celebrate classlessness while equating materia success with moral rectitude results in tension, contradiction, and paradox, al of which create the "complicated story" to which Gay refers. We apply bumper stickers that advise "Live simply so that others may simply live," while avidly devouring the stories of the rich who are famous simply because they are rich.[5] This tension has been and continues to be evident in young adul novels that explore class issues. Authors present us, over and over, with charac-ters who both distrust the rich while aspiring to riches themselves. But like Al-ger's Ragged Dick, few become rich though they may become respectable.

A Lantern in Her Hand

Bess Streeter Aldrich's *A Lantern in Her Hand,* originally published in 1928 bu recently reissued by Puffin Books, is in some respects an overly sentimenta representation of maternal sacrifice and the pioneer spirit. But it is well worth examining because it embodies the cultural tensions inherent in the Americar dream and the role of class in that dream. Streeter's ambivalence about class and its markers is made evident in a number of subtle ways. On one hand she cel-ebrates a community where "there have been few lines drawn."[6] On the othe hand, she often uses a secondary character's educational background as a short-hand of sorts to reveal his or her value. Rather than fully developing a charac-ter through events that might establish merit or worth, she instead mention that he graduated from Dartmouth or Rice. And that, apparently, is all we nee to know to find this character admirable. Aldrich's ambivalence is most evi-dent, however, in her depiction of her main character, Abbie Deal.

Abbie, whose widowed mother and siblings have immigrated to Illinoi in the 1850s, loves to hear tales of her father's family's lost wealth, a fortune tha produced a fine town home and two country residences in Scotland in the early nineteenth century. Streeter describes in exquisite detail the day-to-da hardships of the impoverished pioneer family and in equally exquisite detail ten-year-old Abbie's attempts to relieve the hardships of her life with stories o ier family's past riches that she dreams of regaining, telling herself over and over, "Someday she, too, would be lovely, gracious, and wealthy."

Abbie's decision to marry Will Deal instead of the wealthy, young doctor who has courted her fairly ensures that her life will be one of hardship. And it is. Though she becomes moderately comfortable, she never becomes wealthy. Will and Abbie migrate to Nebraska, where land is cheap, and for the first thirteen years of their marriage live in a sod house, often struggling simply to feed their growing family. Though Abbie is eventually forced to abandon the dream of wealth and gracious living for herself, she refuses to do so for her children, insisting that "the children must have some of the best *things* in life . . . . She must not let them grow without good *things*" [italic ours] (109). Abbie's notion of what constitute the "good things" is solidly grounded in both class distinctions and classicist assumptions about culture. The phrase "fine things" can be read as code for the long-cherished distinction between high- and middle-brow (popular) culture. Within this framework, taste becomes a way of both recognizing and reinforcing class status. Abbie wants her children to appreciate Shakespeare (and has them memorize speeches from his plays when they are very young), art, and classical music. Correlative to her desire to have her children appreciate these finer things is her desire that they not form alliances with those who don't hold Abbie's values. She worries that one of her neighbor's sons shows too great an interest in one of her daughters and dismisses him as "stolid, crude, and virile . . . . Emil was no mate for Margaret with her love of the niceties of life" (120).

In her depiction of secondary characters Streeter's ambivalence toward class is equally evident. A clearly negative figure is the wealthy young doctor Abbie rejects in order to marry Will, negative because he drinks and womanizes and is able to avoid serving in the Civil War by paying Will to do his service for him. An even more negative figure is Christina, mother of the virile young Emil. Christina is a German pioneer woman who moves to Nebraska with her husband at the same time as Abbie and Will. She is a staunch friend to Abbie throughout her life, even saving her life at one point, and yet she is clearly intended as an example of the life not well lived. At various points in the novel she is depicted as "Dutchy, narrow, and ignorant" (184).[7] Abbie, though she relies on Christina and knows she owes her life to her, nevertheless dismisses her as someone who "had no finer feeling" (100).

In contrast to Christina is Sarah Lutz, who also comes to Nebraska at the same time as Abbie. Sarah and her husband, unlike Abbie and Will, do achieve wealth, and throughout the novel Sarah's stylishness is favorably contrasted with Christina's frumpiness. While Abbie can appreciate Christina's steadfastness and chastises her daughter when she ridicules Christina, she clearly prefers the company of Sarah—who seems selfish and shallow—for no other apparent

reason than Sarah *is* more stylish. Though Abbie and Will are never as materially successful as either of their neighbors, Abbie never rejects her girlhood
dreams of achieving wealth and those "finer things," if not for herself, then for
her children, and the prologue makes clear that her sacrifices bear fruit. Her
two sons become successful, one a lawyer and the other a banker. One daughter marries a successful doctor and is able to pursue painting, an endeavor for
which Abbie never had time. Another, who has inherited Abbie's talent for
singing, becomes a professional musician, while the third takes Abbie's experience as a school teacher one step further and becomes a college professor.

Finally, the most tangible marker of Abbie's successful infusion of her
dreams and goals into her children and grandchildren involves the pearls Abbie's
mother gives her on her wedding day. Belonging originally to Abbie's wealthy
paternal grandmother, they represent all that Abbie's family has lost and what
she hopes to regain. Her mother gives them to Abby as an insurance policy of
sorts, telling her," Y'ell never starves as long as you have 'em" (45). Significantly,
the older woman, having experienced both great wealth and severe poverty, is,
unlike her daughter, unwilling to equate wealth with happiness, telling Abbie
"it wasn't the wealth that brought us happiness" (45). Abbie pays lip service to
her mother's words, saying "when you follow your heart you don't need pearls
to make you happy" (46), yet the pearls represent all that she longs to regain.

Ironically, Abbie never wears the pearls herself. She doesn't achieve the
wealth that would make them a suitable accoutrement to her lifestyle. And her
oldest daughter, to whom she tries to give them, rejects them. When they *are*
worn, it is by one of Abbie's granddaughters, Katherine, a child of privilege
whose life of ease is the antithesis of her grandmother's. Though Katherine is
seemingly nonchalant when Abbie presents her with the pearls, her nonchalance
is pretence. She has absorbed the stories Abbie has told her of her aristocratic
great-great-grandmother and the values represented by that ancestor's life. On
her wedding day Katherine surprises Abbie with the portrait of her great-great-
grandmother, the one that hung in the family mansion in Scotland and which
Katherine's father, Abbie's son, has managed to track down and purchase. Sadly,
the recovered portrait brings Abbie no joy, only reminding her of "all the wonderful things I planned to do when I was young . . . and never did" (240). Significantly, all those things have little to do with what Streeter is ostensibly cele-
brating, the hardworking, family-oriented, community-minded, pioneer spirit.
Rather, they have to with living a life of material ease that allows one to wear
beautiful clothing, have beautiful objects, and spend one's time exploring the arts.

Lyddie

While *A Lantern in Her Hand* can be read as a text of contradictions, one that
both critiques and endorses class privilege, Katherine Paterson's *Lyddie*, pub-

lished in 1991, is a more straighforward deconstruction of the implications of class structure in the United States.[8] As such, Paterson interrogates two essential components of the American dream: first, that movement from one class to another can be accomplished with relative ease, and second, that that movement is primarily the result of individual effort rather than communal cooperation. Over the course of the novel, the main character, Lyddie, learns that both class and gender constitute forms of slavery whose bonds are as difficult to break as those imposed by race in nineteenth-century America. When the novel opens, Lyddie is thirteen and living on a hard-scrabble farm in Vermont. Her father has left, heading west, ostensibly in an effort to improve the family's fortunes. Her emotionally fragile mother, though physically present, is emotionally distant, and it is Lyddie, the oldest child of four, who has taken on the responsibility of holding the family together. When her mother can no longer bear life on the farm, she abandons it to live with her sister and brother-in-law, leaving Lyddie and her younger brother, Charlie, to survive as best they can. They do survive, though barely, and so are shocked when they learn that their mother has rented out their land and hired out Lyddie to work as a chamber maid at an inn and Charlie at a mill.

At the inn Lyddie learns that being at the bottom of the socio-economic heap means more than struggling simply for enough food to eat, as she and Charlie had done. It also means giving up the autonomy that she has cherished. Approaching the inn, she realizes that "Once I walk in that gate, I ain't free anymore." But before walking through that gate, she encounters what at first appears to be an example of upper class privilege: a young, well-dressed woman descending from a carriage. The quality of the woman's clothes leads Lyddie to assume she is a lady, a woman of the leisure classes. Later she is disabused of this notion when her new mistress complains "of the guest who made herself out to be a lady when she was nothing but a factory girl putting on fancy airs" (22). The episode is significant for a number of reasons. First, it reveals the extent to which class position has historically been identified by outward markers such as dress.[9] Second, it illustrates the confusion that results when members of a lower class appropriate upper-class markers for their own use. Third, it reveals, in the landlady's reaction to the well-dressed factory girl, the hostility that results when class lines are breached. Finally, it suggests the possibility of class mobility. When the well-dressed factory girl appears at the inn a second time and tells Lyddie that she can make a better life for herself in the mills in Lowell, Massachusetts, the older girl's prosperous appearance convinces Lyddie that she speaks the truth.

Lyddie resolves to seek a brighter future when her mistress becomes angry with her for taking a day off to visit her brother and their old homestead. That resolve is strengthened when she encounters a slave who is using her family's cabin as a refuge as he waits for transport on the Underground Railroad to

Canada. Though brief, Lyddie's encounter with the escaped slave Ezekiel is transformative. He makes clear to her that slavery takes many forms. One can be enslaved by gender, something Lyddie implicitly acknowledged earlier when she referred to herself as "doomed to be female" (23). But one can also be enslaved by poverty, by class. When Ezekiel says "So many slaves," Lyddie recognizes that he is including her in this group. She immediately rejects the label: "'I ain't a slave.... I just—I just—' ... Whatever she said only made it seem worse" (41). Lyddie's use of "ain't" is telling, especially when contrasted with Ezekiel's command of standard English acquired from his constant reading and rereading of the Bible. Throughout the novel Paterson makes clear that language functions as a classmarker and that education is one way of achieving class mobility. Slowly Lyddie recognizes that freedom is problematic when one is riddled by debt, forced to work for no pay, and has no education to rise above her station.

Consequently, Lyddie makes her way to Lowell where she finds work in the mills. Once there, she is faced with contradictions that force her to explore the confusing gap between appearance and reality. The young women who work in the factory may dress well, but they work long hours in unhealthy conditions, are forced to live only in those boarding houses approved by the Lowell corporation, and are expected to attend church on Sundays. The material conditions under which Lyddie works further complicates her understanding of freedom and class: debt may make one a slave, but a salary doesn't necessarily make one free.

Yet for much of the novel Lyddie enacts Franklin's precept that if one works hard enough, riches will be inevitable. Her already strong work ethic coupled with her desire to save money and free her family from debt so they can return to their farm, pushes her to take on more and more looms at the factory. But her bank account grows more slowly than she wishes, and the stress on her body leads to both illness and injury. More severe is the psychological toll: Lyddie isolates herself from the other factory girls and thus loses the camaraderie and support they offer. Though her very basic reading skills have improved while living in the boarding house, and reading gives her great pleasure, she nevertheless is too exhausted after her work in the mills to join the other girls in their study groups. She also refuses to join the efforts of those young women who are trying to form a union in order to improve the conditions under which they work. Making her paycheck her god, she is transformed in a way that even she recognizes is not healthy. When she finds herself reluctant to send her own mother a dollar, she "marveled that there had been a time when she had almost gladly given a perfect stranger everything she had, but now found it hard to send her own mother a dollar" (116).

Sexual harassment, her mother's death in an insane asylum, and the need to care for her younger sister all force Lyddie to reevaluate the life she has been eading. She wonders "why she is working so hard" (148), and her sister Rachel's presence and affection makes her realize "[h]ow dry her life had been before Rachel came" (138). Her supervisor's sexual harassment of her and another factory girl she has mentored leads Lyddie to reconsider the value of the union she has resisted joining. And when she defends a co-worker who is being harassed by her supervisor and is, as a consequence, accused of "moral turpitude" and fired, she realizes that "[i]n silence the battle had been lost" (168).

Over the course of Paterson's novel, Lyddie is forced into several painful recognitions that force a change in her world view. She learns that poverty can enslave one and that being poor and dependent results in one being treated like "a maggot" (164). She then learns that simply earning money and working hard cannot ensure happiness. Finally, she learns that collective actions increase the possibility that all humans will be treated like "proper persons" (149) and that helping others is its own reward. Lyddie returns home to consider her future, and realizes that the only way to free herself from the slavery imposed by poverty and gender is by acquiring an education. The ending of the novel makes two things clear: first, that Lyddie will ultimately return to her hometown and marry the Quaker farmer who loves her, and, second, that she will do this only after she goes to school at Oberlin, the first college in the United States to admit women.

Rebecca Barnhouse has offered an excellent critique of the use of literacy in young adult historical novels, arguing succinctly that the historical accuracy of these novels is diminished when fictional characters acquire a literacy that actual characters were unlikely to have achieved.[10] While her point is valid, it ignores the extent to which all historical fiction is shaped by and reflects the values of the culture that produces it. American culture has long stressed, even perhaps romanticized, education as a tool for self-improvement and the achievement of class fluidity, and so we should not be surprised that it appears as such in young adult historical fiction.

The Midwife's Apprentice

Such a problematic situation occurs in Karen Cushman's *The Midwife's Apprentice*, published in 1995.[11] Cushman's novel captures much that can be verified about medieval life: the situation of abandoned or orphaned children, the role of midwives in a medieval village, the role of superstition, and the day-to-day struggle for survival of those without friends and families. But the novel also contains elements that clearly indicates the culture of its origin. Brat, the main character, early on recognizes that being perceived as someone who can read is a social advantage. When the opportunity arises for her to learn to read, she grabs it. Her relationship to the written word, though it may not be historically accurate is, nevertheless essential to the development of her character's growing sense of self and thus the plot of the novel.

Brat, who over the course of the novel undergoes several name changes is sleeping in a dung heap when the novel opens, a disgusting place but one that offers warmth and shelter for her "unwashed, unnourished, unloved, and unlovely body." Without family to support her, she scrapes by doing day labor and finds shelter where she can. Such a life has left her with no expectations no hopes; "she dreamed of nothing, for she hoped of nothing and expected nothing" (2). The human tendency, whether instilled or inherent, to assert superiority over those less fortunate than themselves means that no matter where she lands, she is at the bottom of the social heap even in the small, impoverished villages where she takes shelter. Cushman writes that "[i]n every village there were boys. . . . Always they were the scrawniest, or the ugliest, or the dirtiest, or the stupidest boys, picked on by everyone else, with no one left uglier stupider, than they but her" (3). The above passage contests the notion that those at the bottom of the social structure feel an instinctive bond for one another. Rather, it implicitly endorses the belief that that survival is always of the fittest and makes clear that if Brat is to survive she must make a place for herself, something she can only do by acquiring skills that will make her a necessary part of a community.

The opportunity to do this occurs when the midwife Jane offers Brat a home in exchange for her labor. Though what the parsimonious Jane offers is scanty at best, it is, nevertheless, more than Brat has had. More important than the food and shelter Jane offers is the gift, unwittingly given, of identity Though Jane renames Brat Beetle (as in dung beetle), she also gives Beetle a more important gift: Beetle becomes the midwife's apprentice and as such has a recognizable place in the life of the village. Jane's own role in that community is an important one. Until medicine began to be professionalized in the 18th century, midwives held a place of the utmost importance in community life. Their skill in delivering babies and treating other female health issues was valued and respected. As the village midwife, Jane holds more power and authority than other women. At a time when women's options were more often than not limited to marriage or the convent, midwives had an enviable autonomy. Jane maintains her own home, determines her fees, picks and chooses her clients, and even engages in sexual relationships without fear of any reprisal other than embarrassment when discovered.

Gradually, as Beetle's most basic needs are met, she recognizes the power Jane has over her own life and sets out to learn the secrets of the older woman's skill, recognizing that, though she cannot articulate it, those skills bring autonomy. Though Jane tries to keep Beetle out of the cottages when she is delivering babies, Beetle gradually recognizes that the older woman does so "not because she [Beetle] was stupid, but to keep her in ignorance of the midwife's skills and spells" (14). Jane needs Beetle's help but recognizes a future competitor in the young girl and is determined to maintain a monopoly on her trade.

In spite of her attempts to keep Beetle ignorant, the girl acquires knowledge and is soon "surprised at how much she knew" (15). Reinforcing Maslow's hierarchy of needs, once Beetle no longer has to worry about food and shelter, she "found her mind empty and [cast] about for something to figure out" (17). Beetle's shift in focus is important because it forges a connection between intellectual curiosity or development and the material conditions of an individual's life. Beetle's experience makes clear that material condition shapes the extent to which we interact with or are engaged by the world. This awareness implicitly critiques that idea that strength of will alone is necessary to achieve success.

When Beetle's stomach is no longer empty, she begins to display a curiosity about others in the village. More significantly, she begins to exert an influence, although a covert one, in the villagers' lives. Once she has some security, she uses her intellect to avenge the various wrongs done to her by villagers' who had made her their whipping girl. Using the skill she acquires from local woodcarver and playing on the villager's superstitions, she slowly exposes their very human frailties, such as adulterous relationships and dishonest trade practices. That she is able to do indicates that she has acquired both some power and some confidence.

The crisis for Beetle, who renames herself Alyce,[12] comes when the knowledge she has slowly been acquiring proves inadequate and she is unable to deliver a child on her own. Shamed, she flees the village that has become her sanctuary. From this point on the novel becomes an exploration of the psychology that prevents individuals from claiming a place within a community. At the end of Katherine Paterson's *Lyddie,* Lyddie recognizes that it has been her own "narrow spirit" (181) that has kept her from doing all that she might. Similarly, Alyce recognizes that fear of failure has deprived her of the closest thing she's had to a home. She decides to return to Jane, determined to "try and try again . . . to try and risk and fail again and try again and not give up" (116–117). That both Lyddie and Alyce locate their failures in themselves can be interpreted in several ways. We can read this as a reinforcement of the aspect of the American dream that credits radical individualism as the sole factor in assigning either success or failure to any given person. We can also read it as an acknowledgement that the desire for social advancement, to move from one social status to another, can manifest itself only when the most basic needs for food, shelter, and group membership are first met.

Fever 1793

Laurie Halse Anderson's *Fever 1793* arises questions about how socially constructed notions of class as well as its ideological underpinnings are complicated and contested in the face of natural disaster. The impetus for these questions is the yellow fever epidemic that struck Philadelphia in 1793 and in "three months killed nearly five thousand people, ten percent of the city's population."[13] Mattie Cook, the narrator of *Fever 1793,* will initially strike a chord with adolescent readers: she wants to sleep in; her mother wants her get out of bed. She is easily bored. When she dawdles over chores, her mother chastises her with stories of her girlhood when "we were up before the sun" (2), stories that Mattie, like most adolescents, understandably resents. But this rather stereotypical pattern of parent / child interaction is broken by Mattie's ambitions that are hardly those of typical teenager. Mattie's widowed mother runs a coffee house built by her late husband, a carpenter she married against the wishes of her wealthy parents. In so doing she subverted one of the essential components of rigidly stratified class structure, that one should marry members of one's own class.[14] When Mattie's mother's both chooses her own husband and marries *out* of class, her actions reinforce the ideal of the United States as a place where class is fluid and self-invention a possibility.

But rebellious though she was in her own choice of mate, Mattie's mother nevertheless still clings to some traditional notions of both class and gender. She disapproves of Nathanial, the painter's apprentice for whom Mattie cares, dismissing him as a "scamp" and a possible "scoundrel" with no "future" (30). Mattie refutes these charges, not by reminding her mother of her own controversial choice of mate but rather by asserting that Nathanial is "a gentleman" (35). Mattie is more than a teenager infatuated by a man her mother finds unsuitable. She is a girl with a plan, and that plan, one that Ben Franklin might well have approved of, is to improve her family's material position through expansion and acquisition. When Mattie, her grandfather, and her mother discuss what they might do with their "windfall," increased profits due to an influx of new customers who have fled other coffee houses in the center of the city (37), Mattie, who wants to own "an entire city block" (12), reveals an entrepreneurial spirit that makes her sound very much like a young Donald Trump:

> First we should buy another coffee urn, to serve customers with more haste . . . Next is to expand into Mr. Watson's lot. That way we could offer proper meals, not just tidbits and rolls. You could serve roasts and mutton chops. And we could have an upstairs meeting room for the gentlemen like the coffee houses down by the wharves . . . . And we could reserve space to sell paintings and combs and fripperies from France. (38)

Mattie's ambitions, certainly an important expression of the American dream, are obstructed initially by her mother's inclination to "bury the money in the backyard to benefit the worms" (37) and then by the outbreak of the yellow fever which first kills one of her family's servants, Polly, and then strikes Mattie's mother. As of result of these incidents Mattie is forced to grow up very quickly. Polly's death requires Mattie to take on the serving girl's work. Though she has previously characterized herself as someone whose mother forces her to work as "as a mule"(12), the significantly more demanding work load of a serving girl forces Mattie to ask herself, "How did Polly do this every day?" (22)

As the fever spreads through Philadelphia, it becomes clear that class, which has historically protected those at its upper levels from the grittier aspects of life, offers no protection from the disease or even assurance that those in the upper classes will treat their own with any humanity. Self-preservation becomes the main goal of the healthy, and those who threaten that objective are literally cast away. Returning to the city after she has recovered from her own bout of the fever, Mattie notices what appears to be a bundle of rags on "the marble steps of a three story house" (118). When she tries to stop and help what turns out, in fact, to be a young man in "well tailored clothes,"(119) the driver of her cart refuses saying, "He is past helping. . . . His family tossed him out so they wouldn't catch the fever" (119).

Though Mattie is understandably pained by such scenes, as well as those that more directly affect her (such as the death of her grandfather), they are interspersed by comic ones. Anderson makes clear that not just disease but the inclinations of the human heart can also effectively breach class strictures; thus, when comedy does occur, its object is the inability of the upper classes to protect themselves from their own impulsive behavior that disregards social expectations. When Mattie asks her African American servant Eliza whether a girl from an upper class family, a girl who has treated Mattie shabbily, has died from the fever, Eliza's answer paints a darkly comic picture.

> "Miss Colette came down with an awful case of the fever. You know how they are. They call in this doctor and that doctor. Spend money, fuss and holler. Nothing helps. The girl is burning up. The whole family gathers at her bedside thinking she's going to Jesus, when she sits up straight in bed and starts screaming, 'Loueey! Loueey!' Turns out this Louis is her husband."
>
> "But she was engaged to Roger Garthing."
>
> "Um-huh. And listen. This Louis was her French tutor. They had eloped just before she got sick. So everyone starts to scream and carry on, the younger daughter had a temper tantrum 'cause it turns out that she was sweet on this Frenchie, too. The mother faints and their little dog bites the doctor." (186–87)

Ironically, the epidemic becomes a way for Mattie to make progress toward achieving her dream of expanding the family business. To do this, she must go even further toward challenging cultural notions of gender and class than her mother did by marrying out of class. Mattie challenges notions of race by redefining her relationship with Eliza, who at the beginning of the book is a black family servant but by the end a partner in the coffee business. Because the epidemic breaks down both internal and external barriers to aspiration, Mattie can expand beyond what her mother thinks is possible. Though Mattie's ambition is evident at the beginning of the novel, it is restricted by her mother's financial caution and her desire to recapture her own class position by having Mattie marry more advantageously than she has. But though Mattie talks a good game and resists her mother's attempts to make her into a lady, traditional notions of rank and gender are more deeply inscribed on her than she knows.

The epigrams with which Anderson heads each chapter make clear how difficult it is for Mattie (and by extension, any of us) to escape from a culture's programming. Drawn from the conduct manuals that were popular for and among women in the seventeenth century,[15] these books advised behavior intended to reinforce traditional notions of class and gender. Chapter Five, for example, begins with an epigram from Hannah More's *The Young Lady Abroad or Affectionate Advice on the Social and Moral Habits of Females* that reads, "A low voice and soft address are the common indications of a *well-bred woman*" [italics ours] (24). Another chapter opens with a sentence from Gervase Markham's *The English Housewife,* setting forth "the first and most principal" asset for a desirable wife is "to be a perfect skill and knowledge of cookery . . . because it is a duty well belonging to women" (6). Mattie looks forward to the day when shopkeepers address her as "Ma'am" (12) as a sign both of her maturity as well as an acknowledgment of her place in the community. But when Mattie has recovered from her own bout of the fever and is told by an older woman that she can now help others, she responds, "How can I help anyone? I am just a girl" (115). Just as Katherine Paterson's Lyddie realizes that it is her own "narrow spirit" that limits her aspirations, so must Mattie realize that she is more than "just a girl."

The impetus for Mattie to escape her self-imposed restrictions is the example of Eliza, her African-American servant. It is Eliza she seeks out after her grandfather has died and she cannot find her mother. And it is Eliza's example, as a member of the Free African Society that offers nursing and other forms of assistance to all regardless of race that opens Mattie's mind to the possibility of new forms of community.[16] Asserting that "We are all better off together" (185), Eliza offers Mattie a new model for making one's way through the world, even succeeding in it, based on both cooperation and individual choice. At the novel's end, Mattie's mother has returned to the coffee shop and a reversal in roles for mother and daughter is anticipated. Mattie recognizes that her mother, weak-ned by fever, is unlikely ever to resume her position of authority in the coffee house. Though saddened by her mother's weakness, it is that very weakness that, in part, assures Mattie that "everything has changed" (218). This realization allows her to assert that she "would set her own course" (217). She does so by implementing new business methods (free samples as a marketing tool!) and making clear that she will marry Nathanial when she deems the time is right.

Out of the Dust

Karen Hesse's *Out of the Dust*, like the other novels discussed in this chapter, can be read as a both a critique and corrective to the American dream's promise of class mobility.[17] As in *Fever 1793*, *Out of the Dust* begins with a family already struggling to maintain their way of life when it is faced with natural disaster. In Hesse's novel, the dust storms and drought of the 1930s chip away at the Kelby family's hope of supporting themselves, much less prospering on their small farm in the Oklahoma Panhandle. As in the novels discussed above—*Lantern in Her Hand, Lyddie, The Midwife's Apprentice,* and *Fever 1793*—Hesse makes clear that hard work doesn't ensure success and that social mobility and self-determination, two cherished components of the American dream, can be undermined by forces beyond human control. And when humans not only do survive but flourish, it is because they have worked with others to enhance their mutual prospects. Hesse frames the free verse musings of Billie Jo Kelby, her protagonist, with subtle references to noteworthy events and personages from the Great Depression. References to kidnapping of the Lindbergh baby, the birth of the Dionne Quintuplets, Franklin Roosevelt, and the CCC camps locate Billie Jo's family tragedy (the death of her mother and baby brother from an accidental fire and the crippling of her own gifted musician's hands) in the context of more highly publicized ones.

Hesse's juxtaposition of Billie Jo's sufferings with those of others reinforces two points about class already made earlier. First, membership in the upper class cannot shield one from tragedy. The kidnapping and subsequent murder of Charles and Anne Lindbergh's baby boy suggest this, as does the affliction of Franklin Delano Roosevelt with adult polio. Second, in both *Fever 1793* and *Out of the Dust* we encounter characters whose efforts to improve or simply maintain their class status is done so at the expense of equally cherished American notions of family: the death of the young man in *Fever 1793* whose family throws him out of his home reminds Mattie that wealth is not a protection from disease. And when Billie Jo notes the birth of Dionne quintuplets, readers (at least those of a certain age) are reminded of the subsequent exploitation of those children, first by their parents and then by the Canadian government, for material gain.

Hesse's corrective to the "feel-good" cultural narratives that equate an individual's hard work with material success is to offer family and community, imperfect and flawed though they may be, as the only safeguards against disaster. He novel begins in a community already suffering the effects of years of poor crop yields. Billie Jo's second monologue, "Rabbit Battles," illustrates both the personal and environmental problems the community faces as well as its responses to them. Two men complaining about the damage rabbits have done to their crops decide to compete to see who can kill the most rabbits. Billie Jo's initial reaction to this is one of disgust: "Grown men clubbing bunnies to death. / Makes me sick to my stomach" (6). Yet, as her teacher points out, the rabbits are forced to eat the crops because of the farming practices that plow under what the rabbits previously fed on, practices that we now realize led to the erosion that, combined with years of drought, led to the Dust Bowl. And though the men's contest undermines their friendship so that "they can't be civil to each other" (7), the product of that competition, the rabbit meat "went to families that needed the meat" (7).

Hesse peppers the novel with similar incidents of community members, often at odds with one another, nevertheless offering the support necessary to ensure that all survive. Though Billie Jo's family hasn't had a decent crop in three years, her mother still donates "three jars of applesauce and some cured pork and a feed sack nightie she's sewn for our coming baby" (16) to those whose need is greater. Likewise, when a migrant family seeks shelter from one of the frequent dust storms in the local school house, they are referred to as "Guests" (20) and told they "could stay /as long as they wanted"(12). The students all make an effort to help the homeless family, and the family offers what they can in return:

> Every day we bring fixings for soup
> and put a big pot on to simmer.
> We share at lunch with our guests.
> the family of migrants who have moved out from dust
> and Depression . . . .
> The man, Buddy Williams,
> Helps out around the school,
> Fixing windows and doors,
> and the bad spots on the steps
> cleaning up the school yard
> so it never looked so good. (121–22)

Tempting thought it might be to argue that Hesse romanticizes family and community, her stripped-to-the-bones prose and unwillingness to ignore the pain family members inflict on one another make clear that this is not her intent. Rather, she suggests that in a world where little is certain, people must cling to those around them if they are to survive, much less flourish.

In none of the novels discussed in this chapter do the riches that Benjamin Franklin promised for those willing to work hard materialize. Each novel depicts instead an individual or family struggling to survive. Ironically, even sadly, those struggles are made more difficult by the self-doubt characters experience when their efforts lead neither to social mobility nor riches. The pain of this self-doubt is assuaged only when characters realize that individual effort will take one so far, that if they have failed to achieve the riches Benjamin Franklin saw as a sure thing, perhaps the system they worked within and the ideology they unquestioningly accepted is as much to blame as they are. Abbie Deal recognizes this after years of struggle on the Nebraskan prairies when her efforts do not result in the riches she assumed as a young woman she would achieve: "And the minister at home said you could do anything with your life. But that was not so. Life did things to you."[18] The realization that she has only limited control over her life later leads Abbie to greater sympathy for those who do not achieve even the limited success she and Will have. Confronted with her well-educated youngest daughter's smug assertion that "one could accomplish in this world whatever task he set himself to do" (183), Abbie muses on her own difficulty accepting this notion.

> A great sympathy would surge up in her heart for one whom life had used harshly . . . . When you get older, you get more sympathetic for the under-dog. When you grow out of youthful years you have more charity for folks who haven't succeeded. (183).

A greater sympathy for those whose dreams of success are not achieved despite their efforts, a realization that success and often survival depend on working cooperatively rather than in isolation, and a recognition that cooperative efforts require constantly redefining and reconfiguring traditional notions of family, gender, race, and ethnicity—these are the themes that regularly appear in young adult historical novels that wrestle with our culture's often conflicting notions of class. Even more importantly is the awareness that "even if personal experience showed them that the myth of mobility had a certain substance . . . the vision of climbing very high on the ladder was a mirage."[19] The characters in all the novels discussed in this chapter may improve their lives somewhat but never to the extent they had first imagined. Like the main character in Horatio Alger's *Luck and Pluck,* they learn that while pluck is required to succeed, luck is often a "principal key to success."[20]

NOTES

1. J. Hector St. John de Crevecoeur, from "Letters from an American Farmer." In *Rereading America: Cultural Contexts for Critical Thinking and Writing,* Gary Colombo, Robert Cullen, and Bonnie Lisle, eds. (New York: Bedford/St. Martin's, 2004): 304.

2. Benjamin Franklin, "Advice to a Young Tradesman," quoted by Peter Baida in *Poor Richard's Legacy: American Business Values from Benjamin Franklin to Donald Trump, 1990.* (New York: William Morrow, 1990), 23.

3. Peter Gay, *Pleasure Wars: The Bourgeois Experience: Victoria to Freud,* v. 5 (New York: W.W. Norton and Company, 1998): 15.

4. Horatio Alger, *Ragged Dick* (New York: Signet, 1990 [1867]): 295.

5. Note, for example, the celebrity of figures like Paris Hilton, who, though she has not finished high school, appears on countless magazine covers and on TV shows simply because she is rich.

6. Bess Streeter Aldrich, *A Lantern in Her Hand* (New York: Puffin Books, 2004 [1928]): 29; hereafter cited parenthetically in the text.

7. "Dutchy" is an obvious ethnic slur is used by Streeter throughout the text without any discomfort.

8. Katherine Paterson, *Lyddie* (New York: Puffin Books, 1991): 18; hereafter cited parenthetically in the text.

9. Consider, for example, the sumptuary laws enacted in the middle ages that were intended to maintain class distinctions by allowing only upper classes to wear certain fabrics or colors. Consider also the efforts of such groups as the Quakers to subvert the relationship between class and dress by mandating that its members dress "simply."

10. Barnhouse, *Recasting the Past.*

11. Karen Cushman, *The Midwife's Apprentice,* (New York: Clarion Books, 1995): 1; hereafter cited parenthetically in the text.

12. Historically the act of naming or renaming oneself has been a way for marginalized members of a society to assert their right to self-determination. For example, when finally freed, many slaves rejected the names their owners had assigned them. (Malcolm X has included a full discussion of this in his *Autobiography*.) Beetle's decision to name herself Alyce is important because it marks her recognition that she can claim some control over her life.

13. Laurie Halse Anderson, *Fever 1793* (New York: Aladdin Books, 2002), 244; hereafter cited parenthetically in the text.

14. The notion that one might pick one's own spouse and marry for love is relatively new to western culture, and it is interesting to think of how this notion of individual choice has historically played itself out for men and women.

15. Such texts have continued to attempt to regulate female behavior. See, for example, *Fascinating Womanhood* (1965) by Helen Andelin (New York: Bantam, Revised and Updated, 1992) or *The Rules: Time-Tested Secrets for Capturing the Heart of Mr. Right* by Ellen Fein and Sherrie Schneider (New York: Warner Books, 1995).

16. Anderson points out early in her novel that at the time of the yellow fever epidemic, most Africans-Americans were free (8). Few, however, owned businesses. The Free African Society, founded in 1787 by two black ministers, was intended to fight slavery and assist former slaves. During the epidemic "society members worked night and day to relieve the suffering of the yellow fever victims" (247).

17. Karen Hesse, *Out of the Dust* (New York: Scholastic, 1997); hereafter cited parenthetically in the text.

18. Aldrich, *A Lantern in Her Hand,* 103.

19. Peter Gay, *Pleasure Wars,* 15.

20. Horatio Alger, *Luck and Pluck* (New York: Pavillion Press, 2003 [1869], 15.

· 7 ·

Sugar and (Lots of) Spice

In every outthrust headland, in every curving beach, in every
grain of sand there is a story of the earth.

Rachel Carson[1]

$\mathscr{R}$achel Carson is undoubtedly right in asserting that there is a story in
every grain of sand," and her statement suggests the challenges for authors exploring gender in young adult historical fiction: Whose story to tell and how?
Unavoidably, writers of historical novels bring their own perspectives on any
given issue to their fiction, but they must balance those perspectives with an
accurate representation of how those issues were viewed at the time of the
story they are writing. No matter how adept authors are at this balancing act,
they inevitably insert into their narratives contemporary concerns that may
resonate widely for their readers but were mostly ignored during the era of the
narrative. With no issue is this more true than with gender.

Elizabeth Janeway has said, "If every nation gets the government it deserves, every generation writes the history which corresponds with its view of
the world,"[2] a statement that helps us to understand why the stories of women
and girls remained submerged for so long. Cultural constructions of gender sti-
led female voices and limited their choices in life, and, as a result, historians
demonstrated little interest in them.

Therefore, it is hardly surprising that earlier writers of historical fiction used
mostly male protagonists, who were free to venture into the world while their
female counterparts stayed home. While the girls and women busied themselves
with domestic chores, the boys and men were confronting exciting challenges
with pluck and courage, exercising their budding manhood and engaging young
readers in their adventures. But the foregrounding of feminist issues in the late
twentieth century has spawned a fair number of historical novels that feature

121

strong adolescent girls, literary descendants of the determined young women created by Scott O'Dell in *Island of the Blue Dolphins* and *Sing Down the Moon*. Regardless of when these novels are set, whether the Middle Ages or the first quarter of the twentieth century, they share a tendency to represent young females coming to grips with the restraints imposed by their gender, trying to reconcile their desires for self-determination and voice with the restricted choices their culture offers.[3]

More specifically, the novels discussed in this chapter explore how gender roles, previously seen as normative but now viewed as oppressive, shape a character's understanding of her place in the world. Each of the novels discussed below shows a young woman going through a process of first learning what her culture expects of her as a female, then resisting the restrictions of those expectations and, finally, engaging in a process of negotiation that allows her satisfying sense of self and moral agency. The process of negotiation often involves passive resistance, subversion, and manipulation of the existing code of femininity. Young readers reared to value straightforward assertiveness may be critical of these strategies; the use of them, nevertheless, results in lives for the protagonists that allow more self-expression and control than first expected. More importantly, these strategies are not simply fictional devices but are rather grounded in the historical reality of women's lives.

Catherine Called Birdy

Karen Cushman's *Catherine Called Birdy*, for example, presents a protagonist whose feistiness is bound to appeal to many young readers.[4] Yet while they may be attracted to her strong will, they may likely be repelled by much of what she takes for granted in her life. Her story, told as a journal, opens on this note of frustration: "I am commanded to write an account of my days. I am bit by fleas and plagued by family. That is all there is to say"(1). The family member who "plagues" her most is her casually abusive father, who assumes that at fourteen his daughter Catherine, nicknamed Birdy, is ready for marriage and that it is *his* prerogative to choose her husband. Both the age at which Birdy is to be married and her lack of choice in the matter will strike readers reared to believe that marriage is based on love and individual choice as presumptive and cruel.[5] But as an historical novelist, Cushman must accurately represent thirteenth-century attitudes toward parents, children, women, and marriage while balancing that representation with a plot and a character that will hold the interest of contemporary young adult readers.[6] She does this by creating a protagonist with a passionate desire for self-determination and then proceeds to show what happens when that determination conflicts with her culture's expectations for females of a particular class. Birdy resents the "lady lessons" and "lady tasks" imposed on her and resists the training that she rightly believes will leave her "docile, dumb, and accomplished" (24). She well knows the intended result of the desired behavior: a marriage that will enrich her father.

Over the course of the novel, though she often fantasizes about escape, Birdy gradually accepts that she cannot avoid marriage. Her journey to acceptance—characterized by accommodations, negotiations, and a growing awareness that life is more complicated than she originally believed—make this novel fascinating. Birdy initially chafes against anything that will make her into the lady her mother wants her to be. She takes to writing a journal for two reasons. First, Edward, the brother she loves, believes that her doing so "will help me grow less childish and more learned" (2). But more compelling than the possibility for greater maturity is her mother's promise that Birdy may "forgo spinning as long as I write this account" (2). However, though Birdy is released from spinning, she is not allowed to avoid those other skills her mother feels a woman must have, such as sewing. She rebels against these as well, making clear that she is resisting not only female roles but class-based ones as well:

> Here in my prison my mother works and gossips with her women as if she didn't mind being chained to a needle and spindle. . . . If I had to be born a lady, why not a *rich* lady, so someone else could do the work and I could lie on a silken bed and listen to a beautiful minstrel sing while my servants hemmed. Instead I am the daughter of a country knight with but ten servants, seventy villagers, no minstrel and acres of unhemmed linen. It grumbles my guts. (5)

Unable or unwilling to believe that her mother derives any pleasure from her life, Birdy resists the older woman's attempts to teach her the skills necessary to managing a manor. Her rebellion against her mother's lessons in domesticity, which often takes the form of hiding in a stable or throwing botched embroidery into the privy, intensifies in the face of her father's attempts to marry her off. Attempting to determine her marketability, he questions Birdy, and his questions reveal what made a female desirable in thirteenth-century England:

> "Exactly how old are you, daughter?"
> "Have you all your teeth?"
> "Is your breath sweet or foul?"
> "Are you a good eater?"
> "What color is your hair when it is clean?"
> "How are your sewing, your bowels, and your conversation?" (4)

Though Birdy wishes to escape this life of "hemming and mending, fishing for husbands" and would prefer "crusading, swinging my sword at heathens and sleeping under starry skies" (8), she comes to realize that marriage is inevitable. This realization, coupled with growing awareness of her own limitations, is hardly joyous. Rather, it is born out of a newfound understanding that her society allows her few other options.[7] Commenting on the life of a martyr who chose death over marriage, Birdy asks herself, "Would I choose to die rather than be forced to marry? I hope to avoid the issue, but I do not think I have it in me to be a saint" (54).

The achievement of self-knowledge and a realistic sense of what the world offers is an important theme in young adult literature as well as an indicator of a character's growing maturity. As such, the question Birdy asks herself about what she can endure is important because it reveals that she has achieved a degree of self-knowledge. Accepting that marriage is unavoidable, she begins to observe how the females around her manage to achieve some control over their lives and, occasionally, power over others. She notes, for example, that her good friend Lady Aelis "liked to complain . . . but did as she pleased when no one could see. . . [and] told me she gets away with things because she looks so docile and innocent while she does just what she wants" (30). Birdy further observes that though her mother seldom contradicts her father directly, she "in her quiet way does as she wishes" (107), quietly subverting his power in the process. Madam Joanna, an elderly cousin of the King, a woman Birdy imagines to have led a life of glamour and freedom, gives her more direct instruction. Her advice helps Birdy recognize that her fantasy of "a beloved friend, beautiful as summer, who would rescue me" (104) is just that—a fantasy. Madam Joanna, describing her own strategy for living, tells Birdy: "I flap my wings at times, choose my fights carefully, get things done, understand my limitations, trust in God and a few people, and here I am. I survive and sometimes even enjoy" (106). The behavior of Aelis, Joanna, and Birdie's mother is a form of passive resistance. Though initially anathema to Birdy's desire to speak out loudly and clearly, it is a natural outgrowth of one of the medival ideologies of gender, which enjoined women to silence and submission. Birdy's resistance to this misogynistic notion is demonstrated when she engages in a dual of wits with Agnes, a visiting girl, over a female's use of her voice. Agnes maintains:

> "A silent woman is always more admired than a noisy one."
> "It is also said that 'A woman's tongue is her sword,'" I countered, "and she does not let it rust."
> "Maids should be mild and meek, swift to hear and slow to speak," said Agnes.
> "Be she old or be she young, a woman's strength is in her tongue," I said.
> Agnes pointed her nose at me. "One tongue is enough for two women." (116)

Readers will see Birdy's position in this debate as a predictable extension of her personality, but by including the debate itself, no matter in how abbreviated a form, Cushman provides for young readers a more complex understanding of the Middle Ages. Traditional scholarship has long characterized the discourse of the Middle Ages as essentially misogynistic, but it is more accurate to recognize that there was a well-developed resistance or counternarrative to that ideology, one that Birdy, in her opposition to Agnes, articulates.[8] Birdy never overcomes her aversion to needlework, but, as she pays greater attention to the lives of the women around her, she shows a greater interest in some activities seen as the special province of females such as gathering and preparing herbs for medicinal uses. Her ability to mix herbs and to provide relief from pain to others is, she gradually realizes, a kind of power. Her use of this power, however, is not always benevolent; for a man who irritates her she mixes a laxative into a remedy for his hangover.

Though Birdy accepts that marriage is her fate, she resists her father's assumption that she will have no choice in her husband. Here again the issue of class enters into the novel. When Birdy realizes that peasant girls have more say in their choice of husbands than she does, she asks: "Why can villagers have a say in whom they marry and I cannot?" (129). Unable to participate in the negotiations her father conducts with potential suitors, Birdy contents herself with directing her energies toward alienating those suitors she finds especially noxious. Her efforts in this regard range from blackening her teeth to setting on fire the privy in which a particularly unappealing suitor "with a backside the size of a millpond" (93) is in residence. These attempts provide much of the comedy of the novel. But always underlying this comedy is Birdy's sobering awareness that she has been "raised only to breed and die" (199).

The crisis in the novel comes when Birdy's father chooses a husband she finds completely unacceptable, one who makes earlier suitors suddenly seem desirable. After her first encounter with the suitor she names "Shaggy Beard," Birdy describes in explicit terms those qualities that make him repugnant to her:

> The man was a pig, which dishonors pigs. He blew his red and shiny nose on the table linen, sneezed on the meat, picked his teeth with his knife and left wet grease where he drank from the cup we shared. . . . I think he ate too much, for he made wind like a storm and sounded like a bladderpipe left out in the rain played by a goat. (109)

But table manners, or lack thereof, count for little to Birdy's father when balanced against what Shaggy Beard possesses, "a manor [that] lies next to mother's, and my father lusts after it" (109). After negotiations over a suitable dowry are completed to the satisfaction of Birdy's father, he tells his daughter, "You will be quiet, agreeable, and obedient. And you will wed the pig" (72).

Exacerbating Birdy's pain at her father's choice of husband is her mother's complicity in the arrangements. Even though Birdy's mother "has no great love for Murgaw the Shaggy, [she] seems overcome by his title, and his wealth and his land" (123). Her mother's acceptance of a fate Birdy views as worse than death seems to paralyze the younger woman. Though Birdy's mother is able to postpone the wedding, arguing that she needs Birdy's help through the fall, clearly that is all she will do for her daughter.

The ending of *Catherine Called Birdy* encapsulates the problems facing writers of historical fiction for young adults. As an historical novelist, Cushman must try to accurately portray the conventions of marriage and child/parent relationships during the thirteenth century: Birdy must be married because a young woman in Birdy's postion in the thirteenth century *would* be married. But must Cushman marry her to the odious Shaggy Beard? No, as it turns out. Young adult fiction is essentially an optimistic genre, and if a totally happy ending is not possible, at least a hopeful one is. In an ending that relies a bit too heavily on coincidence, Shaggy Beard is killed in a tavern scuffle. His son Stephen, who—unlike his father—washes, has good table manners and loves learning, wishes to honor the marriage contract with Birdy. Though Birdy knows Stephen only by reputation, his betrothal gift to her, "an enameled brooch of a little bird with a pearl in its beak" (204), convinces her that marriage to him will be like "moving from the darkness into light" (204). And so the novel ends satisfactorily, both for Birdy, who, though still caged by social expectations, is at least not repulsed by her husband-to-be, and for her parents who have done what good medieval parents should do: increased their own wealth and power through their daughter's marriage. By the end of *Catherine Called Birdy*, Birdy has, as her brother wished and as her diary makes clear, matured. She has a realistic sense of what life holds for her as a female and, more importantly, an understanding of how she can subvert her culture's assumptions about gender to gain some control over her life as a married woman.

A Break With Charity: A Story About the Salem Witch Trials

But what of girls whose social status is not as elevated as Birdy's? Or whose desires for voice and power cannot find accommodation within existing social conventions? Do they, like the dreams in Lorraine Hansberry's *Raisin in the Sun*, simply wither up and die? Or might their rage and frustration explode in malevolence and violence? Anne Rinaldi's *A Break With Charity: A Story about the Salem Witch Trials* suggests the latter.[9] Rinaldi's interpretation of this tragic episode in early American history explores themes common to young adult fiction and develops them within the framework of the Salem witch trials: the desire for the affirmation that comes from group membership and the desire for voice and power. This last, paradoxically, can occur only when it does not threaten group membership.

Rinaldi suggests the trials were a consequence of several overarching social factors, both global and local. The first of these was the seventeenth century's unawareness of adolescence as a time separate and different from both childhood and adulthood.[10] Rinaldi, describing Puritan society, states that "people went from childhood into adulthood with no benefit of an awkward age in between" (291). The slave Tituba, analyzing the social positioning of the girls, suggests that the very fact of being neither children nor fully recognized as women marginalizes them in a way their society does not even acknowledge: "Tituba gives them attention they do not get from anyone else . . . some of the girls are no longer children. Yet they are not allowed to be women. They are not married. There is no place for them in this way of life here" (26). Another factor leading to the girls' behavior was Puritan theology, which labeled amusement, the desire for pleasure, as sinful. More significantly, as Rinaldi points out in her afterward, it was intolerant of "everything and everyone who did not subscribe to the very repressive 'norm'" (293). This theology, coupled with "recent outbreaks of smallpox and Indian raids on the fringes of town" (8), created an explosive situation in which a few girls, supported by susceptible adults, were able to wreak havoc on the social fabric and cause the deaths of innocent people.

A Break with Charity is told from the perspective of Susanna English, a member of the gentry and the daughter of loving and (relatively) liberal parents. In spite of her material and familial good fortune, Susanna sees herself as "alone and friendless" (7), longing to be part of the group of girls who meet at the minister's home when he is gone. But her "yearning to be part of it all" (7) is futile. The girls, most of whom are of a lower socioeconomic status than Susanna, hate her because she is "of the gentry" (25) and, as such, embodies what they desire. Ironically, they also hate with equal passion those women who embody what they fear, lives of poverty without men (25), and who, consequently, are of even lower status than they. Frustrated by the narrowness and boredom of their lives, the girls seek entertainment from Tituba, the minister's black slave, a woman able to read fortunes and interprets signs. The chaos that ultimately results in the deaths of twenty-four people begins when they fear being caught and need a scapegoat for their behavior. But what begins out of fear is gradually transformed into an "insatiable appetite for power and attention" (144), two qualities notoriously absent from the lives of adolescents in general and these girls in particular. When Susanna observes that one of the accusers, previously "rather stoop-shouldered," is now standing "erect and proud" (151), she understands the consequences of suddenly being taken seriously, of having power. She notes, too, that appetite and need drive the girls to continue with their accusations: "They knew they could destroy anyone, that the magistrates hung on their every word. They would not stop. They had to keep going" (144). Susanna complicates the girls' relationship to power when she speculates that through their actions, they not only draw power to themselves but also aid those in power—the patriarchy—by ridding the Puritan community of those who violate its repressive norms. Elizabeth Proctor, who with her husband Joseph resists the witch hunts and shelters Susannah after her parents have fled Salem, points out "that those named witches are always just a bit different from others" (189). Her husband adds, "It's as if the afflicted girls are being given instructions on whom to name to cleanse this society of dissenters" (189). Those who are accused of witchcraft are primarily women and include one who "has always been a trouble-maker, putting aside God's ordinance in her manner of dress" (195) by wearing a red bodice, lending credence to Joseph's theory. Further support for Elizabeth and John's theory comes inadvertently from Ann Putnam, the leader of the girls, who callously labels one of the accused as a person who has always "disparaged community decency" (152).

Susanna's own position during this dark period is morally problematic. She knows that the girls' accusations of witchcraft stem from their fear of punishment for engaging in fortune-telling with Tituba. She knows they have not been afflicted by witches and that those accused of witchcraft are innocent. Thus, she has the power to stop the "witch madness" (3) that afflicts her village. Or does she? The afflicted girls, some of whom she has known since childhood, make clear that if she reveals what she knows, she puts her own family at risk. When she accuses the girls' leader Ann Putnam, and Mercy Lewis, who spreads Ann's lies, "They both shrugged" (154). Ann proceeds then to tell Susanna the consequence of revealing what she knows:

> "Do not attempt to tell lies about us, Susanna English, or the rest of your family will be named. You have a sister, remember. And a father. And a brother, due back any day from a sea voyage. . . . I would not interfere, were I you. Or others in your family will be named." I knew I could not speak out now. For these girls did, indeed, have some dark powers. And they could hurt the rest of my family. (56)

Even her mother's imprisonment cannot break Susanna's silence. There are several reasons for this. First and most obviously, she takes Ann Putnam's threat seriously and worries about the consequences for the rest of her family should she speak out. Second, she witnesses the disbelief and social isolation that descends upon one of the girls who attempts to withdraw her accusations. But coupled with these explanations is one that resides more in Susanna herself and the way she has internalized her culture's assumptions about women, their power, and their roles.

Early in the novel Susanna articulates her awareness that she is not a "proper Puritan girl" (9) because she does not accept much of Puritan doctrine. But unlike her father, who freely dissents, she keeps her disagreements to herself because she is a "mere girl" (9). She assumes that her age and her gender render her powerless to register dissent. When she lies to her father, she characterizes herself as a "true daughter of Eve" (48), thus drawing on all the negative cultural stereotypes of women as innately deceitful. When, later in the novel, Susanna does articulate her disagreements with the Puritans to her father, he tells her, "Daughter, it pleases me that you choose to think for yourself" (49). Nevertheless, she keeps before her the fate of women who were exiled from Massachusetts colony for freely expressing their dissenting views.

Susanna's internalization of her culture's misogyny is also evident in her relationships with Abigail Hobbes, a girl who rebels against the restrictions that the Puritans have placed on girls and women. When Abigail leaves her parents' home because she prefers to live in the woods, her parents see her disobedience as stemming from her habit of reading books, complaining to Susanna's parents: "She refuses to go to Meeting. She reads books! Not the Bible! She writes her thoughts down on parchment. Surely this is not proper behaviour for a young woman" (63). Though Susanna herself reads books other than the Bible and has already characterized herself as an improper Puritan, she nevertheless urges Abigail to modify her behavior and "be a true daughter to your parents . . . . They [magistrates] say you are acting like an Indian squaw" (68). Responding to Susanna's advice, Abigail raises the questions that females, socialized to be other-focused, have been raising for centuries: "So now I am to go home and be a docile daughter? And what of my needs? And wants?" (69). Abigail's question is sure to resonate for young female readers facing lives in which they are still expected to put the needs of others above their own. They may be frustrated that Abigail's question is never seriously addressed, but for Rinaldi to treat it as more than rhetorical would give it a weightiness that Salem's society at that time would not have allowed. Eventually, Abigail's subversive behavior brings charges of witchcraft upon her.

After the hangings have begun and when her family is safe in Boston, Susanna decides to break her silence by confessing what she knows about the girls' motives to Joseph Putnam. He then sets in motion the events that eventually rid Salem of its madness. Though Susanna's confession is instrumental, young adult readers should note that her efforts to halt the hanging must be mediated through male power. Neither her own sense of self nor her society's understanding of gender allows her the moral agency that Joseph and her father have simply by being born men.

The prologue and epilogue of the novel are set in 1706, fourteen years after the trials. Susanna has married, had children and, not surprisingly, has gained a more mature and critical awareness of her social role. She describes the girl she was as "Me and yet not me, that young girl" (1). She has come to the Salem Meetinghouse to participate in a ritual of forgiveness. Ann Putnam, now dying, has come to ask the congregants to "beg forgiveness of God, and from all those unto whom I have given just cause of sorrow and offence" (278).

Forgiveness does not come easily to Susanna, and initially she vows not to forgive Ann, wondering why "we women are always assigned the task of peacemaking" (2). But when confronted with the dying woman, Susanna feels something like "a great wall collapsing" (281) and does forgive. Still, though forgiveness does lift a personal burden from Susanna, the consequences of that episode in Salem history, one in which women turned on other women, live on. We learn that Abigail Hobbes, for example, "once free of spirit and brave of heart, who confessed to witchcraft so as not be left out . . . like so many of the girls in the circle now leads the life of a disreputable woman" (279). Abigail, wanting self-determination as a girl, has become a social outcast dependent on the sexual appetites of others for her own survival. As such, she embodies an easily defined category in her culture. And Susanna, who internally rebelled against the strictures of her life, having accepted the socially approved roles of wife and mother, has been placed in a position of bestowing forgiveness on one she earlier feared.

Wintering Well

Lea Wait's *Wintering Well*, set in Maine in 1820, explores the relationship between gender and self-determination in a more explicit way than either *Catherine Called Birdy* or *A Break With Charity*. Each of the above novels focuses on a female protagonist who accepts that her ultimate role in life is that of wife and mother. Birdy, though she fantasizes about a life of adventure, eventually accepts marriage with enthusiasm once she believes the groom will be to her liking. From the start of *Charity*, Susanna has a beau in the offing whom she ultimately marries. Both Birdy and Susanna are straightforward in their admiration of various young men, and there is often a clear component of physical desire in their admiration, especially in Birdy's. She suggests to a more prudish girl, for example, that they watch a peasant load kegs because "he is beautiful as summer and his arms ripple like the muscles on a horse's back and the rain plasters his shirt against his chest."[11]

Marriage, however, is not an issue for Cassie, the protagonist of *Wintering Well*.[12] Only eleven when the novel (which covers a period of fourteen months) opens, she is too young even in the early nineteenth century to be thinking of marriage. But more important to author Lea Wait than marriage is the issue of one's calling. It is an issue of some complexity, involving the relationship between the work to which one feels called, the choices one's culture allows, and the relationship between those choices and one's gender. Cassie, though young, wrestles with the question of her purpose in life and rejects the notion that it is confined to marriage and childrearing. Speaking to her older sister Alice, who is newly wed and newly pregnant, Cassie makes this rejection clear:

> "I wished to know my purpose in life," Cassie said.
> Alice looked at her. "But you do know! Like the purpose of every woman, yours is to marry and care for your husband and children, and ensure that your home is filled with love and faith and caring." (88)

That Cassie even raises the question about her purpose in life indicates that she has not accepted that she will automatically fall into the roles of wife and mother. Within the first few pages of the novel Cassie articulates her uneasiness, even her dissatisfaction, with the domestic roles her sister views as natural, and those around her are well aware of her feelings. One of her brothers notes early in the novel that Cassie "would rather help a young bird back to its nest or watch the birth of a young calf than knead bread or practice her stitches" (4). Her desire to care for the injured is called upon when she inadvertently causes her twelve-year-old brother Will to drop an ax and injure his leg. First an infection, then gangrene sets in, and when Will's life hangs in the balance, Cassie defies her father and brings a doctor to their farm to amputate Will's leg. The discussions between Cassie's parents that precede her defiance and the consequent amputation are heart-wrenching. When Cassie's mother begs her husband to send for a doctor, his response is chilling:

> "What good is a man without a full body? What use to himself, to anyone? Will's leg won't ever be normal. I've seen abscesses like that on animals. If he were a cow, like Susan, we'd be able to end his pain. . . . Why God allows a boy to suffer longer than a cow I do not attempt to know."
> Ma's voice rose in shock. "You can't think of shooting Will as you did an animal?"
> "I won't do it. But I can't say it hasn't crossed my mind as he lies there, moans reaching all of us. Even his smell is throughout the house." (13)

Cassie's father's assumption that his son is better off dead than as an amputee who will burden the rest of his family, cold as it may seem to contemporary readers, suggests an historically accurate attitude toward the handicapped, an attitude prevalent until not so long ago.

Even after the amputation that saves Will's life, when he is on his way to recovery, his father persists in asserting, and within Will's hearing, that there is "[n]ot much use for a cripple on a farm" (44). Sadly, the father's belief that

"Will is a . . . burden and that is his burden and ours" (46) is taken up by Will's older brothers. As a consequence Will learns he has lost not only his leg but his claim to manhood: he is no longer considered by his father and brothers as "one of the boys" (37). He tells his mother that the males in his family, Pa, Simon, and Nathan "hardly look at me now" (52). Nevertheless, as the novel progresses and Will is forced to redefine his purpose in life, it becomes ironically clear that even a crippled boy has more options in life than Cassie.

Initially, motivated by guilt, Cassie takes on the responsibility for Will's care, even steadfastly assisting in the amputation. But although she feels called to help Will during his recovery, she eventually (and understandably) begins to feel oppressed by the responsibility she has undertaken. As she writes in her journal, "Some days I feel as much a prisoner in this room as is Will" (29). As his recovery proceeds and Will's temper worsens, Cassie becomes increasingly frustrated with the restrictions that characterize her life. Significantly, she feels as oppressed by the demands of the domestic sphere as she does by her responsibility for Will:

> I am weary trying to meet his needs and those of Ma and those of the rest of the family. Some days I am proud to be doing what is necessary, the same as a grown woman must . . . I wonder if Ma or Alice ever felt as though the walls of the house were like those of a prison. (35)

Cassie's weariness stems not just from the specific circumstances that temporarily confine her. Rather it is born out of an innate aversion to a life defined solely by domestic tasks. Then a combination of factors release Cassie and Will from the domestic life that frustrates her and seems to provide no place for him. When Will tells the family minister that God has taken away "my dreams" (39), the minister responds, "Then you must find new ones" (39). And when Will's brother-in-law Sam suggests that in the city Will could be fitted with a wooden leg and find work, a move that would allow him more independence, the door is open for the children to redefine their lives. After his father's resistance to Will's going to the city and being fitted for a leg is worn down, it is decided that Cassie will accompany him, to continue to help with Will's physical care and assist her sister Alice as she prepares for the birth of her first child.

Cassie's crisis of self and purpose has two sources, evolving once the initial excitement of city life has worn off and Will becomes increasingly independent. Once fitted with his wooden leg and proficient in its use, he begins to explore other ways to "make my own life" (52). As Will's dependence on her lessens, Cassie, whose sense of self-worth has derived from helping him, is forced once again to question her own purpose in life. In her journal she describes her understanding of her own as yet ill-formed aspirations and hope, once again comparing herself to her sister who has embraced the socially sanctioned roles of wife and mother: "Alice does not have my impatience; she is content with her life, as she says I must learn to be with mine. . . . I can help Will and learn from Alice and perhaps even find a new life, too" (65). Cassie's last phrase suggests that, though willing to help her siblings and learn from Alice, she nevertheless, like Will, still harbors hopes for something beyond the domestic sphere seen as a woman's natural one.[13] But Cassie's attempts to find "a new life" are initially sabotaged by her own reluctance to acknowledge that Will's dependence on her is quickly lessening. "Despite his protests, I do not believe Will is finished needing people" (72), she says. Of course, the "people" she refers to is herself. But once Cassie does accept her diminished role in Will's life, she recognizes that in the city "the air seems full of possibilities" (73). As Cassie opens herself up to these new possibilities, she becomes more overt in her questioning of the traditional gender roles that Alice takes for granted. She writes, somewhat acerbically, in her journal, "Perhaps Alice is correct: All men need a woman to watch out for them. Although if that is so, then who watches out for women, other than God?" (85).

Cassie gradually finds a place for herself that draws on her desire to care for others without being confined to the traditional domestic role that her mother and sister embrace. When Dr. Theobold, the physician who amputated Will's leg, asks Cassie to help care for his young children while his wife is dying, she leaps at the chance. The money she will earn is an obvious enticement, but a more motivating incentive is her recognition that she can help others in ways that extend beyond housework: "I do not mind doing chores when their result makes life better for others. If what I can do makes a difference, can improve someone else's life, if only for a moment, then it is worth doing" (116). Both Will and Alice recognize Cassie's talent for caring for others as well as her dislike of more traditional domestic tasks, as the conversation below makes clear:

> "[S]he's more restless than you, Will. I remember when she was little; she would rather be playing outside, even in wintertime, than practicing her stitches by the hearth."
> Will grinned. "Cassie can sew a straight line but she's not one for spending hours at the task, that's for certain."(117)

The longer Cassie cares for the dying Mrs Theobald, the more she realizes how satisfying it is for her to care for the ill:

> I wish I could have Will's choices. Even though he has but one leg, men speak with him seriously of his future. Alice says my quilt will be much admired, and that pleases me, to be sure. But when I was helping Will, I felt useful and important. The only times I feel my help is valued now is when I am with Mrs. Theobald. I am learning from the doctor, how best to care for someone who is ill. Someday such skills may be useful. (126)

When Mrs. Theobald dies, Cassie continues to care for her children so that the doctor can continue with his practice. But she becomes increasingly interested in the practice, finding "Dr. Theobald's work of more interest than I do his kitchen" (150). Still, she has internalized her culture's gender expectations and cannot completely reject those traditional female tasks. When Will decides one day to accompany the doctor on his rounds in order to determine if he himself might wish to be a doctor, Cassie offers to pack food for the males. Will accuses her of sounding like a little mother, to which Cassie replies, "A doctor is an important person who must think of the needs of others. . . . Dr. Theobold does not have time for household details; those are a woman's tasks" (151).

A year after Will's accident, he and Cassie prepare to return home to attend another brother's wedding. Packing for the trip, Cassie notes, "I have greatly improved my knowledge of cooking these past months. Ma will be pleased at that" (171). But her sense of pleasure is balanced by a concern about her parents' reaction to the plans she and Will have made for their future lives, which they both hope to spend in the city.

Once home, Will announces his desire to develop his skill in woodcarving so that he might create figureheads for ships. His father is at first dismissive, reminding his son, "You are thirteen years old! It is time you took responsibility for your future" (176). But his objections are silenced when Will announces that he has already acquired a commission from a prominent shipbuilder. Pa's resistance to Cassie's plans is greater, especially when she proclaims, "If I were a boy, I'd want to be a doctor, just like Dr. Theobold" (178). But, of course, Cassie is not a boy, and her use of the subjunctive reveals that she recognizes that she must adjust her desires to accommodate her culture's expectations. Her father's reaction is telling: "A she-doctor! I should say not . . . . [W]omen cannot be doctors. Their brains are not strong enough and it would certainly be improper for them to do and see the sorts of things doctors must" (178).[14]

Cassie recognizes—without necessarily accepting—the weight of her father's objections. She settles for what she can get, a life that is traditionally domestic in many respects but which will allow her to develop her desire and talent for helping to heal others: "'I know, Pa,' said Cassie. 'But a woman could a help a doctor. A woman could learn about herbs and medicines and tinctures and potions and how to mix them for patients.'"[15] Eventually, Cassie's pa agrees to allow her to stay in the city, but he does so only after she has reminded him that she will be helping a man and caring for children, two roles historically assigned to females.

Unlike *Catherine Called Birdy* and *A Break with Charity*, *Wintering Well* does not end with a narrator either on the verge of marriage or already married. In part this is because Cassie, only twelve, is too young even in 1820 to have marriage looming on her near horizon. But more importantly, by 1820 females, though they lacked the choices available to young women today, still had more available to them than their earlier counterparts, both fictional and real.

A Northern Light

Another recent young adult novel, Jennifer Donnelly's *A Northern Light*, presents a world in which the choices available to females has further expanded.[16] Donnelly presents a protagonist who, like Birdy, Susanna, and Cassie, struggles to understand the parameters of her world and the extent to which that world allows her self-determination. But Donnelly also differs from Cushman, Rinaldi, and Wait in her willingness to conflate those issues with a more overt treatment of sexuality and sexual desire than the three previous novels do.

Donnelly's *A Northern Light* is set against the background of the murder of Grace Brown, a murder which became the basis for Theodore Dreiser's *An American Tragedy*. Grace, a pregnant factory girl, was murdered by the father of her unborn child, the socially ambitious Chester Gillette. Grace Brown's story is slowly unraveled for the reader by sixteen-year-old Mattie Gorkey, to whom Grace has given her love letters to Chester, making Mattie promise to burn them. Grace then leaves with her lover for the boat ride that will end in her death. As the novel unfolds, Mattie struggles to weigh her commitment to the dead—her mother and Grace Brown—with her commitment and desire to develop her gifts as a writer. The oldest daughter of five siblings, Mattie has promised her dying mother that she will never leave the farm but will stay to care for her father and sisters. As the novel moves from past to present, from the setting of farm to that of the resort hotel where Mattie is finally permitted to work, she struggles to find a way to reconcile the promises she has made to others with her dream, to accept the scholarship she has been offered by Barnard College, where she can develop her talents as a writer.

Her struggles pit her against the cultural conventions—as represented by her father, her aunt Josie, and her fiancé Royal—requiring females to subordinate their desires to the needs of others. Aunt Josie reminds Mattie that "[a] smart tongue does not become a young lady" and that "[n]o one likes a too smart woman" (109). When Mattie asks her wealthy aunt to lend her the money for train fare to New York, Aunt Josie tells her niece she is "selfish and thoughtless" (113) and looks at her niece in such a way "that I suddenly knew just how Hester Prynne felt when she had to stand on the scaffold" (113). Mattie's father, though he dislikes his sister-in-law, echoes her views, adding as a warning that "[m]en only want one thing" (24). The irony of the advice these adults give Mattie is that it runs counter to their own lived experience: Josie embodies the very selfishness and pride of which she accuses her niece, and her father's marriage was based on love, not the "one thing" he tells his daughter men want.

Mattie's gifts are validated and her ambitions begin to be realized through the examples of two women's lives. These women have never met, and they represent two very different models of relating to men and the larger world. Miss Wilcox, Mattie's teacher, represents the world of choice, of resistance to male power as well as the problematic consequence of resistance, whereas Grace Brown represents the consequences of giving up choice and allowing another person power over one's life. The townspeople consider Miss Wilcox "fast." She drives her own car, smokes cigarettes, and has a secret of her own to keep. When Miss Wilcox reads the stories Mattie has written, stories another teacher has dismissed as "morbid and dispiriting" (37), she tells her she has a "true gift . . . a rare one" (38). Her words, intended to be supportive, create a dilemma for Mattie: "And ever since [Miss Wilcox's words] I want things that I have no business wanting and what they call a gift seems more like a burden" (38). What Mattie wants, of course, is a life beyond the farm, one that allows her to read and write, to experience a larger world. But her desire for a more expansive world is mediated through a question women have been asking for years: Is it possible to have both work and family? Watching her friend Minnie with her newborn twins Mattie wonders:

> I stared into my teacup, wondering what it was like to have what Minnie had. To have somebody love you like Jim loved her. . . . I wondered if all those things were the best things to have or if it was better to have words and stories. Miss Wilcox had books but no family. Minnie had a family now but those babies would keep her from reading for a good long time. Some people, like my aunt Josie and Alvah Dunning, had neither love nor books. Nobody I knew had both. (97)

Later Mattie learns two important facts about her teacher that further complicate the questions she has raised about career and family. First, she learns that Miss Wilcox is, in truth, the controversial poet Emily Baxter, whose work has been declared "[an] affront to common decency" (207). The poet herself has been described as "a blight on American womanhood" (207) because of the challenge her work presents to common assumptions about women and their place in the world. Later, when Mattie learns that Miss Wilcox is in flight from a husband who would institutionalize her to prevent publication of more of her poetry, she is forced to consider the cost of resisting her culture's dominant narrative of gender.

Grace Brown, whose body rests in the parlor of the hotel while her death is being investigated, functions in the novel as a cautionary tale, an example of what can happen to a woman who trusts too wholly in a man and who silences her doubts and needs. Donnelly uses the actual letters Brown wrote to her fickle lover and murderer Chester Brown; the letters create a counterpart to what Mattie is tempted to experience with her fiancé, Royal. Read almost one hundred years after Grace's murder, they are heartbreaking: Grace, at home with her family, who are ignorant of her pregnancy, pleads with Chester not to abandon her, apologizes for showing any sign of impatience when he does not respond to her letters, and even goes so far to deny her actual jealousy of other women: "Really, dear, I don't care where you go or who you go with if only you will come for the 7th" (263). Finally, even Grace's patience wears thin and she threatens to expose Chester, sealing her death sentence. But as Mattie reads these letters she begins to reflect on her relationship with Royal, a young man to whom she is sexually attracted. "I stared at Royal's backside," she says. "Royal's was very nice. Round and proud like two loaves of soda bread" (53). However, whatever the virtues of Royal's backside, he shares none of her interests in literature or writing; in fact, he denigrates them. Gradually, Mattie realizes her sexual appetitie for Royal, whose hands feel like "comfort and danger" (192), makes her as vulnerable as Grace Brown, stifling any of her doubts about whether he actually loves her. When she finally realizes that the letters she holds will reveal that Grace's death was a murder, not an accidental drowning, Mattie is forced to make decisions about her right and need to assert her own voice. She ponders the lives of both Miss Wilcox and Grace, saying to herself, "Just look where your voice got you, Miss Wilcox . . . and look where Grace Brown's got her" (362).

Mattie, nevertheless, chooses to follow Miss Wilcox's example rather than that of Grace, who, in apologizing for her needs, put herself at the mercy of a man who did not deserve her love, hoping he would rescue her from the shame of unwed pregnancy. Mattie breaks her promise to her mother and decides to go New York to become a college student and, she hopes, a writer. Finally, she also breaks her promise to Grace Brown. She does not burn the dead girl's letters but chooses instead to leave them where the police will find them, knowing they will implicate Chester Gillette in Grace's murder. Her reflections on the lives of the women around her have led Mattie to believe it is a bad thing to break a promise, but I think now that it is a worse thing to let a promise break you" (374).

Before Mattie boards a train for New York, she does what she can to help those around her fulfill their dreams. She sends her father part of her savings to pay off the balance on a mule. She gives another part of her savings to her friend Weaver, an African-American, whose college savings were lost in a fire, so that he can pursue his dream of attending Columbia. Mattie's desire to support those around her reveals a theme that characterizes much of the young adult historical literature dealing with gender.

All of the novels discussed in this chapter focus on young females who are able to negotiate mainstream culture's gender expectations because of the support and examples—both positive and negative—that older women embody. As their sense of self become stronger, these girls reach out to provide support to others. Birdy negotiates with her father so a peasant girl can get the cottage she needs in order to marry. Susanna gives food and clothing to an older woman marginalized by her village because she does not fit Salem's notion of what constitutes good housewifery. Cassie, by modifying the domestic expectations for women in Maine in 1820, carves out new ways for females to exist.

White Lilacs

Caroline Meyers adds a new dimension to this pattern in *White Lilacs* by depicting a culture marred not only by rigid class distinctions but by racism as well.[17] In this novel, older women do more than provide examples to young girls; they actively reach out to support them. The importance of this theme cannot be overstated because it provides an essential counternarrative to the radical individualism embodied in such American canonical works as the Leather Stockings series, *Moby Dick*, and *Huckleberry Finn*.[18]

White Lilacs begins, literally, in the Garden of Eden, the name given by the grandfather of the narrator Rose Lee to his own carefully cultivated garden in Freedomtown. This African-American community is located in the middle of a larger white one, and following the Biblical narrative, the novel chronicles the expulsion of the Blacks from their paradise. But there is a twist. Unlike the Biblical narrative in which human sin causes the expulsion of Adam and Eve, the citizens of Freedomtown are blameless. They are forced to leave their beloved homes because of the greedy and powerful white community, which plans to resettle them in the area known as the Flats, land near an open cesspool. Rose Lee tells the story of her community's resistance, attempts at negotiation, and finally, surrender to the wishes of the more dominant community. This bleak story, based on the annexation and destruction in 1922 of the black community Quakertown by the larger community of Denton, Texas, nevertheless shows how the bonds between old and young and, occasionally, black and white can salvage something good out of what seems unsalvageable.

Twelve-year-old Rose Lee accompanies her grandfather whenever she can to his job as a gardener for a wealthy white family. She helps with his chores and, when she can steal a few minutes for herself, draws her surroundings using lined paper and stubs of pencil. She attempts, like her gardening grandfather and quilting grandmother, to create beauty out of the only materials available.[19]

When Rose Lee is asked to fill in for one of her cousins in her grandfather's employer's kitchen, she becomes a valuable conduit of information for the black community. The racism of her white employers, which implicitly denies their servants' humanity, allows them to speak freely in front of Rose Lee, as if she has no ears to hear. But, of course, she does, and she listens to their plans to annex Freedomtown for a city park. Thus, she is able to convey this information to her own family, who then do what they can to preserve their community. Their attempts at reasoned negotiation, embraced by the older generation, as well as aggressive attempts to claim their rights, embraced by Rose's older brother, fail, but Rose Lee is not left without hope. Though her employment as a kitchen worker for the white Bell family is demeaning, it also positions her to meet whites who resist the racism of their fellows.

The first of these is Miss Firth, a Philadelphia Quaker who has taken a job teaching at the Dillon Academy for Young Ladies. At a luncheon at which Rose is a server, plans are discussed to move the inhabitants of Freedomtown to the Flats. Mrs. Bell, Rose's employer, blithely comments, "I cannot think of a single soul who would have the slightest objection to this plan" (12). Miss Firth responds drily, "Except the Negroes" (12). On a later visit to the Bell's home, Miss Firth learns that Rose Lee draws and asks to see her notebook. After viewing it, she tells the young girl, "You are very talented, Rose Lee. Do you know that?" (35). She then invites Rose Lee to join a drawing class she plans to teach in the summer. In so doing, she gives Rose Lee a twofold gift: she recognizes a talent no one else has acknowledged, and she presents a model of racial relationships totally new to Rose Lee. But the time and setting of *White Lilacs* determine that Miss Firth's role in Rose Lee's life will be limited. When she speaks out at a Fourth of July celebration, telling the crowd that " I want to talk to you this afternoon about the rights of Negroes in this community who have served you so faithfully and well for so many years" (133), she is quickly escorted from the stage and soon after is fired from her job. Still, for Rose Lee, who is serving pie at the picnic, the experience of hearing for the first time "a white person, a white *woman* speak out for Negroes like that" (134) is transformative.

Just as transformative, perhaps even more so, is Miss Firth's effect on Catherine Jane Bell, the daughter of Rose Lee's employers and a girl firmly ensconced in the privileges of race and class. Though she and Rose Lee played together as children, their friendship is eroded by the racism and classism characteristic of southern life in the first part of the twentieth century. But inspired by Miss Firth, Catherine violates her parents' order not to communicate with the older woman. More importantly, Miss Firth's example of speaking out inspires Catherine Jane to help Rose Lee's brother escape from the Ku Klux Klan, to which Catherine Jane's brother and father both belong. The plot to help Henry escape the Klan, whose members have already tarred and feathered him, is further aided by another older woman, a black one, Rose Lee's Aunt Susannah.

Susannah functions as another model for dealing with racism. She has left Freedomtown to attend college and begin a career as a teacher after graduation, but she returns to visit her brother's family after breaking her engagement to a white man whose family has threatened to disown him if he marries her. Despite the pain of her broken engagement, she is not one to mope. She attends church wearing a tight, bright red dress and high heels, and she freely laughs at her ineptitude in domestic tasks. Although she has intended this visit as a healing interlude for herself, her presence also has a therapeutic effect on Rose Lee. Susannah's willingness to challenge gender stereotypes and take control of her own life provides an exhilarating example of black female power and Rose Lee is in dire need of just such an example. Susannah's decision at the end of the novel to help her nephew escape, to sell her emerald engagement ring and to use it as a down payment for a home in the Flats, coupled with her decision to take a teaching job in this broken and despairing black community, suggests to Rose Lee the value of not giving up and of working from within for social change.

An overview of this chapter shows that females' choices have expanded over time as have their methods for subverting and resisting oppressive social structures. Birdy and Susanna accept that to be female is to be married and to be confined to the domestic sphere. Their goals are to finds ways to "survive, sometimes even enjoy." Within their limited sphere these young women claim moral agency in any way they can, usually through passive resistance or by using the men in their lives as their mouthpieces. Novels set in the nineteenth century and after depict young women exploring callings that take them out of the domestic sphere. Cassie in *Wintering Well* finds ways to use her skills for healing outside the home; Mattie in *Northern Light* flees her home and her fiancé to pursue a career as a writer; Rose Lee develops her skills as an artist. Though few of these characters are as assertive as contemporary young readers might wish, they do find ways to resist social structures that subvert their sense of justice. The methods they use are subtle but ultimately effective and an accurate reflection of the strategies women have been forced to rely on through much of history.

NOTES

1. Rachel Carson, "Our Everchanging Shore," excerpted by Elaine Partnow in *The Quotable Woman* (New York: Anchor Books/Doubleday, 1978), 308.

2. Elizabeth Janeway, "Reflections on the History of Women." In *Women: The Changing Roles (The Great Contemporary Issues).* (New York: Ayer Company, 1973).

3. Young adults tend to oversimplify both history and psychology because they often make two incorrect assumptions about those who have preceded them. First, the

assume that that their ancestors knew nothing about sex. Second, and more importantly, they assume that their predecessors never chafed against convention or tradition.
Any text that suggests otherwise and thus leaves them with a more complicated view
of history is beneficial in this regard. Sue Miller for example, in her recent novel *The
World Below,* locates her inspiration for that novel in a passage she came across in her
great-great-grandmother's diary written in 1869: "It has rained all day. I washed in the
morning. I worked on Mrs. (illegible) dress. I am doomed to be disappointed in everything I take pride in. I sometimes wish I was under the sod sleeping the sleep that
knows no waking."

4. Karen Cushman, *Catherine, Called Birdy* (NY: Harper Trophy Editions, 1994);
hereafter cited parenthetically in text.

5. The notion that marriage should be based on love is a relatively modern one
that does not begin to emerge until the seventeenth century. Prior to that, marriage
was seen, at least in the upper classes, as a means for increasing wealth or cementing
political alliances. Acknowledging this, Birdy says, "[M]y father . . . seeks to improve our
position through my marriage bed" (33).

6. In *Recasting the Past: The Middle Ages in Young Adult Literature,* Rebecca Barnhouse
takes issue with the diary format of this novel, arguing that Catherine's literacy was improbable at a time when few adults, much less adolescent girls, could write. Although
we agree that Catherine's literacy is not probable, it is not impossible. Ultimately, we
ask for a "willing suspension of disbelief" for a novel that in so many other ways accurately represents life for a girl of this class.

7. For females of Birdy's class, the only option other than marriage would have been
joining a convent. For women who wished to avoid the rigors of marriage and childbirth, this was often a viable choice even if their "calling" was weak or nonexistent.

8. Young adults can be introduced to the issue and its implications by reading and
discussing Chaucer's "Prologue to the Wife of Bath's Tale" or the works of such medieval
women writers as Christine de Pisan.

9. Anne Rinaldi, *A Break with Charity: A Story about the Salem Witch Trials* (New
York: Gulliver Books, 1992); hereafter cited parenthetically in the text.

10. Acceptance of adolescence as a life phase distinct from childhood and adulthood
did not gain general acceptance until the beginning of the twentieth century. Prior to
this it was often assumed that children reached the age of reason by the time they were
six years old and could, hereafter, be expected to make the adult decisions. Those who
did not were subject to the same penalties as adults. In Karen Cushman's *Catherine
Called Birdy*, Birdy is shocked when she attends a thief hanging to realize that the
thieves in question are no more than twelve years old. In Lea Wait's *Wintering Well,* set
in Maine in 1820, a thirteen-year-old boy is sentenced to several months in jail for
stealing apples. For an extended discussion of the development of adolescence as a category, see Philippe Aerie's classic study, *Centuries of Childhood: A Social History of Family Life* (NY: Vintage, 1965). Michael Barson and Steven Heller, authors of *Teenage Confidential* (San Francisco: Chronicle Books, 1998), focus mainly on American culture,
speculating that it was the publication of Booth Tarkington's *Seventeen* in 1915 that sig-
naled popular cultural acceptance of adolescence as a distinct category. They also point
out that there was not even "a name for them [adolescents] before the 1920's."

11. Cushman, *Birdy,* 115.

12. Lea Wait, *Wintering Well* (NY: McElderry Books, 2004); hereafter cited parenthetically in the text.

13. Throughout the nineteenth century it was assumed that men and women should occupy different spheres of influence. Men's sphere was the public world, outside the home, while the cult of true womanhood demanded that women occupy the private domestic sphere where they would reign as the "Angel in the House." Much scholarship is available discussing this division and its implications, but young adult readers might find most accessible the introduction to the nineteenth century in the *Norton Anthology of Literature for Women.* Or they may choose to read Coventry Patmore's poem "The Angel in the House" as an example of literature promoting this ideal.

14. The idea that women's brains as well as their reproductive organs could not stand the strain of too much education or intellectual stimulation was used as a rationalization for depriving them of higher education and intellectual pursuits for hundreds of years. For an extended treatment of this idea in nineteenth-century America as well as the medical practices that were used to enforce it, see G.J. Barker-Bentfield's *Horrors of the Half-Known Life: Male Attitudes toward Women and Sexuality in the Nineteenth Century* (NY: Routledge, 1999). Young adult readers interested in a fictional enactment of these theories can be directed to Charlotte Gilman Perkin's chilling short story, "The Yellow Wallpaper."

15. In her "Historical Notes," Wait points out that "By definition doctors and surgeons were male." She also points out that women "practicing as midwives performed vital services for women . . . [but] by 1820 male doctors in most towns and cities of New England had convinced women that doctors were best qualified to assist during childbirth" (185). Wait also includes another item of possible interest to young adult readers: that Elizabeth Blackwell, "the first American woman to receive a medical degree, did not do so until 1849" (185).

16. Jennifer Donnelly, *A Northern Light* (NY: Harcourt Inc., 2003); hereafter cited parenthetically in the text.

17. Carolyn Meyer, *White Lilacs* (NY: Gulliver Books, 1993); hereafter cited parenthetically in the text.

18. Readers interested in pursuing the different, often contradictory treatments of individualism and community in American literature by nineteenth-century male and female writers are encouraged to read as companion pieces Judith Fetterly's *Resisting Reader: A Feminist Approach to American Fiction* (Bloomington, IN: Indiana UP, 1981) and Leslie Fiedler's *Love and Death in the American Novel* (NY: World Publishing, 1960).

19. Her efforts will remind adult readers of Alice Walker's exploration of the relationship between race, gender, and class in her essay "In Our Mother's Garden" and in her short story "Everyday Use."

The Beckoning Shores

Give me your tired, your poor,
Your huddled masses yearning to breathe free,
The wretched refuse of your teeming shore,
Send these, the homeless, tempest-tossed to me,
I lift my lamp beside the golden door!

Emma Lazarus
from "The New Colossus," 1883

*W*hen Emma Lazarus wrote the famous lines now engraved on a plaque over the main entrance to the Statue of Liberty, she could have hardly foreseen that her poem would become synonymous with the enormous sculpture, not erected until three years later. Nor could she know that Lady Liberty, as the Statue was eventually known, would become a beacon of welcome for about 200 million immigrants who have sailed past her into New York Harbor. They have come for various reasons: jobs and land; freedom from religious, ethnic, and political persecution; and reunification with family members who preceded them. The journey from their native lands was often perilous at best. Most brought little but their wishes for a better future, hoping that in this Land of Freedom and Opportunity they could begin new lives.

Many did indeed find in the United States the answer to their most optimistic dreams, but others among the huddled masses were met with less than the promised welcome. Each wave of immigration aroused alarm among earlier immigrants and their descendents, who viewed the newcomers with suspicion, some fearing that these "foreigners" would take away jobs and move into neighborhoods where their presence would send property values plummeting—issues that continue to plague the United States down to the present.

Even among those immigrants who found more hospitable receptions, problems remained. How many of their former traditions could they maintain? What restrictions should these immigrants place upon their children, who were becoming too "American"? How could they bridge the difficulties posed by a new language? In more recent years, the concept of "melting pot" has been gradually replaced by the metaphor of "salad"—a mixture richer for the many ingredients that comprise its whole—and immigrants have been encouraged to value and maintain much of their culture, but the adjustment to a new country is rarely easy. Young adult historical literature about immigration addresses all of these issues—the difficulty of the voyage to America and of making a place for oneself in a new culture while simultaneously hanging on to native traditions and values.

Maggie's Door

Among the earliest immigrants were the Irish. *Maggie's Door,* by Patricia Reilly Giff, traces the voyage of two young Irish adolescents to the United States in the wake of the potato famine, alternating the point of view between its two main characters, Nory Ryan and her neighbor Sean Red Mallon.[1] The door of the title refers to their mutual destination, the Brooklyn home of Nory's sister Maggie, who has married Sean's brother Francey and emigrated to America.

The novel is a sequel to *Nory Ryan's Song,* a tale set in Ireland that relates the earlier circumstances in the life of the Ryan family when the potato famine began during the mid-1840s.[2] The only mode of escape for these starving peasants was emigration, and a tidal wave of Irish immigrants soon flooded the United States—two to three million in the years after 1845. Like many immigrants to follow, they spoke only the language of their native land—Celtic, in this case—a limitation that complicated their adjustment.[3] Those who came were usually undernourished and poor, weakened and apprehensive—but determined to survive.

Maggie's Door portrays the desperation among the Irish at the peak of the famine. Nory's mother has died, and "one by one," the rest of the family leaves, "trying to escape the hunger that gnawed at their stomachs and even their bones" (6). Even Nory's little brother Patch is on his way, a passenger with Sean's Mam (mother), both riding in a cart that Sean pulls.

Their departure is not only physically but emotionally difficult. Flashback scenes fondly remembered by both Nory and Sean hint at the pleasures of their lives before the famine. Poor as their families were, there were occasions for merriment. Now this mass emigration is splitting families and causing heartbreaking worry. Nory's younger sister Celia had promised before she left for America with her grandfather, "We will send for you and Patch. Together we will get to Maggie's door in America" (8). But the reader is not so sure, for the voyage of Sean and Nory is marked by disasters.

The opening chapters follow the two friends as they make their separate ways from their homes in Maidin Bay to Galway, where they hope to board ships to carry them across the Atlantic. But Sean is waylaid by an English lord and sent on a fruitless errand. The English, in fact, are portrayed as deliberately contributing to this mass Irish migration—and it is a historical fact that they demanded the prompt payment of rent from their starving tenant farmers during the famine in an attempt to drive them off the land. Once the Irish left, the British could then "tumble" their cottages and use the land for grazing their flocks. Both Sean and Nory's family are the victims of this cruel policy.

When Sean returns from his futile errand, he fails to find his cart where he left it and, not knowing what else to do, follows the road to the port of Galway, unaware that Nory is close behind. Nory, who has injured her foot and wrapped it in a now bloody rag, comes unexpectedly upon the cart where Sean's mother has pulled it off the road to hide it from thieves, breaking the axle in the process. Believing that Sean must be dead, his mother decides to return to Maidin Bay, to "die at [her] own hearth" (60) and Nory must carry Patch the rest of the way, limping on her injured foot. The scene establishes Nory as a devoted family member, demonstrates her determination in the face of what seem insurmountable odds, and portrays the reluctance of the older generation to sever their ties to their homeland.

Sean arrives first in Galway. Lacking a ticket for passage on a ship, he signs on as a cook's apprentice; also, he is told, he must act as ballast on the ship between Galway and Liverpool, the point of departure for America. He accepts, although he hears someone say, "Ballast? I wouldn't do that if I had to lie down dead in the street instead" (45). The statement by the unidentified man signifies the deplorable conditions that many of the immigrants suffered on their voyage across the Atlantic. Many passengers died at sea, and those who completed the journey often arrived more dead than alive. Those like Sean who acted as "ballast" suffered perhaps the most, confined to a dark hold with no sanitary facilities.[4]

Nory, still carrying little Patch, arrives in Galway shortly after Sean, both unaware of each other's proximity. Nory is, however, reunited with her grandfather, Granda, who explains that Nory's sister Celia and her father Da have already sailed for America, forced to board a ship according to the departure date stamped on their tickets. Granda has insisted that he be the one to wait and search for Nory. Clutching a cracked cup decorated with roses that another immigrant has given her, Nory, accompanied by Granda and Patch, board a ship to Liverpool, their departure point for the United States and Maggie's door. It is the vision of what lies behind Maggie's door that buoys them as they set sail. "The cup with its wee roses we'll keep for a sip of tea at Maggie's," says Granda (77) prior to their departure.

Reilly Giff spares no unpleasant detail in portraying the conditions under which the Irish immigrants live during the six-week voyage: scant, bug-infested food, lack of privacy, constant illness, and ceaseless noise: "women sighing, crying out in their sleep, babies wailing, one of them day and night, and poor Granda coughing. But the worst was the vomiting that went on and on" (84). Balancing these excruciating sensations are the immigrants' bright visions of what awaits them in America: "We will sleep on a silk mattress with the softest pillows made of goose feathers" (81), envisions one; "There will be potatoes in Brooklyn, fine white ones" (110), says Nory, and Patch announces, "There will be a stream. It will have a great salmon that will swim up to see us" (121).

Nory has learned about healing from Anna, a neighbor in Maidin Bay, and she has carried aboard a little bag of seeds and crushed flower petals whose use is supposed to offset a range of illnesses. When one of the immigrants, a girl about her age, grows ill, Maggie is able to cure her of "ship's fever" with the supplies she carries. But she is unable to help Granda, whose cough grows worse and whose body shrinks to loose skin and sharp bones. Another passenger explains to Nory that perhaps Granda's "time" has come. On the third day of their journey, when Granda turns to Nory and says, "I must go home," one knows that his death is imminent, especially when he adds, "If I go too far, I will never go back" (121). When next Nory climbs to his berth, her grandfather has stopped breathing. She buries him at sea, his spirit—it is implied—winging its way back to Maidin Bay, perhaps to meet up with the spirit of Sean's Mam. Nory is disconsolate, not only at her loss but at her failure to cure her beloved granda. Consequently, she throws her small bags of seeds and petals overboard. Dismayed at the possibility that "[m]aybe she had given Granda the wrong cure, done the wrong thing" (129), she tells herself that she'd "never try to cure anyone again" (128).

But she does. Unbeknown to her, Sean has been working in the ship's kitchen as a cook's apprentice, his boss a brutal, drunken man. In the midst of a violent storm that sickens the passengers and tosses the kitchen pots, pans, and dishes helter skelter, Sean finds and rescues a small girl whose parents are traveling first-class. Several days later, the little girl invites him into their cozy cabin and reads to him from an edition of Aesop's Fables. Time passes too quickly, and later, when Sean opens the door, the cook is waiting for him in the passage outside. Furious and thoroughly drunk, the cook hauls Sean back to the kitchen and throws him against the hot stove. "[Sean] heard the hissing as one arm hit the red-hot stove; he heard the sound his own voice made" (134).

Another cook's assistant has heard about Nory's ability to cure, but when he seeks her help, she at first refuses, her memory of having failed Granda fresh in her mind. Then she remembers something her mentor Anna once said: "*Even if the cure doesn't work, it means something just to make the poor soul feel better*" (130), and she allows herself to be led to where Sean is hidden. When she recovers from the shock of seeing her old friend, her knowledge of cures returns to her, and she fashions a cast to cover the burnt arm. "We will dance on the cliffs of Brooklyn," she promises the boy (140).

Nory's cure works, and she and Sean are on deck together to catch the first glimpse of their new country. As the ship approaches New York Harbor, the captain orders the immigrants to clean up the hold where they have been living, to "throw out the old straw bedding and anything else that is not clean" and to wash themselves "because a doctor will be coming aboard" (144) and they "will be sent back to Ireland if he doesn't like the way [they] look" (145).[5] As Nory watches Patch's filthy coat float away in New York Harbor, Sean assures her, "Everything will be new for us, and there will even be a coat for Patch by the time winter comes" (145).

Soon they are on their way to Maggie's door, riding in a carriage paid for by the father of the child Sean had rescued. The child also gives Sean her book of fables, an implication that Sean will indeed become skilled at the language of his new country and learn to read. As Nory and Sean ride toward Brooklyn, Nory sees that there are no diamonds in the streets as she had expected, and there are no cliffs; instead, houses crowd narrow streets littered with boxes and papers. But Nory is undaunted. She carries her small bag with the cracked cup, her mother's wedding gown, and a few seeds and dried leaves scattered in the fabric. Beginning a new life, she has not abandoned her Irish heritage. She will grow the seeds that remain to make new cures, and the reader trusts Nory's determination to find success in this strange new place.

The novel ends on an optimistic note when the carriage pulls up to Maggie's door and Nory's family comes tumbling out. At last the family is reunited. "How long we've watched for you, waited for you," Maggie says (153), and Nory closes the story with the affirmation that "We are here. . . here at last" (154). Had Reilly Giff chosen to follow Nory into her new life, the ending might have been tempered by the harsh discrimination the Irish encountered upon their arrival in the United States, by stereotypes of them as drunken and lazy, by window signs in commercial establishments that read, "Help Wanted. No Irish Need Apply." But for now, Nory is joyous, and her strength promises that she will find happiness in this new world.

Dragon's Gate

Other authors are less forgiving. Laurence Yep, for example, in *Dragon's Gate*, shows America not as the promised land of opportunity but instead as a "death trap" for the thousands of Chinese who immigrated to California to work on the transcontinental railroads.[6] Set in the years immediately following the Civil War, Yep's novel begins in China, where Otter lives with his mother. In his village his family is considered wealthy; the source of their wealth is his father and uncle's manual labor in the United States. Otter and the other inhabitants of his village refer to those Chinese living in the United States as "Guests of the Golden Mountain" (53), implying that they lead, as guests generally do, lives of ease and comfort. The irony of the word "guests" gradually unfolds as the reader is slowly made aware of the disparity between what Otter and the other villagers believe life in the United States is like for the Chinese and the grim reality of those lives. The images of a cosseted existence usually associated with the status of "guest" are soon replaced with images of brutal and ill-paid labor.

When Otter's father and uncle return to visit China, they are treated and behave as royalty: they are feted with feasts, and they bestow gifts on the villagers. More significantly, in spite of the lives of servitude they lead in the United States, they refer to it as a place where "[e]verybody there, they free. Everybody there, they equal" (33). Such pronouncements instill in others, like Otter, a desire to leave their village to immigrate to this land of great opportunity where they themselves can become "guests." Ironically, they come to America willingly through the legal apparatus of contracts that exploit them, for example, by manipulating the different ways in which the Chinese and Americans measure time and thus determine an hour's worth of labor.

When Otter is forced to flee China after he accidentally kills a man, he must confront the disparity between his dreams and reality. He is also forced into the more painful recognition that his father and uncle have been complicit, by misrepresenting their lives, in enslaving him and other Chinese. When Otter attempts to leave his work station as a protest against oppressive work conditions, the overseer orders him back. Otter defies this order: "I was born free. I am free. This is a country where you fight to be free" (174). Otto's boss Kilroy[7] responds to this challenge by brutally whipping Otter in front of the other workers, Chinese and American, making clear that if Otter is to regain his freedom, he will, indeed, have to fight. Over the course of the book, as Otter endures long hours of back-breaking work, near starvation, the death of his uncle and the blinding of his father, he comes to grips with what the United States is for the lower classes, especially the nonwhites: a place where the environment is savaged, where promises are broken, and where, as on George Orwell's *Animal Farm*, some people are more equal than others.

But through his sufferings he matures and develops the capacity for heroic action. He also learns some valuable lessons that complicate his experience. His friendship with the overseer's son teaches him that not all Americans are bigoted, and his organization of a strike teaches that through collective action the

ppressed can strike a blow for freedom. In short, he begins to see the shades
f grey associated with moral maturity. He also acquires what W.E.B. DuBois
as called "double-consciousness."[8] Otter's uncle, Foxfire, explains this phe-
omenon to him by saying that one of the inevitable consequences of his com-
g to the United States and experiencing another culture is that he will now
e all of life not just through "Tang" eyes but Western eyes as well. When Ot-
r tries to convince his uncle that the "sooner we get away, the better"(197),
oxfire explains that though they can physically leave the United States, they
e inevitably and irrevocably marked by their encounter with a culture that
es them as inferior, and he is referring to a marking much different than the
ars left on his back by the overseer's whip: "You don't understand, boy. You
n never go home now. When you go to Three Willows [their home in
hina], you'll see things through western eyes. . . . Once you guest on the
olden Mountain, you change inside. Only some of the guests don't realize it's
appened" (197). When Otter asks his uncle how he views his life in Califor-
a, Foxfire sadly answers, "I see things with Tang eyes" (197).

As a consequence of his new vision, Otter realizes the naiveté of his ear-
er image of the United States. But he also refuses to give up on his new coun-
y, recognizing in it the potential for dreams to be realized. When the railway
nnel is completed in 1867 and he is asked if he now will go home, he replies,
Not yet. My uncle had high hopes for this country. I'd like to see if he is
ght" (271). But Otter has learned from his experiences on the Golden
ountain that his uncle's high hopes will not be achieved without struggle and
ffering. His experiences organizing the Chinese workers into a labor collec-
ve to oppose inhumane conditions have taught him a valuable lesson: "If you
ep silent, then you lose by default" (249).[9]

n Ocean Apart, A World Away

ensey Namioka gives readers a different perspective on the Chinese experi-
ce in the United States in *An Ocean Apart, A World Away*.[10] Zhang Xueyan,
r Yanyan as she is known, is the daughter of a wealthy Chinese family living
Nanjing. The novel, told in the first person from Yanyan's point of view,
pens in 1921, ten years after the revolution that toppled the corrupt Manchu
ing dynasty. Yanyan's family practices many Chinese traditions; her mother,
r example, totters on bound feet, and when the family gathers for dinner,
e men (including Yanyan's two brothers) sit on one side, the women on the
her. But Yanyan's father has progressive views about the role of women, and
anyan herself is no slave to tradition. Her feet are unbound, her voice is too
ud for a proper young lady, and she rejects the role of a submissive Chinese
ife—or a wife of any kind, for that matter. Instead, she wants to become a

doctor. She is about to finish at the Macintosh School, a missionary academy taught by Americans, and the prospect of professional study excites her.

In the first half of the novel, set mostly in Nanjing, she meets Liang Baoshu, a friend of Yanyan's Eldest Brother. He is half Manchurian and half Chinese, a skilled martial arts student, tall, handsome, and adventurous. Accompanied by Eldest Brother and Baoshu, Yanyan travels to Shanghai to say goodbye to her friend Tao Ailin, who is sailing to the United States with the American family for whom she has been working as a nanny. The girls had met at the Macintosh School, but Ailin had to withdraw when her family's land was taken over by warlords in the lawless period following the revolution, and she could no longer afford the tuition. This section of the novel provides many facts about Chinese history, information that is supplemented in "A Note on the Manchus, Manchuria, and Manchukuo" at the end of the story.

During the railway journey to Shanghai, Yanyan, Eldest Brother, and Liang Baoshu find themselves sharing their compartment with a blond ("straw hair") Western man. Unaware that the foreigner, who seems engrossed in his newspaper, speaks and understands Chinese, Yanyan's brother and Baoshu speculate about the limitations of having Western features. "What happens when these Big Noses catch a cold?" wonders Eldest Brother. "They'd have to put a basin under their chin to catch all the catarrh" (16). Then he adds, "Foreigners are physically incapable of speaking Chinese. . . . Something about the shape of their noses, perhaps" (17). Liang Baoshu is similarly misinformed: "They can't appreciate subtlety in art. . . . Their eyes are set too deep, so they're unable to see the fine shading in a brush painting" (17). As the two men talk, other erroneous preconceptions surface: foreigners need to eat bloody meat at every meal, they are so hairy they must shave twice every day, and their country is so "new" that red-skinned savages grab the unwary and scalp them (17–18). But when the train pulls into the Shanghai station, the Westerner speaks to them in perfect Chinese, reassuring them that there are now no savages scalping people in his country—and that the skin color of the red-skinned natives is not red; it is, in fact, similar to the complexion of the Chinese. Yanyan is mortified, but the Westerner seems unruffled. He gives them his business card and explains he is a professor of Oriental History at Cornell University in Ithaca, New York, adding that he and his family have been living in Nanjing during the last year but will be returning home soon.

The journey to Shanghai intensifies the attraction that Yanyan feels for Baoshu, especially after he defends her and Eldest Brother from armed thugs who corner them in an alley. It also evokes Yanyan's envy over her friend's opportunity to travel halfway around the world—but she is determined to remain in China and study to be a doctor. Upon her return home, she finds herself unexpectedly confronted with a chance to practice the healing arts when Baoshu is wounded by a policeman's bullet and escapes by leaping over the family's sheltering wall. The bullet has lodged in his shoulder, but Yanyan is able to dig it out, and she hides Baoshu in the family's storage shed. Only later that night, when the Police Chief pays a visit to all homes in the neighborhood in search of the unidentified fugitive, does Yanyan learn that Baoshu is a member of a secret society plotting to restore the Manchu dynasty.

After Baoshu has recovered and left the family's compound, he arranges a secret meeting with Yanyan and urges her to come away with him to Manchuria. "What a glorious team we would make! You've always wanted adventure, Yanyan. Here is your chance!" he says (73), knowing that Eldest Brother has taught Yanyan the martial arts and that she has been a skillful student. But Yanyan needs time to think. However tempting the offer (and her attraction to Baoshu is stronger than ever), she is torn by her desire to become a doctor.

Suspecting that Yanyan is still taken with the young adventurer, her father offers her the chance to study abroad, effectively separating his daughter from a lover deemed inappropriate, a not uncommon parental ploy to terminate a young, ill-advised romance. Yanyan remembers the Westerner with the straw-colored hair, the professor at Cornell. Perhaps she could attend his university. Should she go with Baoshu or accept her father's offer to study in America? Both options sorely tempt her:

> If I went with Baoshu, I would very likely have to give up my plans to become a doctor. . . . But what an adventure it would be, the two of us working together and braving dangers! . . . I might even help with the wounded if one of the conspirators got hurt. [But] if I gave up going to medical school, my practice would never go beyond digging out bullets.
>
> Studying in America, that would also be a great adventure! I thought of my friend Tao Ailin, and her experiences [opening a restaurant with her new husband] in the city called San Francisco. Her life sounded hard, but so exciting that I almost writhed with envy as I read her letters. (76)

Ultimately, Yanyan opts for America. If she were to go with Baoshu, she reasons, she'd be acting only to please Baoshu. Unlike the traditional Chinese woman, Yanyan wants to follow her own dream. And the question of her journey to America is resolved when the family learns that Professor Pettigrew, the Westerner on the train, is a friend of an American teacher at the Macintosh School, and they are leaving for America shortly. Yanyan is invited to join them; she will enroll at Cornell as a special student for the first semester and live in off-campus housing. If she does well, she will be admitted as a regular student in the spring.

The second half of the novel follows Yanyan, whose American name is Sheila, as she adjusts to life in Ithaca, New York. Strictly speaking, she is not an immigrant but a true "guest," but she confronts some of the same problems as those who come from their native countries to settle in the United States. But unlike Otter, who has the solace of being surrounded by his countrymen, initially Yanyan finds herself the only Chinese in a community of Caucasians. She is lonesome in her rooming house, unaccustomed to the harsh climate of upstate New York and the scratchy woolen clothing of female Western dress. She misses her silken tunics and Chinese food, and she is repelled by the boarding house foods: corned beef and cabbage, macaroni and cheese. She finds her studies difficult, especially since she has resisted the advice of her advisor and insisted on taking physics, a second-year course, despite (or because of) his warning that "sciences such as physics are not really suited to the female mentality" (112).

Many things about her new country amaze her. There are no Indians in feathered headdresses, women can own property (her landlady possesses a large three-story house), and strangers on the street who see her studying a map of the city offer friendly help—which at first seems threatening to Yanyan. Ithaca's transportation system, with its buses, trolleys, and trains—but no rickshaws—further confuses her.

Idiomatic English expressions also leave her baffled. When she is warned about pickpockets, she wonders why anyone should pick *her* pocket, a very ordinary one, and for what? When one of the roomers explains that he is a teller at a bank, she is again perplexed. What is he supposed to tell? And to whom? What does her landlady mean when she says she must "pull [herself] together" and get her housework done sooner? (129).

Yanyan is also taken aback when she confronts stereotypes about the Chinese. During a visit to the Pettigrews, another guest mistakes her for a maid, ordering her to fetch a cloth to wipe up her spilled drink. Then she turns to her hostess. "I'm so glad that you finally broke down and decided to hire yourself some help," she says sharply. "Chinese girls can work very hard, but is her English adequate? Can she understand you well enough to follow orders?" (145). Annoyed, Yanyan snaps back, "I can muster up enough English to follow orders and mop up your spilled drink" (145). She does not fill the role of the "meek and downtrodden" (122) Chinese woman that men in her own country—and foreigners as well—expect.

Yanyan's landlady nurtures her own stereotypes, surprised that Yanyan wants to send out some laundry, as "all Chinese are expert at laundering" (95). One day, when Yanyan goes to the Chinese laundry to pick up her clean clothing, another customer scolds her for putting too much starch in his shirt. His response to Yanyan's explanation that she is not an employee of the laundry but a university student is both offensive and puzzling: "Well, I'll be doggoned! I did hear there were Chinks at the university" (121). Yanyan can make no sense of the dog that is gone, but she correctly suspects that *Chink* is a derogatory term for a Chinese person.

Other stereotypes are less innocent, more hurtful. Yanyan overhears her teaching assistant in physics conversing with a friend during lunch one day and is dismayed at their conversation—about her! "That Chinese girl is not only clumsy, she doesn't have the proper mental discipline for a subject like physics," he says. To which his companion replies, "Those Orientals have brains that are fundamentally different from ours. Even the shape of their skull is different!" (120). These incidents, coupled with the observations of Eldest Brother and Baoshu about the Westerner on the train, illustrate how racial differences are often given negative interpretations that have no factual basis.

Yanyan's life brightens when she meets four other Chinese students, and, like many immigrants, she is more interested in bonding with her countrymen than in making Western friends. She is particularly attracted to L.H., a male sophomore in her physics class majoring in astronomy. He is thin and a little stooped, very different from the tall, muscular Baoshu of whom she still thinks fondly and whose romantic image has lodged in her chest like a "bullet." She learns from L.H. that Chinese men in America use their initials for a name, whereas the women must adopt English names. This annoys Yanyan, who not only dislikes her English name, Sheila, but sees that this difference makes the status of male students different from female students.

When the Chinese students invite her for a meal, she accepts eagerly, although she senses hostility on the part of Celia, also a sophomore. The others are attending Cornell on scholarships, and when Yanyan says that her father is paying for her education, Celia's hostility sharpens. "Your family must be really rich!" she says. "I hope you won't despise this poor food we're serving here" (136). Class differences, which can cause the wealthier to look down upon those not so fortunate, can also work in reverse: the less fortunate, envious of those who enjoy freedom from financial worries, can try to exclude the more fortunate from their circle of friends.

Despite Celia's hostility, Yanyan's friendship with L.H. continues to grow. He admires her propensity for doing the unexpected, such as taking the physics course in her first semester and, despite her difficulties, sticking it out for the second semester. Yanyan finds his approval refreshing:

> So far, I'd found that people became annoyed, even angry, when you did something unexpected. They wanted you to conform to their idea of what you should be. Chinese were expected to be experts at laundry, girls were expected to do exquisite embroidery, and Westerners with big noses were not expected to be able to speak Chinese. People liked you to be predictable because it made them feel safer. (148)

One night, when L.H. walks her home, he is suddenly set upon by three towering athletics who want L.H. to do their math homework for them. When he refuses, they assail him—but they have not anticipated Yanyan's martial arts skills. After she attacks two of them, they all take off. Later, L.H. explains that he looks weak, a tempting target for bullies. "Besides," he adds, "since I'm Chinese, people won't rush to help me when they see me attacked" (153). His statement dramatizes just how difficult it is to be the "other" in a foreign culture and how much is demanded of the outsider. But, L.H. says, if the bullies continue to ask him to do their homework, he will continue to refuse. Yanyan realizes that despite his slender build, he is "tough" inside, and her admiration for him grows.

Over Christmas vacation, the other Chinese students plan to stay in New York, but their arrangements exclude Yanyan. "Too bad my cousin doesn't have room for another person. But I'm sure Sheila has plans to go somewhere else. She can afford to travel much farther than New York," says Celia (162). Finally, Yanyan accepts Ailin's invitation to come to San Francisco. When she meets Ailin's husband, whom she assesses as "not outstandingly handsome" (168), she is nonetheless struck by the "humor and gentleness" she sees in his eyes when he looks at his wife. "She had chosen well," Yanyan decides, and that decision—that striking good looks are secondary to other desirable qualities in a man—signals that Yanyan is maturing.

With Ailin as her teacher, Yanyan learns to cook some Chinese dishes. She also learns that Ailin, unlike Yanyan, has no plans to return to China. Yanyan wants to complete her studies at Cornell, including her medical training, but "there is nothing in this country that holds me here," she says (173). However, her experiences with Ailin and James give her a fresh perspective on her feelings for Baoshu, especially when she remembers how James had looked at his wife with "love and pride. Without her help, the restaurant could not have succeeded. She was a full partner" (176). She is seeing the world through Western eyes, finally understanding what had caused her to reject Baoshu: he wanted her, "but what he wanted was a follower and a companion to share his adventures" (177).

Thus, it is no surprise that when Baoshu, now a diplomat representing the Manchu government in exile, shows up in Ithaca at the Pettigrews, Yanyan eyes him warily, especially as he waxes passionate about establishing an independent Manchurian state. "China would be broken up into pieces," she objects, aware of the "glitter in his eyes, a hunger for excitement. Stability might be boring for someone like him" (186). When they leave the Pettigrew's home, Baoshu once more tries to persuade Yanyan to come away with him. "We'll have many dangers and obstacles to face," he says. "Doesn't that tempt you?" (189). Earlier, in China, the adventure was indeed a temptation, and part of Yanyan longed to join the handsome Baoshu. But now she rejects him outright: "Don't you see, Baoshu, adventures are for children. I'm an adult now, and I want to become a doctor" (189). Suddenly L.H. appears on the scene, ordering the taller, stronger Baoshu to "leave Sheila alone" (190). Resolute even when Baoshu threatens to toss L.H. into the gorge by which they are all standing, L.H. steps between the adventurer and Yanyan, saying that for Baoshu to do so would earn Yanyan's "contempt," the one thing Baoshu cannot tolerate. L.H. has quickly understood Baoshu's character, and "something inside Baoshu seemed to collapse" (191). When Yanyan hears his retreating footsteps crunching on the snow, she sinks down upon the cold ground, weeping. L.H. pulls her to her feet and wraps his coat around the two of them, she leaning upon him for support. "But the support wouldn't always be one-sided," Yanyan realizes. "I had saved L.H. from the bully football players, and in the future, he might accept my help again. Baoshu, on the other hand, would always insist on being the strong one" (193). L.H. has helped to extract the image of the handsome adventurer from Yanyan's heart, once lodged there "like a bullet," and now the healing can begin. Whether L.H. and Yanyan return to China or remain in the United States, Yanyan's experiences in America have provided a passage for her into adulthood. Like Foxfire in *Dragon's Gate,* she now understands two different cultures. No longer does she think in terms of Big Noses—nor does she accept the stereotypes that Westerners have of Chinese. However painful some of her experiences away from her sheltered life in China, she has gained the "double-consciousness" of which W.E.B. DuBois speaks.

Esperanza Rising

Like Yanyan, Esperanza Ortega has known a privileged life, the only child of Sixto, a wealthy rancher, and Ramona, her beautiful, doting mother. *Esperanza Rising* is her story. Author Pam Munoz Ryan has drawn on the experiences of her maternal grandmother to create this narrative, using a tightly controlled third-person viewpoint told from Espanaza's perspective.[11] Growing up on El Rancho de las Rosas (the Ranch of the Roses, named for Papa's lush rose garden) in Aguascalientes, Mexico, Esperanza cannot imagine living anywhere but there, or with any fewer servants, or without the circle of the people who adore her (8). However, she discovers too soon that she will be transplanted to another place, that she will live without servants and her adoring family and friends.

In the early chapters, Esperanza is proudly aware of her elevated position. For years she has enjoyed a childhood friendship with Miguel, the son of the family's housekeeper, Hortensia, and her husband Alfonso, the gardener. But now that she is on the cusp of adolescence, she tells Miguel that they stand on different sides of a deep river that neither can cross, for she assumes that the class differences that separate them are inflexible. After that, he mockingly calls her "*Mi reina,* my queen" (18).

Her grandmother, Abuelita, reminds her that "there [is] no life without difficulties" (14), but the pampered child can hardly comprehend actual difficulties beyond the accidental breaking of an egg. Still, Abuelita continues to offer valuable advice. She is teaching Esperanza to crochet, and when she rips out the girl's uneven stitches, she tells her granddaughter, "Do not be afraid to start over" (15). Esperanza knows that her grandmother's advice applies to more than crocheting, but she is little prepared to start over and face the hardships that ensue when events take a tragic turn.

Although it is ten years after the Mexican Revolution, there is still resentment again the large landowners like her Papa Sixto, and when he fails to return from a day out on his ranch working the cattle, on the eve of his daughter's thirteenth birthday, Esperanza fears that he has come to harm at the hands of bandits. Her worst fears are confirmed when Alfonso and Miguel return late that night with her father's body. His birthday gift to her—a beautiful doll in its own sturdy valise—has been purchased and wrapped in advance, and when Esperanza finally agrees to open her presents days later, it is the doll that she treasures.

Her family's life is further disrupted by her father's stepbrothers, both powerful figures in town, one the mayor, the other the banker. In settling the estate, Esperanza's mother learns that she has inherited the house and its contents, but the family lawyer tells her Mexican custom disallows women from inheriting land. Sixto has left his wife the house but the actual surrounding land to Luis, one of his stepbrothers who was the banker on the loan. Luis first offers to buy the house from his sister-in-law, then—when she refuses—proposes marriage after a year's wait. Her rejection is met with a warning from Luis that she will regret her decision because he can make life "very difficult" for her. This is no idle threat: days later, the family awakens to find their house on fire.

The next morning, Luis reappears to repeat his proposal and to promise he will build a bigger, better house. Mama murmurs a tentative agreement to reconsider his offer. When Esperanza protests loudly, Luis says that he will immediately look into a boarding school that will teach the girl to behave like a lady. Ultimately, left with few viable alternatives, Mama decides to take Esperanza and secretly leave for the United States, accompanying Hortensia, Alfonso, and Miguel. Alfonso's brother has arranged for a cabin and fieldwork on a large farm that employs him. They must leave Abuelita behind, as she has injured her ankle the night of the fire and cannot make a rigorous journey yet.

She can, however, help by arranging the necessary travel documents through her sisters in the convent, as all the original papers have been lost in the fire, and she promises to join the others when she is able. "Don't be afraid to start over," she repeats to Esperanza. Then, referring to the zizag pattern of the blanket they have been crocheting, she adds, "Mountains and valleys. Right now you are in the bottom of the valley . . . but soon you will be at the top of a mountain again" (49, 51). She further reassures her granddaughter by reminding her of the story they have read about the phoenix, the young bird reborn from its own ashes. "We are like the phoenix," she says. "Rising again, with a new life ahead of us" (50).

But the journey to California seems to pull Esperanza further into the valley. First, she must lie hidden in a wagon beneath a load of guavas, and when she and the others finally board the train, she is dismayed to find herself surrounded by peasants who do not look "trustworthy." After all, she reminds herself, she is Esperanza Ortega from El Rancho de las Rosas. To comfort herself, she lifts her new doll from her valise but quickly hides it again when a barefoot peasant girl tries to touch it. Mama is more understanding and reprimands her daughter for her bad manners. "When you scorn these people," she says, "you scorn Miguel, Hortensia, and Alfonso. And you embarrass me and yourself. As difficult as it is to accept, our lives are different now" (70). To compensate for Esperanza's bad manners, Mama makes a little yarn doll for the peasant girl, who clutches it with surprised pleasure.

Esperanza receives another lesson about her new status in life when Mama makes friends with a peasant woman also traveling in their car on the train with a crate of live hens. Mama learns that the woman sells eggs to support herself and her eight children, and soon, she is confiding her own difficulties that have culminated in this journey. Esperanza is appalled at the easy friendship. "Mama," she whispers, "do you think it is *wise* to tell a peasant our personal business?" (77). Mama whispers back, "It is all right, Esperanza, because now we are peasants, too" (77). When the egg woman gets off the train, she gives Mama two hens and then drops a coin into the hand of a woman begging at the station.

Watching the woman through the train window, Miguel observes, "The rich take care of the rich and the poor take care of those who have less than they have" (79), adding that those with Spanish blood, those with the fairest complexions, are the wealthiest. Esperanza disparages the remark as an old wives' tale, reluctant to admit that there might be some truth in what Miguel has said. Besides, she reasons, they are all going to the United States, where skin color has no link to privilege and status. She has much to learn about both class and race.

They are met in Los Angeles by Alfonso's brother Juan, his wife, Josephina, and their children. Everyone piles into Juan's truck for the long ride to the company camp where they will live in a cabin next to Juan's family. When they take time out to stop for lunch, Esperanza stretches out on the ground, just as she used to do with Papa, but now, instead of hearing the heartbeat of the earth, as she once had, she hears only the prickly sound of dry grass.

She tells herself to be patient, just as her father had once told her, and let the fruit fall into her hand. Instead, she begins to feel as if she is drifting upwards, and, unable to "find the place in her heart where her life [is] anchored" (92), she blacks out. It is Miguel who rushes to comfort her, holding her hand and admitting that he, too, misses Papa.

When they resume their journey, they have not driven far when they stop for a young girl that Juan's family knows. This is Marta, who lives with her mother and picks cotton at a neighboring farm. Upon learning about Esperanza's luxurious life in Mexico, she becomes hostile. Esperanza learns from her that some of the workers are talking about striking, a foreign concept. As if to emphasize the reasons for striking, Marta points out several camps that house different populations: Okies, Japanese, Filipinos, and Mexicans. She explains that the company owners don't want their workers banding together for higher wages or better housing because they think the Mexicans won't mind having no hot water as long as they think no one else has any.

The camp where Esperanza will live in California comes as another jolt. Because there is no housing for unmarried women, Mama and Esperanza must claim to be Alfonso's cousins and will share two small rooms with them in a shack that Esperanza judges as inferior to the horse stalls back at her ranch in Mexico. The shack is drafty, requiring that its walls be lined with cardboard and newspaper to keep out the wind. The toilets, all housed in a separate wooden building, provide no privacy, a further cause for dismay. Esperanza clings to the notion that her Abuelita will recover soon and come to America with enough money to buy a big house, that her current circumstances are only temporary. But Mama tries to accept the turn that fate has dealt them and sings as she goes about settling in, telling her daughter that their choices are reduced to being happy in the camp or being miserable. She herself chooses to be happy and encourages Esperanza to do the same.

Later on the day of their arrival, Esperanza learns that her job at the camp will be to watch Alfonso's year-old twins with help from his daughter Isabel and each day to sweep the wooden platform used for meetings and dances. Furthermore, Isabel will start school the following week and all the laundry duties will fall to Esperanza. Humiliated by her lack of experience and proficiency in performing these chores, she admits, "It is not easy for me" (120).

Gradually she masters the tasks, gratified by Mama's approval and praise. And she continues to crochet the blanket that Abuelita has started for her, stitching up to the top of the mountains and down into the valleys. Then Miguel and Alfonso provide another bright spot in her life some time later when they surprise her with a bed of roses rescued from Papa's garden. They have kept the roots damp during the train journey and transplanted the bushes behind their new quarters around a little shrine to Our Lady of Guadalupe.

Although Esperanza is adjusting to her new life, the threat of losing their modest living quarters and their work looms over them as migrants from Oklahoma, refuges from the Dust Bowl, arrive in waves. There is also the threat of strikes incited by people such as Marta and her mother, although everyone in their camp has agreed not to strike, knowing that many others are waiting to replace them. But as a friend says, many Mexicans still have the revolution in their blood, and they all want the same things, enough food for themselves and their children.

The possibility of strikes is diverted when a dust storm hits, coating everything with a layer of brown powder. Mama and Hortensia have been trapped in an open shed where they have been packing grapes. The men are stranded in the fields. Although by nightfall everyone returns home, Mama develops a cough that grows worse and worse with each day. She is a victim of Valley Fever. An American doctor, "light and blond," makes several calls, telling Esperanza that when some people move to this area and aren't used to the air, the dust spores can get into their lungs and cause an infection. Mama's illness signifies the difficulties of migration for adults. Just as Granda lost the strength to leave Maidin Bay, Mama cannot fight off her infection. She begins to have trouble breathing and finally must go to a county hospital in Bakersfield, for the doctor says that she is not only weak but depressed, and she needs round-the-clock nursing to recover.

In light of Mama's life-threatening illness, Esperanza resolves to write to Abuelita, reasoning that if sadness is making Mama sicker, then happiness would help cure her. However, the family has depleted their small savings on doctor bills and medicines, and Abuelita most likely has no access to her own money, on deposit in the bank owned by Esperanza's uncle. Now no longer "Esperanza Ortega from El Rancho de las Rosas" but a desperate peasant girl, Esperanza loses no time in formulating a plan to earn enough money to bring her grandmother to California. A neighbor woman has offered to watch the babies, and Esperanza will work in the sheds, hiding her youth behind layers of clothes and a new hairdo so that each week she can save a little money to bring Abuelita to California.

When Christmas comes, Esperanza no longer desires finery and toys. Instead, she wants Mama to get well, she wants more work, and—looking at her hands, now dry and cracked from her work with the crops—she wants soft hands (175). But instead of getting better, Mama, still in the hospital and now weakened by her long bout with Valley Fever, develops pneumonia. The doctor must isolate Mama so that she cannot catch another disease from visitors.

Unable to visit her mother, Esperanza find solace in the company of other peasants. She has come a long way since she shrank from the peasant girl on the train. She shares dried beans with those in need and gives some children a piñata she has bought in town. But fear of other desperate migrant workers lingers as talk surfaces that "ten times the people here" will arrive from Oklahoma, Arkansas, Texas, and other places (196). Still, there are moments of rejoicing, such as when Miguel secures a job in the machine shop at the railway, a longtime ambition that gives him an opportunity to use his knowledge of motors. But the pleasure from such times is short-lived. By now the strikers are well-organized, sabotaging the workers' efforts by hiding snakes and rats in the produce, razor blades and shards of glass in the field bins. An angry rattlesnake is even discovered in a crate of asparagus stalks.

The strikers' disruptions result in immigration "sweeps" designed to rid the farms of the strikers. Mexicans with the proper papers are trapped, and even American citizens of Mexican heritage who have never been to Mexico are also deported. Esperanza is highly troubled: "Something seemed very wrong about sending people away from their own 'free country' because they had spoken their minds" (208).

Finally, the fog and grayness of winter in the valley dissipates, and the clear air hints of spring. Esperanza is still learning about life in her new country, but not all she learns is comforting. For example, Miguel always drives a distance to the Japanese market instead of shopping at more conveniently located American stores, and his explanation is distressing: the store owner treats Mexicans with dignity, "like people" (186), he says. Pressed for more explanation, Miguel describes how Americans stereotype Mexicans, perceiving them all as "uneducated, dirty, poor, and unskilled . . . as one big, brown group who are good for only manual labor" (187). Esperanza has heard about the special sections in the town's movie theater for Negroes and Mexicans, and she knows that in town parents do not want their children going to school with Mexicans. She decides that living in the company camp has its advantages, because all the children—white, Mexican, Japanese, Chinese, Filipino—go to school together. "It didn't seem to matter to anyone because they were all poor" (188). Esperanza's thoughts confirm that racial bigotry is as much a matter of class as skin color.

Nor are those the only instances of racial and ethnic discrimination. Miguel's cousin Isabel, the only third-grader with straight A's, is not chosen as Queen of the May at her school, where the teacher's selection is supposedly based on who is the "best girl student" in the third grade. Instead, a blonde blue-eyed girl is chosen, as usual. What is unusual is Esperanza's reaction. Telling Isabel that being Queen of the May would have lasted for only a day, she gives the heartbroken girl her beautiful doll—the last gift she received from Papa—so that Isabel will have something to treasure that "will be yours for a long time" (228). But the valise that held the doll is not empty. Each week, Esperanza hides money orders there, slowly accumulating enough money to bring Abuelita to California.

Then Esperanza hears that a new camp is being built for people from Oklahoma, with inside toilets and hot water—and a swimming pool. The Mexicans will be allowed to use the pool—but only on Friday afternoons, before the pool is cleaned on Saturday mornings. Piling injury on insult, Miguel loses his job at the railroad to some men from Oklahoma with no experience with motors. His alternative: to dig ditches or lay tracks. Needing the pay check, Miguel chooses the latter.

This latest affront brings Esperanza's anger to the boiling point. "Nothing is right here. . . . You cannot work on engines because you are Mexican. . . . They send people back to Mexico even if they don't belong there, just for speaking up. We live in a horse stall. And none of this bothers you?" (221).

Miguel's response reveals the differences between them:

> In Mexico, I was a second-class citizen. I stood on the other side of the river, remember? And I would have stayed that way my entire life. At least here, I have a chance, however small, to become more than what I was. You, obviously, can never understand this because you have never lived without hope. (222)

Then he adds in Spanish, quoting Papa, "Wait a little while and the fruit will fall into your hand" (223). But Esperanza's patience is exhausted. "I don't want to hear your optimism about this land of possibility when I see no proof! . . . Are you standing on the other side of the river? No! You are still a peasant!" To which Miguel snaps, "And you still think you are a queen" (224).

The next morning he is gone, telling his father that he is headed to northern California to look for work on the railroad. Esperanza is guilt-stricken, sure that her words drove Miguel away. But her heavy heart is made lighter when Mama is released from the hospital after a five-month stay, still weak but home again. To give Mama a bit of cheer, Esperanza goes to her valise, intending to show Mama the money orders she has saved so that Abuelita can join them. Shocked, she finds the valise empty. Miguel has stolen the money orders. How could he do such a thing? The answer is soon forthcoming when she is told that she must go with Hortensia and Alfonso to meet Miguel's bus at the station in Bakersfield, leaving Mama asleep in the shade outside their cabin. As she waits for the bus from Los Angeles, the clerk's "hard, sharp words" of English assault her ears; in the camp, everyone speaks Spanish, but Esperanza resolves to learn English someday. Then Miguel's bus arrives, and he is not alone. He has traveled back to El Rancho de las Rosas and returned with Abuelita, communicating with her through the nuns.

Mama is both teary and grateful when she is reunited with Abuelita, who hears from Esperanza all that has happened to them in the intervening year. The girl tells her story in the language of field-workers, in spans not of seasons but of harvests: grapes, potatoes, asparagus, and peaches. Abuelita has arrived during plums. Now the grapes are ripening for another harvest, and it is almost time for Esperanza's birthday. But first she displays the blanket she has crocheted, which by now is so large it could cover three beds, an enormous spread of mountains and valleys.

A few days before she turns fourteen, she persuades Miguel to drive her to the foothills, where they ascend to a small plateau. Esperanza lies on the ground as Papa had taught her to do and this time, she feels the earth's heartbeat. She glides above the earth, unafraid of slipping away. She "knows that she [will] never lose Papa or El Rancho de las Rosas, or Abuelita or Mama" (249). They will always exist in her memory. She is like the phoenix:

> She soared with the anticipation of dreams she never knew she could have, of learning English, of supporting her family, of someday buying a tiny house. Miguel had been right about never giving up, and she had been right, too, about rising about those who held them down. . . . Esperanza reached for Miguel's hand and found it, and even though her mind was soaring to infinite possibilities, his touch held her heart to the earth. (250–1)

Esperanza Rising is aptly titled. The young girl has risen above the loneliness and frustrations inevitably linked to the immigrant experience. The difficulties she has encountered have made her stronger, her heart lighter. She has learned much, not all of it positive, but in a year, she has matured by leaps, no longer the pampered "queen" but a determined and loving young woman. The novel closes with a scene in which Esperanza is teaching Isabel to crochet. As she unravels her pupil's uneven stitches, she says to Isabel, "Do not ever be afraid to start over" (253).

Those words summarize the experiences of the immigrants in the novels discussed above. When they leave their native land to start over, they must draw on courage to face unfamiliar customs and language, class and racial prejudice, and a lower station in life. They will know sad times in the valleys, moments of triumph on the mountains, but if they are strong, they will find the American Dream within reach. If they are patient, the fruit will fall into their hands.

NOTES

1. Patricia Reilly Giff, *Maggie's Door* (Wendy Lamb Books, 2003); hereafter cited parenthetically in text.

2. As Reilly Giff explains in an Afterword to *Maggie's Door*, an obscure fungus, *Phytophtora infestans,* rotted the potato crops that were the sole sustenance of millions of peasants and produced a devastating famine.

3. Reilly Giff sprinkles an occasional Celtic word or phrase in her characters' dialogue and supplies a list of such terms and their meanings in the novel's prefatory material.

4. Most of these immigrants were actually serving the timber trade barons who shipped their plentiful lumber from Maine back to England but had to bring their ships home empty. The captains initially took on rock, sand, or bricks for ballast on the return voyage, but eventually an idea developed that passengers willing to cross the ocean would do just as well for ballast; furthermore, they would be easier to load and unload. Even better, they, unlike rocks, would pay to travel. By the time the Great Famine began, ship owners were making money on both legs of the trip: timber one way, and emigrants the other. As demand grew for more ships (and more profit), vessels—coffin ships—that had no business being on the water were refitted and put out to sea, their holds full of Irish refugees. Sean Red Mallon was one of these.

5. For a vivid portrayal of the difficulties of leaving Ellis Island and gaining admittance to the United States during the nineteenth century, see Karen Hesse's *Letters from Rifka* (New York: Henry Holt, 1992). *Maggie's Door* skips over this hurdle, sending Nory and Sean on their way in quick order.

6. Laurence Yep, *Dragon's Gate*. (NY Scholastic, 1993): 181; hereafter: cited parenthetically in the text.

7. One can't help but suspect some ironic intention on Yep's part in designating the cruel overseer "Kilroy," the same name used by liberating GIs during WW II to indicate their presence in countries occupied by the Axis powers.

8. W.E.B. DuBois, *The Souls of Black Folk* (Boston: Bedford Books, [1903] 1997): 38. DuBois describes "double-consciousness" as a "sense of always looking at one's self through the eyes of others, of measuring one's soul by a tape of a world that looks on in amused contempt and pity. One ever feels his two-ness—an American, a Negro; two souls, two thoughts, and two unrecognized strivings." Though DuBois saw double-consciousness as an inevitable product of racism directed against blacks, it is not far-fetched to see it as shaping the experience of other minorities as well.

9. The idea of oppressed groups equating silence with defeat, even death, has a long history. The slogan of AIDS activists and victims, "Silence Equals Death," can be seen as one of the most recent reincarnations of this idea. Lyddie, in Katherine Paterson's novel of that same name, realizes after she has been accused of moral turpitude, that "in the silence the battle had been lost." (Katherine Paterson, *Lyddie* [NY: Penguin/Puffin, 1991]: 168.)

10. Lensey Namioka, *An Ocean Apart, A World Away* (New York: Dell Laurel-Leaf, 2002); hereafter cited parenthetically in text.

11. Pam Munoz Ryan, *Esperanza Rising* (New York: Scholastic, 2000); hereafter cited parenthetically in text.

·9·

Battle Cries

War is not the normal state of the human family in its higher development, but merely a feature of barbarism lasting on through
the transition of the race, from the savage to the scholar.

Elizabeth Cady Stanton[1]

*E*lizabeth Cady Stanton's assertion that war is not "normal" will strike most
readers as wishful thinking. History itself suggests that war is an inevitable aspect
of human affairs, and, given its unremitting nature, it is hardly surprising that war
has been a subject of ongoing interest for writers from Homer to the present.
Young adult literature is no exception, but what has changed—and changed dramatically in recent years—is, first, how war has been represented; second, whose
experiences dominate the narratives of war; and third, how both the causes and
consequences of war are portrayed. For example, nineteenth-century novels, such
as Lionel Lounsberry's *The Quaker Spy: a Tale of the Revolutionary War* (discussed
in Chapter Two) presented the American Revolution as having noble origins, as
one in which there were clearly defined heroes (the colonists) and villains (the
British and any colonials who sided with them), and as a male activity in which
females' opinions only echoed the positions of their men folk. The sufferings and
death that accompany war were treated as hazards to be addressed with an uplifting call to patriotism. In short, these novels promoted the outlook that World
War I poet Wilfred Owen challenged in his poem, "Dulce et Decorum Est," i.e.,
that it is sweet and decorous to die for one's country.

The social and political contexts of some of these earlier novels may offer an explanation for what often seems to modern readers as a call to un-
thinking, unquestioning nationalism. When Esther Forbes published the New-
berry Award winner *Johnny Tremain* in 1943,[2] the United States was in the

164

middle of World War II. Cultural pressures, subtle but significant, resulted in a narrative for readers—especially young readers who might in a few years be required to serve—in which the United States was represented in its military endeavors as the champion of freedom. This was especially true when not only were American boys dying in Europe and the Pacific but when those staying at home were being asked to plant Victory Gardens, collect tin, and accept rationing of everything from gasoline to sugar. Such narratives helped to establish a tradition of the United States fighting on the "right" side, stories more likely to attract a larger audience than ones that suggested that there might be multiple ways of understanding a war and exploring those perspectives.

Joel Taxel makes a similar point in an analysis of Revolutionary War novels for young readers.[3] More specifically, he compares novels published during World War II when European fascism threatened the entire world with those published in the late 1960s and early 1970s when the conflict in Vietnam had stirred considerable anti-war sentiment. His analysis demonstrates that novels published during the former era view the Revolution as a "defense of America's basic ideological values and beliefs," an emphasis "indicative of a confidence in the righteousness of American history and institutions and a perception of America as the defender of the 'free world'" (78). The "good" characters in these novels are driven by an attachment to high ideals, whereas the villains—always aligned with the Crown or Tories—are base and self-serving, seeking only to advance their narrow self-interests and oblivious to the merits of any cause. In contrast, novels published when many Americans were disillusioned by the war in Vietnam demonstrate ambivalence in the characters' attitudes toward Revolutionary ideology. Nor are the characters portrayed as good or evil according to their respective political alignments; in fact, some who reject Revolutionary ideology are kind and good.

Troy

Recent young adult novels dealing with war are more likely to embrace the complexity of war and in doing so contest traditional notions of patriotism and the earlier tendency to present it primarily as a male experience. Such novels explore in greater detail how war affects not only its frontline participants but those who are left behind and suffer the consequences of war. An excellent example of this more complex treatment of war is Adele Geras's recent novel *Troy*.[4] Based on Homer's *The Iliad* and *The Odyssey* but told solely from the viewpoint of Trojan women, children, and servants, Geras's novel is faithful to Homer's plot, tone, and the representations of his main characters. Readers familiar with Homer's epics know early on, for example, that the destruction of Troy is inevitable, that the Greek gods and goddesses will interfere in human action, and that the novel will end with the Trojan heroes dead and the women and children either fleeing or being enslaved. Paris is a still a cowardly playboy (though going to fat and losing his hair), Achilles is still defined by his rage and his love for his male cousin Patroclus, and Hector is still the devoted family man who bravely goes to his final battle with Achilles knowing he will be defeated. However, these men—the focus of Homer's work—are important in *Troy* only to the extent that their actions affect the lives of those connected to them: women, children, servants, and the elderly.

While Homer's classic begins with the traditional invocation to the muse and uses the elevated language associated with epic poetry, Geras make clear from the start that her shift in focus from the male warriors to those who are marginal to Homer's treatment demands a more colloquial approach.[5] Consequently, she eschews invoking a muse, instead immediately situating her readers in a scene that reminds us of the bloody consequences of war and challenges the conventional notion of the enemy being simply someone on the "other side." In her first chapter, "The Blood Room," the reader meets not a noble warrior whose name has endured through history but rather Charitomene, an old woman who oversees the nursing of the warriors and tries to mend the damage done them. We also meet her young helper, Xanthe, a young serving girl in her early teens who assists the older woman when she is not working for Hector's wife, Andromache.

Through Xanthe's character, Geras makes explicit a theme only implicit in Homer's poem—the secondary status and frequent sexual exploitation of women in war. Whereas Homer portrays the source of Achilles' rage as the loss of his concubine to his fellow Greek Agamemnon, there is no suggestion in the poem that either man's treatment of females is problematic. What is critical to Homer's theme is how an individual's rage, in this case that of Achilles, can damage a larger community. The capture and consequent sexual exploitation of females "belonging" to the enemy is represented as simply one of the perks of war.[6]

Geras, however, emphasizes in *Troy* that any account of lives previously marginalized in war novels must explore all aspects of such suffering. For female characters this involves sexual exploitation, specifically the threat of rape. In addition, Geras makes clear that because of their subordinate status, the threat of rape comes not only from the enemy soldiers but from those ostensibly on the women's side. By doing this, she blurs the conventional notion of enemy. In the first page of the novel Xanthe is shown praying to the gods on Olympus to protect her from a particular Trojan man who carries bodies off the battlefield and to the Blood Room. Though she tries to hold him at bay and to diminish her fear of him with ridicule, telling him to his face that his genitals resemble "boiled squid" (90), he poses a very real threat. When he finally does attack her, it is only his extreme drunkenness as well as her willingness to knee him in the groin that allows her to escape.

Troy is told from the perspectives of multiple characters, all young people, and in each instance Geras's characterization undermines or challenges a previously cherished stereotype of war. The young Trojan Alastor is downright terrified on his first battlefield, unlike Adab, the young Quaker patriot of *The Quaker Spy* who never shows fear or, indeed, any strong emotion other than resolve. Similarly, the emotional repertoire of Johnny Tremain is only slightly more expansive. For example, he shows only slight evidence of sadness when he observes Lexington Green, where eight colonial soldiers were killed trying to hold back seven hundred British soldiers: "The fear that filled him made him nearly sick, and he was ashamed, too, so that the tears sprung into his eyes, and if no one had been there to see him, he would have turned and fled."[7]

When Alastor is injured in this, his first battle, he is taken to the Blood Room, where he is nursed by Xanthe who, literally struck by Cupid's arrow, falls in love with him. But just as the course of true love does not run smoothly for the famous/infamous Paris and Helen, neither does it for Xanthe. Her love is not only unrequited, but she must bear the pain that comes when Alastor falls in love with her sister, Helen's handmaiden Marpessa. Alastor impregnates Marpessa, and at the end of the novel when she is returning to Sparta with Helen and her reconciled husband, Menelaus, Alastor assumes the dress and role of a peasant girl so that he can pursue the girl he loves. It is hard not to view his replacing of his armour with female clothing as a symbolic rejection of the warrior role he assumed so unthinkingly at the novel's beginning. Just as difficult is trying to imagine the famous heros of Homer's poems—Hector, Achilles, or Odysseus— making such a choice. Perhaps more interesting is the significance of the uncertainty of the young lovers' future. This uncertainly lies not in the external circumstance of their lives, the destruction of Troy, or their place in their new home with Helen and Menelaus. Rather it lies in Marpessa herself, who, though pregnant, questions her commitment to a relationship begun in the emotionally charged atmosphere of war.

Unlike earlier novels (again, *The Quaker Spy* comes to mind) where women objected to war only through feeble expressions of concern for the safety of loved ones, Geras allows her women characters full range of expression. They express bitter and extended tirades against the war that has dominated their lives for ten years and also against the gendered nature of war in general. Andromache, wife of the doomed Trojan hero Hector, laments the socialization that encourages young males to embrace war as a way of establishing their masculinity as she watches her toddler son Astyanax:

> She feared for Astyanax. Other women, older women who knew such things, told her this never leaves you. . . . And if your husband is determined that your son should grow into a hero and gives him tiny swords to play with, what then? What can I show him, Andromache thought, that is half

as exciting as chariots and horses? My looms, my wools? Are my lullabies as
thrilling as the stories that he will hear from men who lie and lie and speak
only of glory?[8]

Andromache's fears are justified. By the novel's end she has lost her husband
and watched her young son die when a Greek soldier throws him from one of
the walls of Troy, dashing his brains out on the stones below. She is then carried off into slavery.

Dove and Sword

Like *Troy,* Nancy Garden's *Dove and Sword,* a retelling of the story of Joan of
Arc, complicates the notion of the enemy as well as analyzes and critiques the
gendered nature of war, but goes even further, questioning whether war is ever
the solution to human conflict.[9] The novel is narrated in the first person by a
fictional young woman—Gabrielle—whose mother is a midwife. Gabrielle,
too, wants to be a "healer," but not only a midwife. She aspires to be a physician, an improbable ambition for a village girl in fifteenth-century France
where girls and women are mostly confined to the domestic realm. Inept at
household tasks, Gabrielle enjoys playing at war with the village boys. Soon her
play becomes a reality, for she is the fictional companion to Joan of Arc, accompanying Joan (or Jeanne)[10] into battle.

The novel is structured as a framed tale, played out in Gabrielle's memory, and the Prologue and Epilogue of the frame are set nearly thirty years after Jeanne's battles in Burgundy and her agonizing death at the stake. Gabrielle
is now living alone in a hut at the edge of a convent's walled garden, healer to
the nuns and the villagers in the surrounding area. In the Prologue she receives
a visit from Jeanne's brother Pierre, who informs her that the Pope has sanctioned an investigation into Jeanne's trial for heresy. In the Epilogue Gabrielle
agrees to accompany Pierre to Paris to testify on Jeanne's behalf. Between the
Prologue and Epilogue are twenty-nine chapters that follow Gabrielle's meta-
morphosis from simple village girl to military page and healer.

A central theme of the novel is Gabrielle's evolving views on the role of
women and the morality of waging war. The framing device allows the reader
to understand how Gabrielle has arrived at her final philosophical stance and her
abhorrence of war. Also, by ending Gabrielle's story where it began, the circular
structure echoes the circularity of her development, for *Dove and Sword* closes
with her enacting her initial ambition to heal after detours into battle and love.

Gabrielle's ultimate destination hinges on three aspects of her experiences
as a young adult—her growing awareness of how her gender has positioned
her, an intense romance and its tragic end, and her exposure to the brutalities

of war. As a child, Gabrielle begins to sense that her gender is a disadvantage if she is to realize her dream to become a doctor. She has secretly vowed never to wed, and she is "cheered" when Jeanne breaks off her betrothal to a young man to whom she had been promised. Gabrielle's own life takes a turn when she receives parental permission to accompany Jeanne's mother, Isabelle, on a pilgrimage, during which they will stay at monasteries along the way—"monasteries where the monks grow herbs and study healing" (40).

This pilgrimage begins a "new life" for the girl. Once she and Isabelle reach their destination and learn that Jeanne plans to raise the siege of Orleans, Gabrielle wants to accompany her friend into battle, a wish born of dual motives: she does not want to return to Domremy and "spend [her] life on women's daily chores" (77), and she feels that Jeanne should "have a woman with her, one she knows and who knows her" (78). Although Jeanne has forbidden women to follow her army, she makes an exception for Gabrielle on the condition that she travel dressed as a male page.

Gabrielle's disguise as a male liberates her both literally and figuratively. She feels "freer" without skirts to trip her and frequently enjoys the masquerade, learning, for example, to "swagger" —a boastful gait prohibited to women. And dressed as a boy, she is privy to conversations among the men that she might otherwise not have heard, particularly about Jeanne. When the captains miscalculate and lead their troops in on the wrong bank of Orleans, a fellow page says to Gabrielle, "This is what comes of having a woman lead an army" (115). Both the French and English soldiers revile Jeanne in language that stereotypes females—whore, tart, witch, sorceress—and Gabrielle perceives that Jeanne's gender prolongs her battles: even when surrounded, the English refuse to give up, in part because they will not surrender to a woman.

Still, despite her growing awareness of the disadvantage of her gender, Gabrielle holds tight to her female identity. She vows that she will be "a boy in speech and manner, but her heart will remain a woman's" (175), a pledge that she enacts in both her actions and emotions. Unlike the male soldiers, she mourns the slaughter of the enemy, a show of compassion that earns her a reproach from her master: "You have a woman's tenderness; be careful it does not soften you too much" (180).

Told by a friend that if "a woman is to ride among men as a soldier, she had better wear men's clothes" because men are "beasts" (38), Gabrielle learns that those words speak a painful truth. As she tends a wounded soldier, her doublet opens, revealing her breasts. The man tries to grab her until Gabrielle reminds him that together they follow the Maid on behalf of God and the Dauphin. In a similar incident, an English soldier grabs her tattered doublet with such force that again it opens, and she narrowly escapes being raped. Her own father, learning that she has joined Jeanne's army, fears that she will become a whore.

Despite her encounters with the "beasts," her new life introduces her to many good men, especially Louis, a young nobleman whom she meets on her pilgrimage. He joins Gabrielle in her journey, introducing her to love along the way. Forgetting her earlier determination to remain single, she agrees to marry him. She even forgets that she has earlier forsworn wedlock and wonders how many children she and Louis will have. When Louis is killed in battle, Gabrielle is overcome with grief.

But it is her experiences in war that change her most. Initially, Gabrielle perceives war as a great adventure. When she first see Jeanne dressed as a soldier, she envies her friend her armor, sword, and men's clothes, wishing herself free of her own cumbersome skirts. She feels "more suited" than Jeanne to lead an army into war, for it is she, not Jeanne, who hates spinning and cooking, who has enjoyed playing war with the village boys. With each bloody battle she witnesses, however, she finds war more and more abhorrent. When she finds herself carried away by the fervor of combat and charges into the fray with a knife, she discovers that war is a "passion that seizes a crowd, consuming each individual so that the crowd becomes one person, mindless, bent on a single goal, to kill and maim and take" (165). The mob mentality, she understands, robs soldiers of their individual will. She comes to have "no stomach" for war, a revulsion that is magnified when she sees Louis, his face distorted by hate, swing his ax at a fallen enemy soldier's bare head, splitting it in two. She wonders, "Was this what becoming a soldier had done to him?" (191).

In the aftermath of this battle, she looks into the face of dead English soldiers—her first close exposure to the enemy—and discovers that "their faces were like our men's faces, some round, some long, some old, some pitifully young, some bearded and some plain, with all colors of hair and many shades of complexion" (192). She reflects that God, in whose name Jeanne fights, "cannot be pleased by such a slaughter" (195). The battles she has witnessed have changed her irrevocably, and she reflects on how far she has come "in spirit, as well as distance, from [her] people," suspecting that she can "never" return to her village (204). The realization that one cannot go home again—certainly figuratively and perhaps literally—is a sobering one, part of moving from childhood innocence to adult maturity. She even goes so far as to question the rightness of the Crusades: "If war was evil, surely the Crusades were evil as well, even though the Church called them holy. How could war on God's behalf be good if war were evil?" (261).

Gabrielle comes to value peace over victory, and the novel takes its title from an early scene in which Jeanne, noting her friend's gentleness, dubs Gabrielle the dove of peace, whereas she herself wields the sword of war. Much later, when Jeanne asks if Gabrielle is still Dove or if war has grown more to her liking, Gabrielle replies without hesitation, "Dove."

Having witnessed so much suffering, Gabrielle begins to rethink some of her beliefs. She wonders "bitterly" why, if God is on the side of the French, He allows so many of Jeanne's troops to die. "Could it be that He was punishing us for thinking He was on the side of any who fought?" (239).

When Gabrielle reaches the convent, she is befriended by Madame Christine de Pisan, the woman who has written the famous poem about Jeanne.[11] Madame Christine teaches Gabrielle to read and provides her with books on medicine. She tells Gabrielle that she herself has found peace in study and proposes that Gabrielle also find comfort in work. The nun who has been the healer at the convent is aged, and Gabrielle can learn under her tutelage, replacing her when she is no longer able to work. Madame also proposes that Gabrielle tend the village women, for the midwife lives some distance away. So the young village girl from Domremy becomes educated in the medical arts, hoping to follow in the footsteps of other great female physicians of and from whom she learns. When she becomes discouraged with all there is to master, Madame tells her to "think of the women who will follow you, and those who will follow them, until the day when women may practice medicine as much as men, and as legally" (260).

Gabrielle also struggles to resolve her ambiguous feelings about the part she has played in the war and about her friend Jeanne, who led men into battle "to kill and to maim" (261). Madame helps her untangle her conflicted emotions one day when Gabrielle frees a mouse trapped under their cat's paw, telling the girl that she is "like the Maid [Jeanne] after all" (261). Gabrielle protests, but Madame explains that "the cat had in his paw a helpless being, as the English had France, and you made war on him, as our French have war on the English. Does God frown on you punishing a bully?" (262). The parallel motivates Gabrielle to join Jeanne's forces again when Pierre comes seeking her services as a physician for the troops. During the ensuing battles, Jeanne is captured. The embedded section of the novel follows Jeanne to her tragic death. Although Gabrielle dreads witnessing Jeanne's death and fears that its memory will haunt her forever, she finds a place in the crowd in Jeanne's line of vision, hoping that the sight of her will remind her friend of "a happier time, of the misty valley of her childhood" and show her that "not all was hateful in this world" (327). Fastened to the stake are the words that spell out Jeanne's crimes: "a blasphemer of God, defamer of the faith of Jesus Christ . . . invoker of demons" (328). Gabrielle muses that it is as if her captors have taken all the things good men hate the most and blamed Jeanne for them. Why is this happening? She concludes that Jeanne's gender is responsible:

If you are a soldier and are bested in battle by a woman, must you not think the reason is something more than that she is a better soldier than you? If you think God is with her, you must then think He is not with you—and so it would serve your interest better to think she is a creature of the Devil. (329)

When Pierre visits her at the convent, almost three decades later, Gabrielle has come to admire Jeanne without reservation. She agrees to accompany him to plead Jeanne's case, saying, "I do not like soldiering now, [but] I do not think Jeanne was evil, and all France—all humankind, perhaps—can learn from her cheerful courage" (336). Nonetheless, Gabrielle ultimately condemns war as a solution to disputes:

> No matter how much I have thought and read and prayed and studied, I have in the end not been able to find it right that people choose to kill and maim one another, though I understand, I think, the passion, like Jeanne's that leads them to it, and I respect those who go to the aid of the mouse under the cat's paw. (336)

This is no facile pronouncement but a conclusion reached through suffering and loss, words that transcend the personal. She has made a declaration about a universal issue.

Bull Run and *Soldier's Heart*

Although no character in *Bull Run,* a Civil War novel by Paul Fleischman, makes such an overt pronouncement, the author's outlook implicitly endorses Gabrielle's conclusions.[12] The events leading up to the battle of Bull Run and its enactment are told from the viewpoints of sixteen characters, both Southern and Northern.[13] Their monologues, taken together, leave the reader, like Gabrielle, unable to find it right that people choose to kill and maim one another. The large cast of characters in such a short novel (102 pages) can be confusing, but the novel succeeds in presenting a mosaic of ambiguities about war. Each side enters into battle with naïve visions of an easy victory, ignorant of the inevitable brutality of combat. However just the cause, this novel implies, war is a terrible solution.

Dr. William Rye, a volunteer whose task is to keep a regiment of North Carolina men healthy, has no illusions about the glory of war. His first monologue opens with a cynical, if accurate, observation:

> Man is the deadliest of God's creatures. None could doubt it who's watched the troops train. . . . How intently the men studied the art of killing. With what care their officers refined their skills through drilling, precision parades, mock charges. And yet, when the bugles are in earnest, how shocked we are that men bleed and die, as if we'd not striven day after day toward that very end. (25)

Other characters range from a female slave to a German immigrant fighting for the Union to a sentimental Southern woman who sees the rebel troops as "brave knights" (9). Throughout the novel they speak in figurative language that is both striking and believable. "The cannons rattled the very constellations" (1) and "the slimmest of smiles fled his lips, like a snake disappearing down a hole" (2), says Southern colonel Oliver Brattle. Eleven-year-old Toby Boyce, who joins the Southern effort as a fife player because he wants to "shoot a Yankee," remembers "Grandpap saying that if I ever saw the Devil to cut him in half and walk on between the pieces" (30). And a frustrated General Irvin McDowell, the one actual historical figure in the novel, vents his frustration over the circumstances crippling his command: "I felt myself to be a horse who's ordered to gallop while still hitched to a post" (35). The soldiers are portrayed, with few exceptions, as a drunken, gambling, ill-disciplined bunch, coarse and arrogant, a stark change from earlier novels such as *Johnny Tremain*. The women, left at home, find their duties limited to praying and sending boxes of supplies and hand-sewn clothing. One anonymous woman encloses a note that reads, "I fear I will take my own life" (24). One can only imagine the fear and loneliness behind the battle lines that prompted such words.

Slavery is, of course, an issue that fuels the war, but racism runs rampant even among the Northerners. Slave Carlotta King is incredulous and horrified to learn that escaping slaves who cross the Mason-Dixon Line are "handed back to their owners *by the Yankees*" (45). Gideon Adams, a light-skinned Negro from Ohio, weeps with joy at the President's call for men. He sets up a recruiting station filled at once with black volunteers, but when he arrives at a school house designated as another recruiting station, he finds it ringed with "a crowd of clamoring whites" with clubs, many of them drunk. They shout, "It's a white man's war!" and "Go back to your miserable homes!" (8). When Gideon tries to enlist at another station, he is told in "the most impolite terms" (15) that he cannot serve because of his race. Determined, he cuts his hair very short, buys a larger cap to hide any stray hairs, and joins at another station under the name of Gideon Able. "I was no longer who I was," he accurately reflects (16), for masquerading as a white person has cancelled much of his former identity. However, both his surnames are telling: Adams, of course, alludes to the first of God's human creations, and Gideon is the Biblical name of a mighty general of Israel.[14] And he is nothing if not able, as his determined performance in the service demonstrates. When one of his soldiers mistakenly rejoices over what appears to be a defeat of the Rebels and declares that "we'll be in Ohio in a week," Gideon is repelled by his good cheer. He determines that because he had joined a three-year regiment, he won't "return to Ohio until the Rebels [have] been beaten" (95). However, "to be a Negro living in the midst of whites, unknown to them, is to be a ghost spying on the living"

(39), witnessing abhorrent racism. He reports, "Most of [the Union soldiers] said they were fighting against secession, not against slavery. Some declared they'd rather shoot Negroes than the Rebels" (39). But he continues to stand with his regiment.

As in most wars, stereotypes about the enemy abound. Although admitting he has never known a Southerner, Union soldier A. B. Tilbury boasts that "I'd read enough to know that they were cruel-hearted, war-loving villains" (43). Demonizing the enemy is, of course, a common strategy in the training of troops, lest they stop to ponder the humanity they share with their enemy. Tilbury himself later muses on the common humanity that links Union and Rebel soldiers: "I expect they crouched when they heard a shell coming, same as we did. I almost felt I'd a double across the lines. I took to wondering whether their men were truly all savages, as I'd heard tell" (77).

Tilbury's change of attitude is dramatized in *Soldier's Heart*, another Civil War novel, this one by Gary Paulsen, which begins with the battle of Bull Run and follows Charley Goddard, Union soldier from Minnesota, from the thick of opening battles to his joyless homecoming in 1867.[15] One night on guard duty on the Union side of a river, Charley is contacted by a Rebel soldier on the opposite bank; the two men trade coffee and tobacco, conversing across the water about their mutual satisfaction with the results of the trade. They learn that both are farmers raising similar crops, with more to unite than divide them. The Rebel soldier is the first to articulate what he calls the "stupid" situation: "Here we be, both farmers, talking and trading goods and tomorrow or the next day we got to shoot at each other" (69). Charley survives the war, but returns home scarred by physical wounds and what was then known as "soldier's heart," a condition from which the novel takes its title and that today we label post-traumatic stress disorder.

The ironies about the battle of Bull Run can be applied to most wars. Before the actual shooting begins, congressmen and their wives—all "people of quality" (58)—are driven in carriages to watch the battle from a grassy hill, bringing with them the makings of a celebratory picnic: Virginia ham, softshell crabs, oysters on ice, champagne (69). The scene calls to mind those in the United States who viewed the first Gulf War almost as entertainment, tuning their television sets to images of "smart bombs" smashing into building, the camera at sufficient distance to shield viewers from any human misery, the representations resembling nothing as much as bloodless Pac Man computer games. In the melee that follows the Union rout at Bull Run, the once merry crowds scatter in panic, their expectations of a party as they prepared to watch men being slaughtered now shattered.

The novel makes another universal point when a cheering trainload of Rebels, cocksure that the war is as good as won, are subjected to a lecture by a white-haired schoolmaster riding in the same car. He reminds the soldiers that "every secessionist's swaddling clothes are woven in Maine . . . His hobby-horse is built of Maine cedar, his wedding ring worked by a Rhode Island goldsmith, his Colt revolver made in Connecticut, and his tombstone quarried in the hills of Vermont" (18). His words stimulate a "lively, democratic discussion" among the Rebels, not about the interdependence among men but whether to throw the man off the moving train or at the next station. (In deference to his age, they opt for the latter.)

In all military conflicts, there are those who profit from the suffering. In *Bull Run,* it is the Northern photographer Nathan Epp. As Epp's luck would have it, one of his subjects is shot as he stands for his portrait, but Epp develops the film nonetheless. The picture shows a blurry human shape seeming to step out of the standing man's skin, and Epp promotes it as the first photograph of the human soul leaving a dying body. "After that," he boasts, "I have never gone hungry since" (*Bull Run,* 20). Later, with the Union troops in disarray, he shows the photograph of the dying soldier, and says, "I was pleased to see how the picture cheered the men. It had a similar effect on me, for it brought in forty-nine dollars that night" (*Bull Run,* 48). And when the Union soldiers are retreating, Epp sits under a tree, waiting for the advancing Rebels, who "would be anxious to have their pictures made" (*Bull Run,* 93).

The details of the battle itself are gruesome. Even Toby Boyce, the young fife player so anxious to "kill a Yankee," vomits when he comes upon a Yankee with "no body to speak of below his waist" (*Bull Run,* 96). When the suffering man begs the young boy to kill him, Boyce cannot follow through. "He was a Yank," the boy says. "How I'd longed back home to kill one. Here I finally had my chance. But instead I ran, dodging dead bodies, ran back through the Southern men, past the wagons, past the doctors, and kept on running toward Georgia and Grandpap" (*Bull Run,* 96). One of Dr. William Rye's monologues elaborates on what Boyce was running from. The doctors soon ran out of chloroform and whiskey and had to hold the injured men down while operating. "A small mountain of amputated limbs grew up between our two tables," he recounts, "the feet often still bearing shoes. A few of the hands wore gloves. The sights and the stench were overpowering" (*Bull Run,* 94).

Soldier's Heart echoes the same bloody scene in even more horrific detail. Covered with blood, Charley arrives at the Surgeon's Tent and sees "a pile of arms and legs that stood four feet high and ten or twelve feet long" (*Heart,* 86). Upon examination, a doctor determines that Charley "ain't hit," that the blood covering him is from other men, but instead of being sent back to battle immediately, Charley is ordered to pile up the dead bodies lying around "to stop the wind from the side of the tent" (*Heart,* 89).[16] Working with another soldier, Charley moves the bodies, "stacking them like bricks and angling them at the corners so they would not tip over, until they had a stout frozen wall five feet high and thirty feet long" (*Heart,* 89). Nothing more quickly demystifies war than scenes such as these. Rather than being a glorious chance to prove one's manhood and become a hero, war is an invitation to suffering and brutality.

Under the Blood Red Sun

Soldiers are not the only ones to suffer during war. Anguish is also endured by those far from the battlefields. *Under the Blood Red Sun*, by Graham Salisbury, depicts the plight of a Japanese family living in Honolulu when Pearl Harbor is attacked.[17] Tomikazu Nakaji—or Tomi, a Japanese American boy—narrates the story. He is an eighth-grader at a public school, the son of a fisherman and his wife, both Japanese immigrants. His best friend is Billy Davis, a *haole* or white boy, with whom he shares a passion for baseball. His nemesis is Keet Williams, a bully who torments Tomi at every opportunity, calling him "fish boy" and "buddhahead." Once, just once, Tomi fought back with his fists, and his father warns him often against taking such action again. The memory of his father's words echo in his head: "*If you make trouble and lose face . . . you shame yourself. If you shame yourself, you shame all of us. Be above it, Tomi*" (28). So now Tomi is powerless to retaliate against Keet Williams, even when Keet torments Papa's pigeons—racers and tumblers—caged at the edge of a backyard field. To complicate matters, Tomi's mother works as a domestic for the Williams family, and Tomi's family rents a small cabin on their land.

Tomi's story unfolds in the few months between September 1941 and January 1942. Even before the Japanese attack on Pearl Harbor there is tension between the native islanders and those of Japanese origin or descent. In an opening scene, Grampa, who has suffered a stroke, washes his large Japanese flag and hangs it out to dry. Tomi, appalled, yells at his grandfather for the ill-considered action:

> Papa's worried enough about what the Hawaiians think of us and what the *haoles* think of us. We don't need anyone to think we're anti-*American* too. There's a war going on, you know. And Japan isn't making any friends around here. (3)

But Grampa is a first-generation immigrant, steeped in the customs of his native country, and "looks at things in a certain way. The Japanese way—which was stern and obedient" (5). In the living room of the small house he keeps a family *butsudan*, a little enclosed altar with a picture of his deceased wife in it, and a picture of the Emperor Hirohito on the wall above it. His most prized possession is the *katana,* a samurai sword that has been in the family for over three hundred years, the symbol of generations of honorable living. It is kept under Tomi's bed, wrapped in a silk scarf and stored in a burlap bag.

Unfortunately, Keet has seen Grampa hanging the Japanese flag and later uses his knowledge of the incident to threaten Tomi's friend Billy. "Listen," he says, "I want you to stop hanging around with this Jap. It's disgusting to see you two acting like friends" (10). But nothing, certainly not Keet's words, can separate Billy from Tomi. The two practice their baseball pitches and catches in every spare minute, and Papa even takes Billy and Tomi on his sampan when he goes on a two-day fishing trip with his helper Sanji, the first time a *haole* has ridden on the boat.

The descriptions of the boys' life in Hawaii are idyllic—until December 7, 1941. Billy and Tomi are out tossing their baseball when the bombing begins, the amber planes with a blood-red sun under the wings flying low and smoke billowing up from Pearl Harbor. When the boys run towards Tomi's house, there is Grampa flapping his Japanese flag. His motives are well-intentioned: if the pilots see the flag, they will not drop bombs on the Nakajis' home, but his actions terrify the family. And Papa is at sea, fishing. Have the bombs struck him and Sanji?

Mama tells the boys to bury the flag, but they cannot bury their Japanese identity. Shortly thereafter, eight U.S. Army soldiers arrive, with rifles and bayonets at the ready. The military has received a report that someone in the area was "signaling Japanese fighters" (118). Everyone denies knowledge of any such happening, although Billy later confesses to Tomi that he was so uncomfortable with the lie that he avoided his friend for a while.

The Hawaiian territory is placed under martial law, with strict sunset-to-sunrise curfews and blackouts. Life grow worse for Tomi's family. A U.S. soldier and two policemen appear at the door asking for Tomi's father. Told that he is still at sea, the men inquire about "messenger pigeons" (124) on the property. Despite Tomi's denial that the birds are carrying messages, he and Grampa are ordered to slaughter the pigeons. Following his grandfather's example, Tomi does as he is told, bleeding the birds to death "with quick, clean slits across the throat" (127), reflecting that like the soldiers killed in the surprise attack on Pearl Harbor, "They never had a chance. They just had to take it" (127). But Grampa has the last word. Facing the soldier, he glares into the man's eyes and declares, "We are 'merican. . . . We talk Ing-lish. We no make trouble" (128). It is an enormous turnaround for the old man, so proud of his Japanese heritage but now shamed by the actions of his countrymen.

Nor is that all. Tomi and his mother encounter hostility when they go shopping: Tomi realizes that a lady who glares at them wasn't seeing just a boy and his mother, but "a *Japanese* boy and his *Japanese* mother" (131). The United States declares war on Japan, and the family learns that Papa's boat has been sunk, Sanji killed, and Papa arrested. In fact, all Japanese fishermen have been arrested, suspected of bringing fuel to Japanese submarines. Then Mama is warned by a Hawaiian family friend to stay close to home, "no talk Japanee, no bow like one Japanee, and no wear any kind Japanee clothes, kimono, like that" (136). Mama is quick to respond, telling Grampa and Tomi, "We going through this house to find everything that could bring trouble . . . photograph, letter . . . everything. . . . We going bury 'em" (137). Obeying Mama, they hide almost all the memorabilia of their heritage—Mama's traditional kimono, Grandma's altar, photographs—in the dirt under the front porch. Everything but the *katana*. Grampa takes that into the jungle and leaves it hidden deep in the greenery, after telling Tomi, "That belong to your ancestor. Long time ago. Nobody since then bring disgrace or shame to the name of this family." Then he pauses, watching his grandson. "My country," he says. "My *country*, Tomikazu . . . they . . ." (163). He is unable to finish, for his country has shamed him and betrayed all he believed about it.

Tomi learns that his father may have been imprisoned on Sand Island, an inaccessible and heavily guarded detention center. Is Papa indeed alive? He must find out. Defying the curfew and risking his life, he swims across the harbor to Sand Island, where he sees his father confined behind wire fencing. Although Papa looks "awful," unshaven, grimy, and limping from a bullet wound to his leg, he is able to whisper that Tomi should tell Mama not to worry. The boy swims back under the cover of darkness and finally arrives back home, wet and exhausted, barely escaping an arrest for curfew violation. Later, Grampa is able to ascertain that the imprisoned men have been shipped to the mainland.

A few days later, Grampa himself is arrested, calling his final request to Tomi as he is led away: protect the family honor and save the *katana*. But when Tomi goes into the jungle and retrieves the sword from its hiding place in a hollow log, he is secretly followed by Keet Williams carrying a loaded rifle. Keet commands Tomi to put the *katana* down, and with the rifle pointed at his head, Tomi obeys. But when Keet shoots at the *katama,* nicking the handle, Tomi gathers up his courage and the sword, warning Keet that if he reveals the secret of the *katana,* he—Tomi—will make him "pay for it . . . and not in money" (225). Keet, a coward, disappears into the jungle. Tomi is learning he can use the strength of his mind instead of muscle to face down opposing forces.

Schools closed since the attack reopen in January. On the first day, Tomi's teacher leads the class into a discussion of the reason for war, for all wars. It is desire for power that begins wars, he says. "It's like a drug. Some men can't get enough of it. They want your power and my power and everyone else's power" (234). But people fight back, "fighting to . . . make their own choices, to . . . live a free life" (235). The discussion empowers Tomi. He will not disgrace the family name by scuffling in the dirt, but he will fight for freedom. When he and his friends cross paths with a man who insults them by saying to Tomi, "Hey, Buddhahead—you got a lot of nerve coming out in the open after what you people did" (240), the other boys are inclined to fight. But Tomi stops them. The exchange between the boy and the man indicate just how well Tomi has absorbed the lessons from his father and linked them to his own power to defend himself.

> "You got it wrong, mister," I said. "I was born here. I live here, just like you do. And I'm an American."
> "Beat it, Jap," he said.
> *Be above it, Tomi . . .*
> "American," I said again.
> He narrowed his eyes but didn't say anything more. I eased away feeling . . . strange . . . very strange. Almost peaceful. Spooky, feeling peaceful when somebody hates you. (241)

As Tomi's story ends, he understands his heritage and knows he will pass it on, imagining he will take out the *katana* and polish it carefully. Then he will pass it to his little sister and explain where it came from, what it stands for, and the need to protect it. He will tell her how proud Papa and Grampa will be when they come home and discover that Kimi knows all about it. When they come home, he will hand it to Papa, and he, Tomi, will look firm, like Grampa. And the scene in his mind blazes with pride:

> Papa would hand the *katana* to Grampa, and Grampa would take it and gently turn the blade in the light. Then he would look deep into my eyes. And nod once. (244)

Tomi's story could not have been written in the era during which it took place or in the years immediately following World War II. Although we now recognize treatment of Japanese Americans during the war as deplorable, unjustified, and racist, it was not until forty years later that our government made restitution to the families on whom it had inflicted such suffering. This is a novel for our times. It allows us to look back with shame and insight lacking during the stressful days of the 1940s.

Fallen Angels

Set in Vietnam in 1967, *Fallen Angels,* by Walter Dean Myers, takes its title from a memorial service for a fallen comrade in which all soldiers are described as "angel warriors . . . because they get boys to fight wars."[18] The novel, winner of the 1989 Coretta Scott King Award, is narrated by Richie Perry, a Harlem teenager who volunteers for the service after high school to escape the poverty that has defined his life. Myers creates the Vietnamese jungle—the heat, the dampness, the insects, the rats, the boredom punctuated by attacks by the Vietcong—in vivid and relentless detail.

When Perry is shipped to Vietnam, he has one year of his enlistment left to serve. He is sending money home to help his younger brother Kenny graduate from high school because his father walked out on the family long ago and his mother is "falling apart" (35). Perry feels very protective of Kenny. His thoughts about home and growing up in Harlem are interwoven with the jungle scenes and provide insights into Perry's character. But mostly it is the war that controls the narrative in this novel.

The plot is slow-paced, with "[h]ours of boredom, seconds of terror" (132), simulating the hurry-up-and-wait tempo of military life. Perry notes, "Once I had figured that of the seven months I had spent in the army, four of them had been standing around waiting for something to happen. Vietnam might have been a different place, but the army hadn't changed" (8). During the long days between battles, Perry makes friends with some of the other soldiers, mostly black. Peewee is his closest buddy, and together they plan for when they are back "in the World"—if only they live long enough.

The dark war story is enlivened by occasional moments of humor, many of them provided by Peewee, as when, for example, he tries to convince a new recruit that a soldier can go home early if he kills enough Cong to equal his own weight. In a later incident, Peewee says that another unit consists of better soldiers than his own, and his captain demands, "Where the hell is your pride, soldier?" Peewee's wit is equal to the question: "In Chicago, sir." he says. "Can I go get it?" (271).

There is talk of a truce being hammered out in Paris, and Peewee wants to "get into it" before the war is over. Although Perry isn't "gung ho" to fight, he wants to do his part. The violence of the war hits home when Perry's unit goes into its first battle—into the "boonies"—and Jenkins, a recent arrival, is killed when he steps on a mine. The image of his death haunts Perry: "Seeing him lying there like that, his mouth and eyes open, had grabbed something inside my chest and twisted it hard" (43).

The horrors pile up rapidly. Perry's unit, out on patrol one night, fires into the darkness, shooting "hell" out of another platoon in a tragic incident of friendly fire, and Perry's imagination is haunted by ghastly scenes. "They [the soldiers] all started crowding in on me. The guy with the plasma taped to his helmet, the sergeant crying. . . . a medic putting a tag on a wounded soldier. . . . A body bag. The guys that our artillery blew away didn't have a reason to die. . . They just died because somebody else was scared. . . . We were killing our brothers, ourselves" (106).

Lieutenant Carroll, Perry's likeable commanding officer, is killed in a mission to "pacify" a village where his patrol had earlier received a friendly welcome. But this time, met with Vietcong gunfire, they shoot blindly "into the fearful darkness" (126). When the chopper comes to pick them up, it levels the villagers' huts, sweeping away everything in its path, mostly women and old men running for their lives, the very people the unit had earlier "come to save, to pacify" (127). Perry has a hard time coping with Lieutenant Carroll's death. "It hung around our shoulders and filled the spaces between us" (129), he says. Ordered to write to Carroll's wife informing her of his death, he is flooded with survivor's guilt: "In a way I felt real bad just being alive to write it" (130).

All the Vietamese people become a faceless, nonhuman force—"gooks." A black soldier asks, "How come when you say 'gooks' it sounds like 'nigger' to me?" He understands the dehumanizing implications of such terms, but in his war it is impossible to discern enemies from allies. Approaching villages, the soldiers' fear is palatable. The Vietcong has committed atrocities to ensure that no one, whatever their sympathies, cooperates with the U.S. forces. In one village the VC has killed a person in each hut. The soldiers discover an old woman with bones protruding from her face, a beheaded baby. So much blood and death inevitably panics Perry and his platoon, and they lose control:

> We could have killed as easily as we mourned. We could have burned as eas-
> ily as we put out the fires. We were scared, on the very edge of control, at once
> trying to think of what was right to do and hating the scene about us. (178)

Chaos reigns. The men are shooting at everything; Perry is about to toss a grenade into the village when his sergeant helps calm the men down, letting them be "human again; in all the inhumanity about us, he let us be human again" (178). Nonetheless, when Perry enters a hut and is confronted by an armed Vietcong, he fires his rifle into the man's face point blank, emptying the clip. The image of the dead soldier—"just an angry mass of red flesh where the face had been"— stays with him, a nightmare of looking down at the Cong and feeling his own face torn apart. As Perry reflected earlier, "Maybe the time had passed when anybody could be a good guy" (150). In a later, even more horrifying scene, the soldiers encounter a Vietnamese woman with two children. Peewee begins to make a doll from grass for the little ones when the woman stops and hands one of her chil-dren to a soldier. "The G.I.'s arms and legs flung apart from the impact of the blast. The damned kid had been mined, had exploded in his arms" (231).

Witnessing such brutality, Perry himself is brutalized and almost succumbs to the instinct to kill, kill: "Maybe we would stop pretending that we knew who the enemy was and let ourselves believe that all the Vietnamese were the enemy. . . . The women, the babies, the old men with their rounded backs and thin brown legs. They would be the enemy, all of them, and we would be those who killed the enemy" (229).

Nor do the soldiers know why they are even there, fighting in the swamp
jungle against an enemy indistinguishable from innocent civilians. "The real
question," Perry says soon after his arrival in country, "was what I was doing
what any of us were doing, in Nam" (69). When a television crew arrives to pose
this very question, the men provide clichéd answers that are no answers at all
They "have to demonstrate that America stood for something"; they are "trying
to free the South Vietnamese people to do what they wanted to do"; they're
fighting because they "hate Communism," because their "country asked [them]
to" (77). One of the men supplies "the domino theory" as his answer. None o
these responses, sifted from the media and government propaganda, suffice. Perry
gropes for an answer in a letter to his brother, but is at a loss. "Saying that you
were trying to stop Communism or stuff like that was different than shooting
somebody. It was different than being scared and looking at somebody who wa
maybe as scared as you were" (189). Recognizing the common humanity tha
binds him to the enemy, just as Tilbury and Goddard have done in novels dis
cussed earlier, highlights the barbarous and insane aspect of all wars.

Despite the foregrounding of the war, this is Perry's story, the effect of hi
experiences on who he is:

> I had come into the army at seventeen, and I remembered who I was and
> who I had been as a kid. . . . And now all the dying around me, and all the
> killing, was making me look at myself again, hoping to find something more
> than the kid I was. Maybe I could sift through the kid's stuff, the basketball,
> the Harlem streets, and find the man I would be. (187)

He has plenty of time to "sift" when he is wounded and airlifted to a hos
pital. During his recovery a visiting chaplain comes by and gives a predictable
speech: "You are defending freedom," he says. "You are defending the freedom
of Americans and of the South Vietnamese. Your acts of heroism and courage
are celebrations of life, and all America thanks you" (215). But the chaplain
meaningless words contradict the reasons his friend Peewee gives for battle: kill
the Congs before they kill you, reason enough until they get back to the
World. "Maybe [Perry] was right," Perry concedes. "But it meant being some
other person than I was when I got to Nam" (216).

He is, indeed, "some other person" by the novel's end. He is not exactly
sure who but knows he can never be the person he was when he left Harlem
even though his Mama would expect her son back unchanged. "[B]ut it could
never happen. She hadn't been to Nam. She hadn't given her poncho to any
body to wrap a body in, or stepped over a dying kid" (267). Still groping fo
words to describe the war to his brother, he settles for a blunt fact: "The wa
was about us killing people and about people killing us, and I couldn't se
much more to it. . . . I had thought that this war was right, but it was onl

right from a distance" (269). From his hospital bed Perry reads *Stars and Stripes,* the military newspaper, and notes that in the stories "there didn't seem to be any cost. A hill was taken, or a hamlet, and the only body counts that were given were for the Congs" (305). His visions of coming home a "hero" are sharply ironic, given what the reader knows about the dissent back home. When he is finally on a military transport with Peewee, bound for the United States, the plane loaded with live soldiers and full caskets, Perry's mind wanders back to the boonies and his dead comrades. As he prays for God to care for them, a "fat man complained that they didn't have the wine he wanted" (309). The war that has consumed him, that has caused him to rethink his ideas about foreign enemies and his own country, is trivialized in the man's complaints and the abrupt sentence that closes the novel: "We were headed back to the World" (309).

Any one of these novels discussed in this chapter demonstrates the hollowness and brutality of human beings killing each other for causes that will fade into history. Taken together, they make a powerful statement that columnist Ellen Goodman has expressed with compelling brevity: "There are just wars and there are unjust wars. There are wars that are forced upon us and wars we rashly choose. But there is no such thing, then or now, as a good war."[19]

NOTES

1. Elizabeth Cady Stanton, quoted by Elaine Partnow, ed. In *The Quotable Woman* (New York: Doubleday/Anchor, 1978): 23.

2. Esther Forbes, *Johnny Tremain* (NY: Houghton Mifflin, 1943).

3. Joel Taxel, "The American Revolution in Children's Fiction." *Research in the Teaching of English* 17.1 (February 1983), 61–83.

4. Adele Geras, *Troy* (New York: Harcourt Brace, 2000); hereafter cited parenthetically in text.

5. However, it should be noted that recent translations of *The Iliad*, Stanley Lombardo's being an excellent example, tend to more colloquial language than earlier ones.

6. In her classic text, *Against Our Wills: Men, Women, and Rape* (NY: Simon and Schuster, 1975), Susan Brownmiller documents this assertion in stunning detail.

7. Forbes, *Johnny Tremain*, 7.

8. Andromache's phrase about the men who "lie and lie and speak only of glory" hearkens back to the final lines of Wilfred Owen passionately felt "Dulce et Decorum Est" in which he rails against those who would induce young men to enlist in wars begun by older men. Owen knew whereof he spoke: he died after writing this poem during his second tour of duty at the front lines during World War I and one week before the war ended.

9. Nancy Garden, *Dove and Sword: A Novel of Joan of Arc* (New York: Scholastic, 1995); hereafter cited parenthetically in the text.

10. Garden uses the French for "Joan," referring to her variously as Jeannette (her childhood name), the Maid, and Jeanne. Once she takes up arms to reclaim the French throne for the Dauphin, she is called "Jeanne" almost exclusively. Therefore, this discussion uses the latter name.

11. Garden's Author's Note clarifies that Christine de Pisan was a "real person who really did write a long poem about Joan" (xiii); her interactions with Gabrielle are, of course, fictitious.

12. Paul Fleischman, *Bull Run* (NY: Harper Trophy, 1993); hereafter cited parenthetically in text.

13. The battle of Bull Run was one of the most savage in American history. Although the Union troops expected an easy victory, they finally retreated in stunned disarray from the raw firepower of the Rebels. As Gary Paulsen points out in an Author's Note to *Soldier's Heart* (New York: Dell Laurel-Leaf, 1998), more men were killed at Bull Run in just two hours than in all previous American wars combined, including the Revolution (103).

14. *The New English Bible,* New York: Oxford UP, 1970: Judges: 6–7.

15. Gary Paulsen, *Soldier's Heart* (New York: Dell Laurel-Leaf, 1998); hereafter cited parenthetically in text. In an Author's Note that closes the novel, Paulsen clarifies that Charley Goddard "really existed. He enlisted in the First Minnesota Volunteers when he was fifteen, lying about his age, and fought through virtually the entire war" (103).

16. Paulsen asserts in his Author's Note that this detail is factual (103).

17. Graham Salisbury, *Under the Blood Red Sun* (New York: Bantam Doubleday Dell, 1994); hereafter cited parenthetically in text.

18. Walter Dean Myers, *Fallen Angels.* (New York: Scholastic, 1988): 44; hereafter cited parenthetically in text.

19. Ellen Goodman, "Remembering the 'Good' War," *Boston Globe,* 21 May 2004: 11 (L).

· *10* ·

Conclusions

Those who don't learn from history are doomed to repeat it.

George Santayana

$\mathcal{P}$erhaps Santayana was right. After all, few of us would deny that we can learn from experience, our own and that of others, however long ago they lived. But *whose* history would Santayana have us learn? And what *exactly* should we learn from it? Are the lessons the nineteenth-century philosopher would have history teach us analogous to our own experience or is there a more complicated relationship between ourselves and the past of which we need to be aware?

These are some of the questions authors of young adult historical fiction raise and wrestle with in their novels, arriving at answers that are shaped by their own culture as much as by their ostensible subject matter. The writers of the texts we have focused on in this study have been unmistakably marked by their own history, by their exposure to influences and forces as varied as the Civil Rights movement, protests against the Vietnam war, Second Wave feminism, multiculturalism, and post-modernism, as well as by their own experiences with class, religion, war, and even immigration. The result of these influences and experiences has been a body of fiction that pushes us to redefine historical fiction and, in so doing, to reconsider what kinds of experiences constitute appropriate subject matter.

It has been said that history belongs to the victors. If we understand this to mean that those who control literacy control, by extension, our understanding of the past, then this certainly seems to be the case. Long ago Chaucer's Wife of Bath bemoaned her young husband's taste for misogynistic literature, pointing out to him that if women had been allowed to write history, well then, it would be a different sort of story he would be reading. The stories the Wife wished for, the stories of those who have been hidden from or by history are very ones that today's young adult authors have increasingly embraced. Whereas novels from the nineteenth century to those written in the early 1970s tended to focus on white male experience and to depict people of color and females as supporting players to the starring male cast, recent novels have shifted their emphasis, moving the secondary players to center stage. As a consequence we should not be surprised that so many of the novels discussed here focus on the experiences and perceptions of young females and people of color rather than on experiences of young white males. And as writers shift their focus to voices and experiences previously ignored or suppressed, they make clear that *any* history is made up of multiple perspectives, perspectives shaped by a character's gender, class, race, and religion. Novels like Karen Hesse's *Witness*, which takes a piece of New England history and presents it from multiple perspectives, do more than just convey history as a series of events to readers. Rather, by showing individual opinions and ideologies being formed, shaped, and even sometimes changed, these books convey *how* history is made and, in so doing, make clear the extent to which writing it is an interpretative act.

One of the inevitable consequences of writers shifting their focus to the experience of the previously marginalized is that their books can be read as a critique of some of the United States' most deeply embedded cultural myths. Integral to the American dream is the belief that we are the home of the free and the brave, a classless society where education is the great equalizer and a land of equal opportunity where one's material success occurs in direct proportion to one's work ethic. These long-held and cherished beliefs are often implicit in textbooks. But contemporary young adult historical novels, drawing as they often do on the experiences of those for whom the American dream has not materialized or for whom it has been more nightmare than dream, challenge these myths. Reading about the experiences of the Chinese who built America's railroads after the Civil War but who lived in virtual slavery, or the deaths of four young black girls in the bombing of a church in Birmingham in the 1960s, young readers cannot help but question the foundations of these myths or ask themselves how they are maintained and who benefits from their maintenance.

Marginalized or not, the protagonists in the novels examined in this study *are* dissatisfied with the status quo of their respective worlds. Despite their youth and powerlessness, they find ways to subvert social structures—whether imposed by custom or legal decree—that have diminished their freedom or completely robbed them of it. To escape these confines, they find various routes to self-empowerment: they rebel, openly or secretly, against oppressive forces; they assume less oppressed identities of race and gender, although not without some feelings of loss; they flee to other lands and new opportunities. That which does not defeat them makes them strong, and all these characters emerge in the final pages as more mature, with keener insights into the larger world than the often-blinkered perspectives with which they began their individual stories. None of this, of course will surprise those readers of young adult literature who understand the genre's commitment to an ending that, at the very least, is hopeful. But what should be acknowledged, even appreciated, is how well contemporary authors of young adult historical fiction balance their commitment to hopeful outcomes with their need to maintain historical accuracy. Otter, the protagonist of Laurence Yep's *Dragon's Gate,* suffers greatly, as did many of the Chinese who immigrated to California. He endures physical hardship, the loss of family and, perhaps most important, the loss of his youthful illusion that the United States is the land of unlimited freedom. Nevertheless, his losses are accompanied, even balanced, by a newly acquired awareness of his ability to lead his people and, thus, so doing, influence the course of history. Similarly, though Mattie Cook, the protagonist of Laurie Halse Anderson's *Fever 1793,* loses beloved friends and family during the yellow fever epidemic that overtook Philadelphia and finds her tentative hold on the middle class threatened, she also uncovers a previously unsuspected talent for hard work, management, and community building.

As we have tried to make clear, historical fiction is *not* history. It may offer the human and psychological truths of history, but a novel—any novel—is a work of the imagination, and, as such, it is more than an accumulation of factual data. Ultimately, its power resides in its ability to move and inspire the imagination. But we have also tried to demonstrate that the view of history presented in any historical novel is filtered through the imagination of an author shaped by his or her own era. Readers of historical fiction invariably learn not only about the past but the era in which any given novel was written. This combination of facts and imagination can exert a power that allows a historical novel to transport readers to places and times that have receded into the past. Jet travel, however sophisticated, cannot accomplish what a single historical novel achieves for its readers. The ability of an historical novel to transport readers to years gone by gives it a potentially more significant power as well—the power to transform lives and in so doing make them agents of change.

The poet Denise Levertov has written that "books influence individuals; and individuals, although they are part of large economic and social processes, influence history."[1] The relevance of her statement to our study should be clear: reading historical novels may provide readers not only with a wider knowledge of the past but also an expanded empathy for those who inhabited and struggled with that past. Armed with knowledge of the past and the increased sensibilities that come with that knowledge, young adult readers can enter the world prepared to be makers of history rather than its victims.

NOTE

1. Denise Levertov, as quoted on http://www.wisdomquotes.com/cat_history.html

Suggestions for Additional Reading

$\mathscr{M}$any of the issues that we have examined in separate chapters of this study—race, gender, class, war, religion, and immigration—intersect within a single book. For example, *Esperanza Rising* can be read as a critique of not only immigration but of race, class, and gender as well. Similarly, *Under the Blood Red Sun* comments not only on war but on race, class, and immigration. Therefore, we have not categorized the list below. Nor do we intend this list to be exhaustive. We have omitted many fine historical novels for young adults mainly because they do not focus on the issues chosen as the focus of this study. As for the novels listed below, we recommend them all as fine examples of historical fiction but leave to readers the task of approaching them through their own critical lens.

Burks, Brian. *Soldier Boy*. New York: Harcourt Brace, 1197. Johnny "The Kid" McBane has made a reputation in Chicago as a boxer, but he must leave all that behind when he refuses to throw a fight. He ends up as a recruit in Custer's calvary, fighting Sioux Indians in the battle of Little Bighorn.

Cadnum, Michael. *The Book of the Lion*. New York: Puffin Books, 2001. Edmund is a young apprentice to a metal worker who is incarcerated for his master's crime of counterfeiting. His story is set during the Crusades, and when he is rescued from prison to serve as a squire to a knight, he finds himself part of the Holy War, fighting alongside Richard the Lion-hearted, and witnesses the unholy consequences of this war.

Collier, James Lincoln, and Christopher Collier. *With Every Drop of Blood*. New York: Laurel-Leaf, 1996. This Civil War novel explores issues of race and family loyalty through the story of Johnny Heller, whose Pa returns from the Civil War mortally wounded. Despite a promise made to his dying father to remain home and care for his family, Johnny eventually agrees to sneak provisions to needy Confederate troops. His mission ends in his being captured by an ex-slave, now a Union soldier, and the two boys overcome historical prejudices to forge a friendship.

Crew, Linda. *Brides of Eden: A True Story Imagined.* New York: HarperTrophy, 2003. When itinerant preacher Joshua Creffield arrives in Corvallis, Oregon, in 1903, he attracts a group of female disciples with his fiery sermons and his claim to have direct contact with God. Based on a historical incident, the novel is narrated by Eva Mae Hurt, who is entranced by the preacher's charismatic but dangerous message. But the "secret rites" he performs in his tent with Eva and other young women lead to his downfall and Eva's eventual freedom from Joshua's bizarre fanaticism.

Crew, Linda. *Children of the River.* New York: Dell Laurel-Leaf, 1991. Fleeing the dangers of the Cambodian war, Sundara escapes with her aunt's family from the brutalities of the Khmer Rouge army. Only thirteen, she must leave behind her parents and siblings. When she settles in Oregon with her aunt's family and tries to fit in at her high school, she is torn between her longing to belong to her American peer group and remaining loyal to her Cambodian heritage.

Cushman, Karen. *The Ballad of Lucy Whipple.* New York: HarperTrophy, 1996. Lucy's mother might as well have hauled Lucy off to another planet, so foreign is the life the young girl encounters in Lucky Diggins during the Gold Rush. Longing for her comfortable life in Massachusetts with her grandparents, instead she must help her mother when the eccentric woman opens a boarding house in a tent for miners.

Easton, Kelly. *Walking on Air.* New York: Simon and Schuster, 2004. June is the stepdaughter of an evangelical preacher who attempts to support his family as a traveling preacher during the depression. Her father's rigidity coupled with the family's extreme poverty pushes June to question the Biblical wisdom that has shaped her.

Elliott, L. M. *Under a War-Torn Sky.* New York: Hyperion, 2002. Based on the experiences of the author's father during World War II, this novel tells the story of Henry (Hank) Forester when he is shot down over Alsace, behind enemy lines. Relying on the French Resistance to reach safety, Hank survives many dangers, and his journey reveals not only his courageous character but the horrors that the Nazis inflicted on the French.

Gormley, Beatrice. *Miriam.* Grand Rapids, MI: Eerdmans Books, 1999. Miriam, Moses' older sister, not only saves her brother's life but suggests to the Egypt princess Bint-Anath that she find a wet nurse for the infant, who turns out to be Moses' own mother. The novel alternates its narrative point of view between Miriam and the princess's lady-in-waiting, thus providing readers with an understanding of both the Hebrew and Egyptian cultures. Ultimately, Miriam must choose between her Jewish heritage and the Egyptian palace life.

Hesse, Karen. *Letters from Rifka*. New York: Hyperion, 1993. It is the early part of the twentieth century, and twelve-year-old Rifka, forbidden by doctors to board the ship with her family to the United States, is now traveling alone from Russia to escape persecution by the Czar. She records the rigors of her journey in the margins of a book, a gift of Puskin's poetry given to her by her friend Tovah. Frightened but determined to set foot on American soil, Rifka forges a strong sense of self to survive the ordeal.

Hobbs, Will. *Jason's Gold*. New York: HarperTrophy, 2000. A survival story that takes fifteen-year-old Jason Hawthorn from the streets of New York City to the frozen Klondike in search of gold, to a new land in a hostile climate. During his Arctic adventures, he is befriended by Jack London, then a young writer.

Hurst, Carol Otis, and Rebecca Otis. *A Killing in Plymouth Colony*. New York: Houghton Mifflin and Company, 2003. While exploring a murder that actually took place in Plymouth Colony in 1630, the authors are able to provide valuable insights into parent-child relationships and gender roles in Puritan culture by narrating this story through the eyes of a Governor's son, eleven-year-old John Bradford.

Jocelyn, Marthe. *Mable Riley: A Reliable Record of Humdrum, Peril, and Romance*. New York: Candlewick, 2004. Like Mattie in Jennifer Donnelly's *A Northern Light,* Jocelyn's novel focuses on a young girl, fourteen-year-old Mable, who wishes to be a writer and struggles to find her voice. As she assists her school-teacher sister and meets an older, very independent woman, she finds models of womanhood previously denied her.

Krisher, Trudy. *Uncommon Faith*. New York: Holiday House, 2003. The title of this novel plays on the name of the main character, Faith Common, who challenges mid-nineteenth century notions about gender and race. From the perspectives of various citizens of Millbrook, Massachusetts, the reader learns of one girl's struggle to achieve equal education for all.

Lasky, Kathryn. *Beyond the Burning Time*. New York: Scholastic, 1994. In this retelling of the Salem witchcraft trials, Lasky's novel includes elements as diverse as two neighbors' feud over property and the effect on the colony of being charterless. Mary Chase, the protagonist, is one of the few girls in the colony not affected by the hysteria. When her mother is charged with witchcraft, she and her brother provide the climax of the novel with a daring rescue. Although this is Mary's story, the subtext is clear: theocracy is dangerous and leads to religious repression.

Lester, Julius. *Pharaoh's Daughter*. New York: HarperTrophy, 2000. In this retelling of the Biblical story of Moses, his rescue from the bulrushes, and his growing up in Pharaoh's palace, Lester has introduced new details and created a compelling story based on careful research into the ancient culture of Egypt.

Levitan, Sonia. *Annie's Promise*. New York: Aladdin Historical Fiction, 1993. Set in the waning months of World War II, Levitan's novel explores issues of immigration, religion, and race through the eyes of Annie, a young German Jewish immigrant, who resists traditional notions of gender.

Mazer, Harry. *The Last Mission*. New York: Dell Laurel-Leaf, 1979. In 1944, during the waning years of World War II, fifteen-year-old Jack Raab lies about his age and joins the U.S. Air Corps. He longs for adventure, the chance to be a hero, but gets far more than he bargained for when his unit flies their last mission and he is imprisoned in a German POW camp. Because he is Jewish, his experiences behind enemy lines are more terrifying than he could have imagined.

McMullen, Margaret. *How I Found the Strong*. New York: Houghton Mifflin Company, 2004. Told from the perspective of Shanks Russell, eleven years old when the Civil War begins, this novel chronicles both the years when Shanks' father and brother fight for the Confederate Army and the years immediately following the war when hostility toward freed slaves runs rampant.

Mikelson, Ben. *Red Midnight*. New York: Rayo, 2002. Santiago, the narrator of this harrowing sea adventure, tells of escaping with his four-year-old sister from his native Guatemala, a country ravaged by guerrilla warfare that has destroyed his family and home. The two siblings set sail for the United States in a kayak built by their uncle, surviving a multitude of dangers from military guards and the stormy seas. Although its setting of less than a quarter century ago makes problematic its classification as historical fiction, the civil war in Guatemala has been resolved, and Santiago's story is of brutalities that now belong to history.

Mikelson, Ben. *Tree Girl*. New York: Harper Collins, 2004. Fifteen-year-old Gabriela Flores climbs trees to find the privacy and safety that her daily life in a remote Guatemalan village does not allow. When members of her village are massacred by U.S-trained soldiers during the worst months of her country's civil war, she begins a journey to find her family and a way to deal with the violence she has witnessed.

Miklowitz, Gloria. *Masada: The Last Fortress*. Grand Rapids, MI: Eerdmans Books, 1999. The Romans have fought Judea for four years. Now, in 72 C.E. after a four-year war, they have only to conquer the fortress

Masada, perched high above the Dead Sea. Seventeen-year-old narrator Simon ben Eleazar tells the story of the Romans' relentless attack and, as an apprentice to Masada's only physician, helps victims of the battle. A subplot involving Simon's romantic feelings for a young woman, the beloved of his best friend, adds another layer of interest to the plot.

Miklowitz, Gloria. *Secrets in the House of Delagado*. Grand Rapids, MI: Eerdmans Books, 2001. Narrated by fourteen-year-old Maria Sanchez, a recently orphaned Catholic, this novel reveals the horror of the Spanish Inquisition when a priest places Maria as a spy in the home of the Delagados, a family that converted from Judaism to Catholicism generations ago. Her report to the priest and its consequences provide a turning point in Maria's life.

Napoli, Donna Jo. *Song of the Magdalene*. New York: Scholastic, 1996. Miriam is the daughter of a wealthy Jewish widower in Magdala. We meet her when she is ten and stricken by seizures. As she grows toward maturity, she suffers many sorrows: her lover dies, she discovers that she is pregnant, is violently raped and miscarries as a result, and is exiled from Magdala for her own safety. Only in the final pages does she meet "the healer that the Romans called Jesus" and becomes the Mary Magdalene familiar to contemporary readers.

Nolan, Han. *If I Should Die Before I Wake*. New York: Harcourt and Company, 1994. Through the magic of time-travel, Hillary, a young neo-Nazi, is hurled back to World War II Germany where she becomes Chana, a Jewish girl, and is able to experience the consequences of Nazism first hand.

Oughton, Jerri. *The War in Georgia*. New York: Houghton Mifflin, 1997. Using World War II as a backdrop, Oughton depicts the pain of one family's break-up and the joy of another's formation from the perspective of thirteen-year-old Shanta.

Peart, Jane. *Toddy*. Grand Rapids, MI: Fleming H. Revell, 2000. Peart uses the Orphan Train West series as a vehicle to explore issues of class and gender in this novel set in the Midwest in the last decade of the nineteenth century.

Peck, Richard. *The River between Us*. New York: Dial Books, 2003. Set in a small town in southern Illinois at the start of the Civil War, Peck's beautifully written novel explores how stereotypes of race, war, and gender intersect when embodied in the individual experience of the narrator, Tillie, and her family.

Rinaldi, Ann. *In My Father's House*. New York: Scholastic, Inc., 1993. Rinaldi explores the effects of the Civil War on the family of Willard McLean, whose homes were both the starting and ending place of the

Civil War. Tensions spring from the differing perspectives on the war held by Will and his step-daughter, Oscie.

Salisbury, Graham. *Eyes of the Emperor*. New York: Wendy Lamb Books, 2005. Although underage, Eddy Okubo of Honolulu joins the army shortly before the Japanese attack on Pearl Harbor. Along with a few other Japanese American soldiers, Eddy is sent to an island off the coast of Mississippi to help train attack dogs. It is a dangerous assignment, for the dogs are being trained to attack Japanese soldiers.

Sappey, Maureen Stack. *Letters from Vinnie*. Ashville, NC: Front Street, 1999. The fictional diary of Vinnie Ream, the first woman to be given a commission to sculpt President Abraham Lincoln, describes not just the effects of war on a family divided but also the burdens that traditional notions of gender place on a young woman who wishes to make her way as an artist.

Seely, Debra. *The Last of the Roundup Boys*. New York: Holiday House, 2004. Told from two perspectives, that of Tom, a transplanted Virginian, and Evie, the daughter of a Kansas rancher, this novel explores resistance to traditional gender roles as well as established notions of class as the two narrators' relationship develops.

Sneeling, Lauraine. *Ruby*. Minneapolis, MN: Bethany House, 2003. The first novel in the Dakota Treasures series, this one follows Ruby Torvald and her young sister, Opal, who have received an inheritance from a father who left home years ago. Now he is dying in the Dakota territory. When the sisters travel to the frontier expecting a legacy of gold, they find instead that their inheritance consists of a "saloon" that is mainly a front for a house of prostitution. Relying on God to help them fulfill their father's dying wish, Ruby and her sister struggle to do the right thing

Son, John. *Finding My Hat*. New York: Orchard Books, 2003. Jin-Han narrates the story of his family's immigration to the United States in the late 1970s, an experience marked by his family's move from city to city as they attempt to find a permanent home. This is also a coming-of-age story for Jin-Han, whose tale begins when he is two and concludes when he is an adolescent experiencing his first romantic relationship and the loss of his mother to cancer.

Wilson, Diane Lee. *I Rode a Horse of Milk White Jade*. New York: Orchard, 1998. When Oyuna, a young girl living on the steppes of late 13th-century Mongolia, was a baby, a mare stepped on her foot, permanently crippling her. Nonetheless, Oyuna learns to ride, and, given a chance to choose a horse of her own, selects an old, lame mare. Gradually, the mare's leg heals, and when the horse is taken for service by men for the army of Kublai Khan, Oyuna disguises herself as a boy and joins the army to stay with her mare, setting out on a dangerous adventure.

Yep, Laurence. *Dragonwings*. New York: HarperTrophy, 1975. When Moon Shadow is eight years old, he sails from China to America to join his father, who has dreams of building a plane, the Dragonwings of the title. Moon Shadow's story, beginning at the turn of the twentieth century, intersects with the first flight of the Wright Brothers. Despite the common stereotype among the Chinese immigrants of Americans as "demons," Moon Shadow makes friends with some in the white community, and they defend him against the forces of bigotry.

Yep, Laurence. *The Star Fisher*. New York: Scholastic, 1991. In 1927, Joan Lee moves with her family from China to Clarksburg, West Virginia, in pursuit of the American Dream. What they find is less dream than nightmare, for they are the first Chinese Americans that the townspeople have seen, and instead of a welcome, Joan's family encounters prejudice and persecution. But Joan Lee knows she's an American and has the courage to stand up to ignorance, concluding on the final page that she thinks she's "going to like it here."

Bibliography

YOUNG ADULT LITERATURE

Aidinoff, Elsiev. *The Garden.* NY: HarperTempest, 2004.

Aldrich, Bess Streeter. *A Lantern in Her Hand.* NY: Puffin Books, (1928) 2004.

Alger, Horatio. *Ragged Dick.* NY: Signet, (1867) 1990.

———. *Luck and Pluck.* NY: Pavillion Press, 2003 (1869).

Anderson, Laurie Halse. *Fever 1793.* NY: Aladdin Books, 2002.

Crowe, Chris. *Getting Away with Murder: The True Story of the Emmett Till Case.* NY: Phyllis Fogelman Books, 2003.

———. *Mississippi Trial, 1955.* NY: Phyllis Fogelman Books, 2002.

Curtis, Christopher Paul. *The Watsons Go to Birmingham—1963.* NY: Bantam Doubleday Dell, 1995.

Cushman, Karen. *Catherine, Called Birdy.* NY: HarperTrophy, 1994.

———. *The Midwife's Apprentice.* NY: Clarion Books, 1995.

Donnelly, Jennifer. *A Northern Light.* NY: Harcourt Inc., 2003.

Finley, Martha. *Elsie Dinsmore.* Chicago: Saalfield Publishing, nd.

Giff, Patricia Reilly. *Maggie's Door.* NY: Wendy Lamb Books, 2003.

Gormley, Beatrice. *Miriam.* Grand Rapids, MI: Eerdmans Books, 1999.

Gregory, Kristiana. *The Winter of Red Snow: The Revolutionary War Diary of Abigail Jane Stewart, Valley Forge, Pennysylvania, 1777.* NY: Scholastic, 1996.

Hesse, Karen. *Letters from Rifka.* NY: Hyperion, 1993.

———. *Out of the Dust.* NY: Scholastic, 1997.

———. *Witness.* NY: Scholastic, 2001.

Lasky, Kathryn. *Alice Rose and Sam.* NY: Hyperion, 1998.

———. *Blood Secret.* NY: HarperCollins, 2004.

———. *True North.* NY: Scholastic, 1996.

Lounsberry, Lionel. *The Quaker Spy: A Tale of the Revolutionary War* Philadelphia: David McKay, 1889.

Matas, Carol. *In My Enemy's House*. NY: Aladdin, 1999.

McDonald, Joyce. *Devil on My Heels*. NY: Delacort, 2004.

Meyer, Carolyn. *White Lilacs*. NY: Gulliver Books, 1993.

Miklowitz, Gloria. *Masada*. Grand Rapids, MI: Eerdmans Books, 1999.

Namioka, Lensey. *An Ocean Apart, A World Away*. NY: Dell Laurel-Leaf, 2002.

Napoli, Donna Jo. *Song of the Magdalene*. NY: Scholastic, 1996.

Paterson, Katherine. *Lyddie*. NY: Puffin Books, 1991.

———. *Preacher's Boy*. NY: HarperCollins, 1999.

Pyrnelle, Louise-Clarke. *Diddie, Dumps, and Tot or Plantation Child-Life*. NY: Harper and Brothers, 1882.

Rinaldi, Ann. *A Break with Charity: A Story about the Salem Witch Trials* NY: Gulliver Books, 1992.

———. *Wolf by the Ears*. NY: Scholastic, 1991.

Ryan, Pam Munoz. *Esperanza Rising*. NY: Scholastic, 2000.

Sterling, Dorothy. *Mary Jane*. NY: Scholastic, 1959.

Wait, Lea. *Wintering Well*. NY: McElderry Books, 2004.

Yep, Laurence. *Dragon's Gate*. NY: Scholastic, 1993.

SECONDARY SOURCES

Books

Andelin, Helen. *Fascinating Womanhood (Updated and Revised)*. 1965. NY: Bantam, 1992.

Aronson, Marc. *Beyond the Pale*. Lanham, MD: Scarecrow Press, 2003.

Baida, Peter. *Poor Richard's Legacy: American Business Values from Benjamin Franklin to Donald Trump*. New York: William Morrow, 1990.

Betsworth, Roger. *Social Ethics. An Examination of American Moral Traditions*. Louisville, KY: Westminster/John Knox Press, 1990.

Barnhouse, Rebecca. *Recasting the Past: The Middle Ages in Young Adult Literature*. Portsmouth, NJ: Boynton/Cook, 2000.

Barker-Bentfield, G.J. *Horrors of the Half-Known Life: Male Attitudes toward Women and Sexuality in the Nineteenth Century*. NY: Routledge, 1999.

Betsworth, Roger. *Social Ethics: An Examination of American Moral Traditions*. Louisville, KY: Westminster/John Knox Press, 1990.

Brown, Joanne. *Presenting Kathryn Lasky*. NY: Twayne Publishers, 1998.

Carnes, Mark C., ed. *Novel History: Historians and Novelists Confront America's Past (and Each Other)*. NY: Simon and Schuster, 2001.

Carr, Edward Hallett. *What Is History?* 4th ed. NY: Bedford Books, 1961.

Carr, Jo. *Beyond Fact: Nonfiction for Children and Young People*. Chicago: American Library Association, 1982.

Cline, Ruth and William McBride. *A Guide to Literature for Young Adults*. Chicago: Scott, Foresman, 1983.

Cowart, David. *History and the Contemporary Novel*. Carbondale, IL: Southern Illinois UP, 1989.

Davies, Robertson. *The Merry Heart: Reflections on Reading, Writing, and the World of Books*. Toronto: Viking, 1996.

Dekker, George. *The American Historical Romance*. NY: Cambridge UP, 1987.

DuBois, W.E.B. *The Souls of Black Folk*. (1903) Boston: Bedford Books, 1997.

Egoff, Sheila. *The Republic of Childhood: A Critical Guide to Canadian Children's Literature*. Toronto: Oxford UP, 1975.

Elias, Amy J. *Sublime Desire: History and Post-1960s Fiction*. Baltimore: Johns Hopkins UP, 2001.

Fein, Ellen and Sherrie Schneider. *The Rules: Time-Tested Secrets for Capturing the Heart of Mr. Right*. NY: Warner Books, 1995.

Fetterly, Judith. *Resisting Reader: A Feminist Approach to American Fiction*. Bloomington, IN: Indiana UP, 1981.

Fielding, Leslie. *Love and Death in the American Novel*. NY: World Publishing, 1960.

Fleishman, Avrom. *The English Historical Novel: Walter Scott to Virginia Woolf*. Baltimore: Johns Hopkins UP, 1971.

Foley, Barbara. *Telling the Truth: The Theory and Practice of Documentary Fiction*. Ithaca, NY: Cornell UP, 1986.

Gay, Peter. *Pleasure Wars: The Bourgeois Experience: Victoria to Freud,* v. 5. NY: W.W. Norton, 1998.

Hamer, Dean. *The God Gene: How Faith is Hardwired into Our Genes*. NY: Doubleday, 2004.

Harding, Vincent. *There Is a River: The Struggle for Freedom in America*. NY: Harcourt, Brace, 1981.

Henderson, Harry. *Versions of the Past: The Historical Imagination in American Fiction*. NY: Oxford UP, 1974.

Jacobs, Naomi. *The Character of Truth: Historical Figures in Contemporary Fiction*. Carbondale, IL: Southern Illinois UP, 1990.

Janeway, Elizabeth. *Women: Their Changing Roles (The Great Contemporary Issues)*. NY: Ayer Co. Publishing, 1973.

Leisy, E. E. *The American Historical Novel*. Norman, OK: U. of Oklahoma Press, 1950.

McGlinn, Jeanne M. *Ann Rinaldi: Historian and Storyteller*. Lanham, MD: Scarecrow Press, 2000.

Nilsen, Alleen Pace and Kenneth L. Donelson. *Literature for Today's Young Adults,* 2nd ed. Glenview, IL: Scott, Foresman, 1985.

———. *Literature for Today's Young Adults,* 6th ed. NY: Longman, 2001.

West, Cornell. *Race Matters*. Boston: Beacon Press, 1993.

X, Malcolm (with Alex Haley). *The Autobiography of Malcolm X*. NY: Grove Press, 1964.

Articles

Aronson, Marc. "A Mess of Stories," *The Horn Book* (March/April 1995): 163–68.

Atwood, Margaret. "In Search of *Alias Grace*: Writing Canadian Historical Fiction." *The American Historical Review* 5.5 (December 1998): 1503–16.

Avi. "Writing Backwards but Looking Forward," *SIGNAL* 22.2 (Summer 1999): 17–23.

Beatty, John and Patricia Beatty. "Watch Your Language—You're Writing for Young People!" *The Horn Book* (February 1965): 114–21.

Blos, Joan. "'I Catherine Hall': The Journal as Historical Fiction." In *The Voice of the Narrator in Children's Literature: Insights from Writers and Critics,"* Charlotte F. Otten and Gary D. Schmidt, eds. NY: Greenwood Press, 1989. 276–83.

———. "The Overstuffed Sentence and Other Means for Assessing Historical Fiction for Children." *School Library Journal* 32.3 (November 1985): 38–39.

Brown, Joanne. "Historical Fiction or Fictionalized History? Problems for Writers of Historical Novels for Young Adults," *The ALAN Review* 26.1 (Fall 1998): 7–11.

Campbell, Patty. "The Young Adult Perplex." *Wilson Library Review* 55.3 (November 1980): 214–15, 238.

———. "The Sand in the Oyster." *The Horn Book.* (September/October): 636–39.

Canby, Henry Seidel. "What Is Truth?" *Saturday Review of Literature* 4.23 (December 31, 1927): 480.

Carson, Rachel. "Our Everchanging Shore." July 1958. In *The Quotable Woman,* Elaine Partnow, ed. NY: Anchor Books/Doubleday, 1978.

Casey, Carol. "Carried by Creative Currents." www.childrenslit.com/f_hesse.html.

Chang, Curtis. "Streets of Gold: The Myth of the Model Minority." In *Rereading America: Cultural Contexts for Critical Thinking and Writing.* Boston: Bedford/St. Martin, 2004. 366–75.

Garfield, Leon. "Historical Fiction for Our Global Times." *The Horn Book.* (November/December 1988): 737–43.

Goodman, Ellen. "Remembering the 'Good' War." *Boston Globe,* 21 May 2004: 11 (L).

Hade, Daniel. "Lies My Children's Books Taught Me: History Meets Popular Culture in 'The American Girls' Books." In *Voices of the Other: Children's Literature and the Postcolonial Context.* Roderick McGillis, ed. NY: Garland, 1999. 153–76.

Harris, Violet J. "Continuing Dilemmas, Debates, and Delights in Multicultural Literature," *The New Advocate* 9.2 (Spring 1996): 107–22.

Haugaard, Erik Christian. "Only a Lampholder: On Writing Historical Fiction." In *Innocence and Experience: Essays and Conversations on Children's Literature.* Barbara Harrison and Gregory Maguire, eds. NY: Lothrop, Lee, & Shepard, 1987: 268–72.

Johnson, Deidre. "From Paragraphs to Pages: The Writing and Development of the Stratemeyer Syndicate Series." In *Rediscovering Nancy Drew.* Carolyn Stewart Dyer and Nancy Tillman Romolav, eds. Iowa City: U of Iowa Press, 1995: 29–31.

Lasky, Kathryn. "The Fiction of History: What Did Miss Kitty Really Do?" *The New Advocate* 3.3 (Summer 1990): 157–66.

———. "Keyhole History." *SIGNAL* 21.3 (Spring 1997): 5–10.

———. Presentation to the National Council of Teachers of English, November 1996.

———. "To Stingo with Love," *The New Advocate* 9.1 (Winter 1996): 1–7.

Lettus, Dorothy. Review of *Beyond the Divide. Voice of Youth Advocates* (October 1983): 204.

Loer, Stephanie. Interview with Karen Cushman. http://www.eduplace.com/rdg/author/Cushman/question.html

Lystad, Mary. "The Adolescent Image in American Books for Children." In *Young Adult Literature: Background and Criticism.* Millicent Lenz and Ramona M. Mahood, eds.

Chicago: American Library Association, 1980: 27–32.

Mallon, Thomas. "Writing Historical Fiction." *American Scholar* 61 (Autumn 1992): 604–08.

Macleod, Anne Scott. "Writing Backward: Modern Models in Historical Fiction." *The Horn Book* (January/February 1998): 26–33.

Paterson, Katherine. "Only a Lampholder: On Writing Historical Fiction." In *Innocence and Experience: Essays and Conversations on Children's Literature*. Barbara Harrison and Gregory Maguire, eds. NY: Lothrop, Lee, & Shepard, 1987:263–64.

———. "Where is Terabithia?" In *Innocence and Experience: Essays and Conversations on Children's Literature*. Barbara Harrison and Gregory Maguire, eds. NY: Lothrop, Lee, & Shepard, 1987: 224–33.

Rochman, Hazel. Review of *The Bone Wars*. *Booklist* 91.4 (October 15, 1994): 420.

Romolav, Nancy. "Children's Series Books and the Rhetoric of Guidance: A Historical Overview." In *Rediscovering Nancy Drew*. Carolyn Stewart Dyer and Nancy Tillman Romolav, eds. Iowa City: U of Iowa Press, 1995: 113–20.

St. John de Crevecoeur, J. Hector. "Letters from an American Farmer." In *Rereading America: Cultural Contexts for Critical Thinking and Writing*. Gary Colombo, Robert Cullen, and Bonnie Lisle, eds. NY: Bedford/St. Martins, 2004: 304.

Seto, Thelma. "Multiculturalism is not Halloween." *The Horn Book* (March/April, 1995): 169–74.

Sipes, Lawrence R. "In Their Own Words: Authors' Views on Issues in Historical Fiction." *The New Advocate* 10 no. 3 (Summer 1997): 243–58.

Speare, Elizabeth George. Newbery Award Acceptance Speech. *The Horn Book* (August 1959): 265–70.

Spence, Jonathan. "Margaret Atwood and the Edges of History." *The American Historical Review* (December 1998): 1523.

Sutcliff, Rosemary. "History Is People." In *Children and Literature: Views and Reviews*. Virginia Haviland, ed. Glenview, IL: Scott, Foresman, 1973: 305–12.

Taxel, Joel. "The American Revolution in Children's Fiction." *Research in the Teaching of English*. 17.1 (February, 1983): 61–83.

Trease, Geoffrey. "The Historical Novelist at Work." In *Writers, Critics, and Children: Articles from Children's Literature in Education*, Geoff Fox, et al., eds. NY: Agathon Press, 1976.

Walsh, Jill Paton. "History Is Fiction." *The Horn Book* (February 1972): 17–23.

Index

About the Authors

$\mathcal{T}$his book, *The Distant Mirror: Reflections on Young Adult Historical Fiction*, marks the second collaboration between Joanne Brown and Nancy St. Clair. Earlier, they co-authored *Declarations of Independence: Empowered Girls in Young Adult Literature, 1990–2001*, also published by Scarecrow Press (2002) as part of its series on young adult literature.

Joanne Brown retired her position as an English professor at Drake University in Des Moines, Iowa, in 2002, but continues to be engaged with young adult literature. During her time at Drake, she developed and taught courses in writing fiction, American drama, and adolescent literature. She earned a bachelor's degree in theater from Northwestern University and a master's and doctoral degree in English from Drake University. She has published short fiction, personal essays, and articles on young adult literature (*The ALAN Review, SIGNAL, The New Advocate*). She is also the author of *Presenting Kathryn Lasky*, part of Twayne's United States Authors series on writers for young adults. She has acted in many roles at the Des Moines Playhouse, where she once served as Education Director and taught children's drama. She and her husband, Milton, live in Des Moines. They have three children, six grandchildren, and a spoiled Wheaton Terrier.

Nancy St. Clair received her bachelor's degree from Cornell College in Mt. Vernon, Iowa, and her doctoral degree in English literature from the University of Iowa in Iowa City. She is a professor of English at Simpson College in Indianola, Iowa, where she has just completed a long term as chair of the English Department and served as the Director of the Cornerstone and Senior colloquium programs and is the current director of the First Year Seminar program. In 1996, she won the Outstanding Junior Faculty award, and in 2003 she won Simpson College's research award for *Declarations of Independence*. She has also published articles on women's studies and young adult fiction. She and her husband, Steve, have two daughters, two dogs, seven cats, a rabbit, and a chinchilla.